Embodied Hot Cognitive Vulnerability to Emotional Disorders

Alexandru Tiba

Embodied Hot Cognitive Vulnerability to Emotional Disorders

From Theory to Treatment

Springer

Alexandru Tiba
Department of Psychology
University of Oradea
Oradea, Romania

ISBN 978-3-030-53988-7 ISBN 978-3-030-53989-4 (eBook)
https://doi.org/10.1007/978-3-030-53989-4

This Springer imprint is published by the registered company Springer Nature Switzerland AG
The registered company address is: Gewerbestrasse 11, 6330 Cham, Switzerland

This book is dedicated to Diana and Victor for always believing in me. I would like to express my gratitude to Larry Barsalou whose encouragement has been vital throughout my work in the field of embodied cognition. I also wish to thank Daniel David for his guidance in REBT and early years of my carrier. Further, I would like to thank Aurora Szentagotai for the thoughtful comments and her openness to new ideas. I am also thankful to Joshua Davis and Nicolas Vermeulen who were important sources of motivation. Especially, I thank Laura Manea for her invaluable support and hard work in making these ideas real.

Contents

About the Author

Alexandru Tiba, PhD is currently adjunct senior assistant professor in the Department of Psychology, University of Oradea. He obtained his PhD in Psychology at Babeş-Bolyai University (2011). He attended a formal training in cognitive behavior therapy at The International Institute for the Advanced Studies of Psychotherapy and Applied Mental Health, Cluj-Napoca, Romania. He is a senior clinical psychologist specializing in cognitive behavior therapy certified by the Romanian National Board of Psychologists. He delivers clinical psychology and cognitive behavior therapy services in his private practice in Oradea, Romania. His research falls in the domains of clinical cognitive science, embodied simulation and the development of science-derived psychological treatments. In 2019, he developed The Psychological Science Treatment, a form of primary care psychological treatment based on methods derived from output scientific knowledge. He works primarily on understanding how the embodied simulations are involved in the cognitive vulnerability for emotional disorders. His recent publications inform experimental psychopathology and psychological treatments about the models of embodied simulations.

Chapter 1
Embodying Hot Cognitive Vulnerability to Emotional Disorders

1.1 Problems and Solutions for Existing Treatments of Emotional Disorders

Emotional disorders are mental disorders characterized by frequent and intense disturbed emotions (Bullis et al. 2019). The most common emotional disorders are anxiety and depressive disorders, eating disorders, and borderline personality disorder (Barlow et al. 2014). Yet of 176 diagnoses of mental disorders, 40.3% likely involve an affective/emotional disturbance and 19.3% are guaranteed to involve an affective disturbance (Jazaieri et al. 2013). Anxiety and depressive disorders alone are leading causes of disability worldwide with top recurrence rates and a chronic course (World Health Organization [WHO] 2012). Altogether, the economic burden estimated to the global economy because of mental disorders for this decade is enormous (US$16 trillion; Patel et al. 2018).

There are two main evidence-based treatments used in the treatment of emotional disorders: medication and psychological treatments. There is a consensus that these treatments are better than nothing (Leichsenring et al. 2019). However, when compared with treatment as usual and placebo, recent meta-analyses (Cuijpers et al. 2019) for both anxiety (Carpenter et al. 2018; Gomez et al. 2018; Liu et al. 2017) and depressive (Cipriani et al. 2018; Cuijpers et al. 2019; Driessen et al. 2015) disorders suggest otherwise. When judged to high-quality research standards, the effect of medication and psychotherapy is small and the effectiveness is disappointing (Leichsenring et al. 2019). For other emotional disorders such as borderline personality disorder (Cristea et al. 2017), the effectiveness seems even more disappointing. Moreover, the rates of remission and response are limited by high levels of relapse (Leichsenring et al. 2019). These facts are important reasons to better understand and treat emotional disorders.

Much trust in sorting out these problems was put into translational research. Integrating basic and clinical research may be a viable solution for developing new and more efficient treatments of emotional disorders. There are several problems for

A. Tiba, *Embodied Hot Cognitive Vulnerability to Emotional Disorders*,
https://doi.org/10.1007/978-3-030-53989-4_1

translational research in mental health treatment: (a) artificial diagnostic category, (b) diagnostic-guided treatment, and (c) disciplinary approach (David et al. 2016). Several solutions such as using trans-diagnostic-guided treatments (Dalgleish et al. 2020), theory-based treatment (David et al. 2016), and multilevel interdisciplinary approach (from molecules to behaviors; Bogdan et al. 2013) were proposed in response to these problems. Unfortunately, this research did not result in hoped new treatments (Bogdan et al. 2017).

Another viable strategy, as an alternative to the development of new treatments, would be to improve the existing treatments. Translating data for improving extant psychological treatments encounters two difficulties. One difficulty with translating data to improve the extant treatments is that models guiding psychological treatments were developed based on clinical utility for intervention rather than basic science research (David and Szentagotai 2006). Because they were developed based on clinical utility, many cognitive models guiding the "gold standard" psychological treatments (CBT/cognitive-behavioral treatments) are hard to be articulated from a basic science perspective (e.g., irrational beliefs).

A second problem for translation to improve the existing treatments is that "gold standard psychotherapies" target the change of clinical cognition in a framework that considers cognition separated (yet interacting) from motivation, affect, and behavior (amodal cognition framework; Fodor 1975). When cognition is a separate construct from our body, brain, and experience-based systems, translating knowledge about these systems in treatments encounters a major difficulty. Both basic and clinical early research on cognition were guided by an effort to prove that cognition is a separate entity from our body, sensorimotor and affective experiences, and environment. The dominance of such an amodal framework is understandable, but it builds unbreakable walls between the extensive data about our brain, motivation, affect, behavior, environment, and the clinical cognition models that guide the extant treatments of emotional disorders. Fortunately, converging ideas from philosophy (e.g., Clark 2008; Gallagher 2009), affective (e.g., Barrett and Lindquist 2008; Niedenthal 2007), cognitive (e.g., Barsalou 1999), and brain sciences (e.g., Varela et al. 1991) reached to a different idea about the construction of cognition: cognition is built by reusing our brain and experience-related systems in a dynamic interaction between our body and environment to inform flexible behavior (Barsalou 2008). Moreover, an emerging consensus suggests that it is hard to find exclusive cognitive and affective brain processes that implement specific psychological states (Barrett and Satpute 2019; Barrett 2019; Lieder and Griffiths 2019).

In this book, I argue that a major blockade of the translation research to inform cognitive models and psychological treatments of emotional disorders is because of the dominance of an amodal disembodied perspective of nonclinical and clinical cognition. This view spread from philosophies that guide basic cognitive sciences (e.g., Fodor 1975) into modern models of cognition applied to the treatment of emotional disorders. From an amodal framework, our direct experiences are transduced into amodal symbols, a language-like type of representation stored in a semantic system (Barsalou 1999). When activated, this type of cognition may influence other systems such as emotions, behaviors, or our physiology. When cognition is built on amodal symbols, differences in cognition result from differences in learning and knowledge.

Distorted cognition is at the core of emotional disorders and their psychological treatments. Because distorted cognition was considered from an amodal framework, distortions of cognition were seen as resulting from differences in learning and knowledge structures. Distorted cognition does not result from differences in our brain and body. Accordingly, extant psychological treatments were focused on finding ways to change learning and knowledge that result in distorted cognition. This is the dominant view in most modern cognitive models that guide the treatment of emotional disorders. For instance, relevant models of cognition-emotion integration which informed important psychological treatments based on amodal cognition are the cognitive model of A. T. Beck (Beck 1976; Beck and Haigh 2014), the information processing theory approach (Foa and Kozak 1986), the multilevel theories of emotion-cognition (Barnard and Teasdale 1991), theories of affect-as-information (Wyer et al. 1999), and so on.

Many sciences (e.g., clinical neurosciences) are largely preoccupied with a distinct problem. They try to answer the question of how the differences in our brain and body result in emotional disorders. As I suggest, when modern cognitive models are based on amodal types of cognition, there is an insurmountable incompatibility that blocks the translation of research about our body and brain's affective and behavioral systems into cognitive models that guide current psychological treatments. This is not to deny amodal representation. Yet I argue that when important genetic and environmental risk factors result in salient neuroadaptations (environment-related changes and alterations in our nervous system), these changes are critical for information processing in the context of disturbed emotional experiences.

In this detail, neuroscience studies revealed that threat-related amygdala (hyper) reactivity is a neural biomarker of psychological vulnerability to emotional disorders (e.g., Swartz et al. 2015). Amygdala (a brain structure laying at the basis of our brain) processing is an affective type of processing that occurs in a non-semantic brain space. Thus, the differences in our non-semantic brain result in the differences in our psychological states and vulnerability to emotional disorders.

Although the mainstream models of cognition (focused to find differences in learning, knowledge, and processing as an explanation for distorted cognition) cannot take into account that affective and brain differences result in differences in cognition (except indirectly by biasing attention to negative and accumulating more negative knowledge that bias processing; Beck and Haigh 2014[1]), some new, yet

[1] Some scholars will argue that recently A.T. Beck integrated the biology into his recent generic model. I do agree that Beck admitted since 2008 that biology might be important for distortions of cognition (Beck 2008). Yet in the generic model (Beck and Haigh 2014), Beck suggested that biological propensities to attend to aversive information result in accumulation of negative knowledge structures. Then, when activated, these knowledge structures impact emotional and information processing. This is still an amodal model of cognition. There are not the differences in our brain that result in distorted cognition but the differences in our negative knowledge structures.

increasingly accepted, models do: the embodied models of cognition (Barsalou 2008; Glenberg 2010). Consistent research suggests that cognition may have a special property that has the power to make it of importance for affective and behavioral responses: it can reuse body processes involved in experiences to represent information about those experiences (Niedenthal 2007). In other words, cognition may be based on *embodied simulations*. This idea is neglected in the traditional models of cognition (which try to evidence properties of cognition that dissociate cognition from our perceptions and experiences); certainly not true for all contexts (Barsalou 1999) and all kinds of cognition (Meteyard et al. 2012); and most probably not so important for nonclinical cognition when the (inter-individual) brain varies little. However, the embodiment of cognition may be a core feature of clinical cognition, making specific predictions about how differences in our brain's affective systems and experiences result in differences in our thinking (Matheson and Barsalou 2018).

In this book, I argue that the process of *embodied simulation* provides a solution for the translation of research from affective neuroscience and experimental psychopathology about our brain, body, and experiences into models of clinical cognition that inform psychological treatment of emotional disorders. Given that both basic research and clinical models of cognition applied to treatment include very different "theoretical dialects," I use a backward-forward translation approach principle (Collins 2011; Wartman 2008). The backwards (reverse) translation (from clinical models to basic research) has the goal to identify the mechanisms from models of existing treatment that can be defined in terms of mechanisms from basic research. Forward translation (from basic research to treatment models) asks how these mechanisms can be described back into the clinical models to inform treatment. Thus, clinical mechanisms that already guide evidence-based interventions may be refined by basic and clinical affective and cognitive research about body, brain, and experience systems involved in emotional disorders.

In this process, I start from the model of cognitive vulnerability to emotional disorders from Rational Emotive Behavior Therapy (REBT), the oldest form cognitive-behavioral therapy (e.g., irrational beliefs; Ellis 1958, 1962). Then, I look for processes from basic research and cognitive and affective neurosciences that correspond to vulnerability factors in REBT. In the end, I use a forward translation process to inform the cognitive model of psychological treatment and existing interventions. As a result, I suggest rigid appraisals (the tendency to demand that situations should be as desired in face of adversities) as a central psychological vulnerability to emotional disorders embodied in adversity-related (hyper) reactivity of mesolimbic dopaminergic system. I advance a model of how rigid motivational appraisals function as embodied cognition and how to guide and improve sound evidence-based psychological treatments.

There are many aspects of psychological treatments that could benefit from the translation of insights about affect and behavior from basic and clinical sciences into the mechanisms underlying the generation and treatment of disturbances of emotions (De Raedt et al. 2010). Specifically, a better understanding of the mechanisms underlying pharmacological and psychological treatments based on embodied cognitive vulnerability could help in two important ways. First, it offers a theory-driven integration of medication and psychological treatments. To this end, I describe how medication may treat embodied rigid appraisals. Second, it contributes to refining intervention strategies. New interventions based on changing memory structures, detachment, and exposure procedures applied to embodied rigid appraisals are described.

1.2 An Overview of the Book

In this book, I introduce embodied rigid motivational appraisals as a vulnerability to emotional disorders. In Chap. 2, I describe non-distorted appraisals from an embodied view. In Chap. 3, I describe the embodiment of distorted appraisals. In Chap. 4, I present an alternative route for the development of distorted appraisals: the stress-related neuroadaptations in the affective and regulatory brain. I discuss how stress exposure results in various neuroadaptations in brain functioning and how verbal embodied cognition becomes a carrier of these neuroadaptations in the understanding of ongoing experiences. In Chap. 5, I review evidence for embodied rigid appraisals. Then, in Chap. 6, I advance a model of embodied rigid appraisals and I describe the processes involved in the development of embodied rigid appraisals. In Chap. 7, I present new psychological interventions targeting embodied rigid motivational appraisals that may optimize existing evidence-based treatments.

Excellent works have described embodied hot (emotional) cognition (e.g., Carr et al. 2018; Niedenthal 2007; Winkielman et al. 2015). However, descriptions of cognitive appraisals from an embodied perspective received less attention.

In Chap. 2, I describe embodied non-distorted hot cognition focusing on appraisals. Embodied appraisals are psychological states that have specific affective, motivational, and behavioral ingredients into their composition. Depending on the specific composition and what is in the frontline of conscious experience, an appraisal may be experienced as a *feeling* (e.g., "I feel I cannot manage my anger"), a cognition (e.g., "I believe I cannot manage my anger"), or behavior (e.g., "I have an urge to avoid rather than manage my anger") (e.g., Barrett 2017). The experience-related content and the neural systems involved in the underlying simulations determine the effect of embodied hot cognition on subsequent behavior and emotion. Based on the *activation level* of underlying affective embodiment, an embodied hot cognition can be inactivated (or disembodied when refer to affective embodiment), partially activated (when the underlying motivational or emotional simulations are strong, the appraisal may be felt cognition such as emotional reasoning; Tiba 2018), or completely/fully activated (emotional cognition is consciously experienced as multicomponent affective responses). Depending on *the type and quality* of thc affective brain systems (which brain systems and their states of functioning) and experiences underlying the emotional simulations, emotional cognition can be non-distorted (based on simulations of non-altered affective states) or distorted/rigid (based on simulations of altered affective states). There are unique types of mechanisms that control emotional simulations involved in embodied appraisals: language, environmental stimuli, body, and brain states. Moreover, embodied appraisals are dynamic psychological states: their embodiment changes as the interaction between the organism and environment changes. For instance, the initial appraisals of the relevance and congruence of a situation will change under the emerging emotional experiences that result from appraising the situation. In turn, the emerging affective states will change the underlying emotional embodiment (Kever et al. 2016; Kuppens et al. 2012). Furthermore, the ongoing cognitive elaboration (e.g., rumination, vivid imagery) will also change the emotional embodiments and the resulting emotional experience. Because by embodying appraisals they are at the same time cognition, feelings, and behavior, various methods may be used for changing appraisals (e.g., emotional, behavioral, and cognitive focused methods). For individuals that have relatively the same level of functioning of the affective brain system (as we see it in emotionally non-affected individuals), the features of the affective brain systems involved in emotional simulations probably do not matter too much. Yet vulnerable and emotionally disordered individuals most probably have marked alterations in neural systems that implement affective experiences and their regulation (e.g., hyper-reactivity of affective brain systems). Thus, in some individuals, the brain systems that implement embodied cognition may show very large differences.

In Chap. 3, I describe how distorted hot cognitions are embodied in motivational and emotional experiences. Hot cognitions are cognitions that result in emotions. To result in emotion, embodied hot cognition should be based on embodied simulations of affective experiences. The characteristics of emotional simulations determine the characteristics of resulting emotional experiences. Disturbed emotions are characterized by high intensity, averseness to emotional experience, lack of control, and attempts to control the emotional experience (Bullis et al. 2019). Furthermore, brain activity during disturbed emotions is characterized by hyperactive affective generation neural systems, hypoactive regulatory brain, and deficient coupling between affective and regulatory systems. Although studies did not investigate features of disturbed emotional experiences into distorted appraisals, several studies suggest that a similar brain pattern of emotional dysregulation observed during disturbed emotional experiences may be observed during distorted appraisals. Exaggerated secondary appraisals (catastrophizing and frustration intolerance) and other types of cognition involved in disturbed negative emotions seem to engage hyper-reactive affective generation and hypoactive regulatory brain areas. All these lines of evidence suggest that embodied distorted cognition is a type of cognition involved in emotional psychopathologies. By considering hyper-reactive emotional embodied simulations as central to embodied distorted emotional cognition, differences that confer distorted quality of emotional simulations depend on whether they engage (besides the other multimodal components) hyper-reactive generative affective brain regions usually associated to deficient recruitment of regulatory brain regions or a shift from an inhibitory mode to an emotional amplification mode (upregulation in individuals with exaggerated perceptions of control over adversities).

Chapter 4 presents advancements related to embodied emotional cognition for cognitive vulnerability to emotional disorders. When cognition is based on embodied representations, the differences in affective brain systems are carried into our understanding of our world biasing cognition and resulting in emotional disturbances. In this chapter I discuss how distorted cognition develops based on stress-related neuroadaptations rather than on learning and negative knowledge mechanisms. Distorted negative cognition has been recognized as core vulnerability to emotional disorders (EDs) both by psychological (Beck and Haigh 2014; David et al. 2010; Everaert et al. 2012; Gotlib and Joormann 2010; Mathews and MacLeod 2005; Ouimet et al. 2009; Watkins 2008) and neuroscience-informed perspectives on vulnerability to EDs (Clark et al. 2009; Foland-Ross and Gotlib 2012; Hales et al. 2014; Harmer et al. 2009; Harmer and Cowen 2013; Roiser et al. 2012).

However, these perspectives are radically different about how they view the development of distorted cognition. In psychological perspectives, distorted cognition stems from learning mechanisms. Accordingly, individuals exposed to high levels of stressful life events accumulate (by learning from experience or social interactions) increased amounts of negative knowledge in semantic and episodic storage systems. Some are prone to accumulate more negative knowledge due to genetic predispositions that makes them more attentive to negative information and thus they build up and store more negative memories. Once dysfunctional knowledge (stored in the semantic system) is activated, it distorts our cognition in new situations resulting in dysregulated emotions (Beck and Haigh 2014). The neuroscience-informed perspectives tell another story. Developmental differences in our genetic and brain functioning (e.g., limbic and prefrontal system) directly bias our attention, distorting our cognition (Roiser et al. 2012). Thus, there are the neurochemical imbalances rather than information-dependent dysfunctional knowledge that result in maladaptive distorted cognition. Dysfunctional knowledge is accumulated after periods of distorted cognition.

While psychological models of cognition have difficulties in integrating brain and affective alterations into distorted cognition, neuroscience-informed models somehow neglect knowledge differences in how people react to stressful life events and how they acquire vulnerabilities after exposure to stress. Explaining how people gain cognitive vulnerabilities after stressful life events by taking into account both neuroadaptations and negative knowledge is important for advancing the understanding and the treatments of EDs. Exposure to stressful events results in both negative knowledge and brain alterations. Although research showed that stress-related altered brain responses (e.g., neural hyper-excitability in affective systems) act as dynamic vulnerabilities that later predispose to disturbed emotional reactions and EDs (Hammen et al. 2000; Monroe and Harkness 2005; Morris et al. 2010; Post 1992), a role which overlaps the role of distorted cognition in EDs, this mechanism has not been yet integrated with negative knowledge and distorted cognition. In Chap. 4, I advance the ideas that: (1) proximal cognitive vulnerabilities to EDs are likely to be embodied in stress-induced neuroadaptations in brain regions mediating emotional generation and regulation (exaggerating the affective and sensory neural representation of negative knowledge) in genetically susceptible individuals, (2) the differences in the simulation of affective stress-induced alterations in negative cognition rather than dysfunctional knowledge underlie “pathological” (i.e., as vulnerability to disorders) biased cognition, and (3) cognition is an important vehicle of carrying these alterations in the construction of emotional experience. Although I highlight stress-related alterations as main sources of dysfunctional neural embodiments underlying distorted cognition in EDs, dysfunctional neural embodiments may arise from other sources such as atypical, age-related (Haller et al. 2014) or gender-specific (Bogdan and Hariri 2012) neurodevelopmental processes, inherited differences, or learning-induced plasticity in modal brain regions.

Nonetheless, the neuroadaptations recruited by central embodied simulations most probably result from the interactions between these multiple mechanisms. In individuals with atypical neurodevelopment trajectories that lead to increased affective reactivity and regulatory dysfunction, these alterations may be further accentuated by age-typical social-affective neurodevelopmental processes (Haller et al. 2014), gender-related differences (Bogdan and Hariri 2012), neurochemical processes (Roiser et al. 2012), or by stress-related plasticity. Learning-induced plasticity may add to that by sculpting regulatory and affective regions. Negative life experiences and maladaptive emotions may further push abnormal neural embodiments to an extreme end of emotional reactivity. Persistent and uncorrected use of emotional linguistic cognitions (e.g., ruminations, worries and negative beliefs, appraisals), memories or perceptions as simulation-control mechanisms may extensively recruit *neuroadaptations as embodiments* in the construction of ongoing experiences disturbing emotions and probably maintaining affective sensitization.

In Chap. 5, I review theoretical and empirical arguments for embodied rigid appraisals (e.g., demandingness). Given the studies reviewed, behavioral and genetic evidence suggests that demandingness, when it acts as vulnerability for emotional disorders, is an embodied type of rigid appraisal that is embodied in adversity-related hyper-reactive responses of dopaminergic motivational states in genetically susceptible individuals. Embodied demandingness is a part of a cognitive/behavioral inflexibility phenotype of rigid active (approach or avoidance) coping implemented by over-reactive mesolimbic states associated with dysregulated emotions, increased salience attribution, compulsivity, and sign tracking. I advance the idea that rigid appraisals, when embodied in disturbed motivation, are core trans-diagnostic processes involved in behavioral and emotional pathologies. The chapter describes studies that support demandingness as embodied rigid appraisals. It is concluded that demandingness may be implemented by different neural systems, the neural system selected to implement rigid appraisals being context-dependent. Rigid appraisals impact emotion and behavior when are implemented by simulations of disturbed motivation. Disturbed motivation is recruited as simulations for rigid thinking based on several biased/dysfunctional top-down (deficient recruitment of prefrontal cortex or excessive upregulation by prefrontal cortex) and bottom-up (context, stress hormones, emotional states, epinephrine, glucocorticoid receptors, etc.) simulation-control mechanisms in vulnerable individuals.

In Chap. 6, I describe a model of the development and the change of embodied rigid appraisals (irrational beliefs/IBs). In this chapter, irrational beliefs are conceptualized as embodied rigid and exaggerated appraisals.

Rigid and exaggerated embodied appraisals are appraisals embodied in dysfunctional motivational and emotional states. Paralleling the ABC model proposed by Ellis (1962), there are two types of embodied rigid appraisals: primary and secondary. Primary rigid appraisals are rigid motivational appraisals embodied in craving/dread experiences (intense dysregulated motivational states). Secondary appraisals result from primary appraisals. There are two types of secondary embodied appraisals. Frustration intolerance is a secondary exaggerated motivational appraisal embodied in states of craving for relief from negative states and situations. Catastrophizing (i.e., awfulizing) is a secondary exaggerated emotional appraisal embodied in states of aversive and dysregulated emotional experiences. Based on the level of action of the embodiment, it is useful to delimitate three states of activation of embodied IBs: (a) inactivated or disembodied IBs (IBs are not embodied in affective systems and states), (b) partially activated embodied appraisals, and (c) fully activated appraisals (IBs are experienced as a complex of believing-emoting-behaving). Partially and fully activated embodied appraisals may be modified by interventions targeting cognitive, biological, behavioral simulation-control mechanisms. Fully activated embodied rigid motivational appraisals are triggered automatically or as episodes resulting from dynamic interaction between cognitive, biological, environmental, and affective factors. Chapter 6 is an illustration of how a "virtuous translation cycle" (e.g., Wartman 2008) between affective neuroscience and clinical models gets into action at a theoretical level. Concepts from the theories of existent treatments relevant for affective neuroscience are located (i.e., the revised ABC model on Ellis believing-emoting-behaving). Then, corresponding concepts from affective neuroscience are found (affect model of craving, incentive salience and hope model, animal models of stress-coping, embodied simulation theories). Based on data from affective neuroscience, the clinical cognitive models that guide psychological treatment are informed and refined. This continuous translation process has benefits both for the clinical models that guide existing treatments and for affective neuroscience. This cycle has at the center an *embodied simulation* model of clinical cognition. Thus, the model of clinical cognition that guides the treatment (IBs) is expanded, new mechanisms that result in clinical cognition being revealed. Affective neuroscience benefits as well. For instance, this translation process suggests that adversity-related hyper-reactivity of mesolimbic dopamine is a neural biomarker of psychological vulnerability to emotional disorders. Refining mechanisms based on translational efforts between clinical cognition and basic research may improve existent psychological treatments. Furthermore, these benefits suggest the advantage of adopting an embodied simulation model of clinical cognition for the cognitive vulnerability to emotional disorders.

1.3 Quo Vadis?

Advancing adversity-related embodied rigid appraisal in affective psychopathology leads to several implications for affective science, basic research of cognitive vulnerability, experimental psychopathology, and treatment research and applications. Adversity-related mesolimbic hyper-reactivity is a neural biomarker proposed as neurocognitive vulnerability to emotional disorders. Affective science research should focus on investigating this neural marker in emotional disorders. Furthermore, several lines of research are opened for the scientific study of rigid appraisals. The embodied simulation model suggests that simulations of cravings are the core of rigid appraisals. There are several directions for research. Which are the most important cognitive determinants of embodied rigid appraisals? The model suggests several cognitive and meta-cognitive factors that result in rigid appraisals. Are there incubation effects (as with craving) for embodied rigid appraisals? If so, what are the processes that moderate the incubation? Which are the most important elaboration processes for embodied rigid appraisals? Do secondary appraisals moderate the effect of primary appraisals on emotions? Research should investigate this in detail. Affective determinants of embodied rigid appraisals are proposed as well. Which are the affective determinants of embodied rigid appraisals? I propose several treatment applications. In Chap. 7, I describe new interventions applied to the change of embodied rigid appraisals. Further research should investigate the best way to deliver these interventions. Although they are new interventions, they are already proven interventions for craving. Moreover, for each intervention I point to clinically proven ways that can be applied based on existing therapy procedures in cognitive behavior treatment. Nonetheless, research should investigate which medication, together with which psychological interventions are appropriate for which type of patients in the treatment of embodied rigid appraisals. Interesting possibilities for the development of precision treatment of emotional disorders are proposed. Would the presence of a quickly assessed neurocognitive marker such as embodied rigid appraisal differentiate between patients that respond to certain medication? Answering these questions may prove the advantage of an embodied simulation model of hot cognitive vulnerabilities and its acceptance in the mainstream theories and treatments of emotional disorders.

References

Barlow, D. H., Sauer-Zavala, S., Carl, J. R., Bullis, J. R., & Ellard, K. K. (2014). The nature, diagnosis, and treatment of neuroticism: Back to the future. *Clinical Psychological Science, 2*(3), 344–365.

Barnard, P. J., & Teasdale, J. D. (1991). Interacting cognitive subsystems: A systemic approach to cognitive-affective interaction and change. *Cognition and Emotion, 5*, 1–39. https://doi.org/10.1080/02699939108411021

Barrett, L. F. (2017). *How emotions are made: The secret life of the brain*. Boston, MA: Houghton Mifflin Harcourt.

Barrett, L. F. (2019). In search of emotions: Review of the neuroscience of emotion by Adolphs and Anderson. *Current Biology, 29*, R1–R3.

Barrett, L. F., & Lindquist, K. A. (2008). The embodiment of emotion. In G. R. Semin & E. R. Smith (Eds.), *Embodied grounding: Social, cognitive, affective, and neuroscientific approaches* (pp. 237–262). Cambridge University Press. https://doi.org/10.1017/CBO9780511805837.011

Barrett, L. F., & Satpute, A. B. (2019). Historical pitfalls and new directions in the neuroscience of emotion. *Neuroscience Letters, 693*, 9–18. https://doi.org/10.1016/j.neulet.2017.07.045

Barsalou, L. W. (1999). Perceptual symbol systems. *Behavioral and Brain Sciences, 22*, 577–609.

Barsalou, L. W. (2008). Grounded cognition. *Annual Review of Psychology, 59*(1), 617–645.

Beck, A. T. (1976). *Cognitive therapy and the emotional disorders*. International Universities Press.

Beck, A. T. (2008). The evolution of the cognitive model of depression and its neurobiological correlates. *American Journal of Psychiatry, 165*, 969–977.

Beck, A. T., & Haigh, E. A. P. (2014). Advances in cognitive theory and therapy: The generic cognitive model. *Annual Review of Clinical Psychology, 10*, 1–24.

Bogdan, R., & Hariri, A. R. (2012). Neural embedding of stress reactivity. *Nature Neuroscience, 15*, 1605–1607.

Bogdan, R., Nikolova, Y. S., & Pizzagalli, D. A. (2013). Neurogenetics of depression: A focus on reward processing and stress sensitivity. *Neurobiology of Disease, 52*, 12–23.

Bogdan, R., Salmeron, B. J., Carey, C. E., Agrawal, A., Calhoun, V. D., Garavan, H., … Goldman, D. (2017). Imaging genetics and genomics in psychiatry: A critical review of Progress and potential. *Biological Psychiatry, 82*(3), 165–175. https://doi.org/10.1016/j.biopsych.2016.12.030

Bullis, J. R., Boettcher, H., Sauer-Zavala, S., & Barlow, D. H. (2019). What is an emotional disorder? A transdiagnostic mechanistic definition with implications for assessment, treatment, and prevention. *Clinical Psychology: Science and Practice*, e12278. https://doi.org/10.1111/cpsp.12278.

Carpenter, J. K., Andrews, L. A., Witcraft, S. M., Powers, M. B., Smits, J. A. J., & Hofmann, S. G. (2018). Cognitive behavioral therapy for anxiety and related disorders: A meta-analysis of randomized placebo-controlled trials. *Depression and Anxiety, 35*, 502–514.

Carr, E. W., Kever, A., & Winkielman, P. (2018). Embodiment of emotion and its situated nature. In A. Newen, L. de Bruin, & S. Gallagher (Eds.), *The Oxford handbook of 4E cognition* (pp. 529–551). Oxford University Press.

Cipriani, A., Furukawa, T. A., Salanti, G., Chaimani, A., Atkinson, L. Z., Ogawa, Y., … Geddes, J. R. (2018). Comparative efficacy and acceptability of 21 antidepressant drugs for the acute treatment of adults with major depressive disorder: A systematic review and network meta-analysis. *Lancet, 391*, 1357–1366.

Clark, A. (2008). *Supersizing the Mind: Embodiment, Action, and Cognitive extension*. Oxford University Press.

Clark, L., Chamberlain, S. R., & Sahakian, B. J. (2009). Neurocognitive mechanisms in depression: Implications for treatment. *Annual Review of Neuroscience, 32*, 57–74.

Collins, F. S. (2011). Reengineering translational science: The time is right. *Science Translational Medicine, 3*(90). https://doi.org/10.1126/scitranslmed.3002747

Cristea, I. A., Gentili, C., Cotet, C. D., Palomba, D., Barbui, C., & Cuijpers, P. (2017). Efficacy of psychotherapies for borderline personality disorder: A systematic review and meta-analysis. *JAMA Psychiatry, 74*, 319–328.

Cuijpers, P., Karyotaki, E., Reijnders, M., & Ebert, D. D. (2019). Was Eysenck right after all? A reassessment of the effects of psychotherapy for adult depression. *Epidemiology and Psychiatric Sciences, 28*, 21–30.

Dalgleish, T., Black, M., Johnston, D., & Bevan, A. (2020). Transdiagnostic approaches to mental health problems: Current status and future directions. *Journal of Consulting and Clinical Psychology, 88*(3), 179–195. https://doi.org/10.1037/ccp0000482

David, D., Lynn, S. J., & Ellis, A. (2010). *Rational and irrational beliefs: Research, theory, and clinical practice*. Oxford University Press.

David, D., Matu, S., Mogoaşe, C., & Voinescu, B. (2016). Integrating cognitive processing, brain activity, molecules and genes to advance evidence-based psychological treatment for depression and anxiety: From cognitive neurogenetics to CBT-based neurogenetics. *Journal of Rational-Emotive & Cognitive-Behavior Therapy, 34*(3), 149–168. https://doi.org/10.1007/s10942-016-0233-3

David, D., & Szentagotai, A. (2006). Cognition in cognitive behavior psychotherapies. *Clinical Psychology Review, 26*, 284–298.

De Raedt, R., Koster, E. H. W., & Joormann, J. (2010). Attentional control in depression: A translational affective neuroscience approach. *Cognitive, Affective, & Behavioral Neuroscience, 10*, 1–7.

Driessen, E., Hollon, S. D., Bockting, C. L., Cuijpers, P., & Turner, E. H. (2015). Does publication bias inflate the apparent efficacy of psychological treatment for major depressive disorder? A systematic review and meta-analysis of US National Institutes of Health-funded trials. *PLoS One, 10*, e0137864.

Ellis, A. (1958). Rational psychotherapy. *The Journal of General Psychology, 59*, 35–49.

Ellis, A. (1962). *Reason and emotion in psychotherapy*. Lyle Stuart.

Everaert, J., Koster, E. H., & Derakshan, N. (2012). The combined cognitive bias hypothesis in depression. *Clinical Psychology Review, 32*, 413–424.

Foa, E. B., & Kozak, M. J. (1986). Emotional processing of fear: Exposure to corrective information. *Psychological Bulletin, 99*, 20–35.

Fodor, J. A. (1975). *The language of thought*. Harvard University Press.

Foland-Ross, L. C., & Gotlib, I. H. (2012). Cognitive and neural aspects of information processing in major depressive disorder: An integrative perspective. *Frontiers in Psychology, 3*, 489. https://doi.org/10.3389/fpsyg.2012.00489

Gallagher, S. (2009). Philosophical antecedents of situated cognition. In P. Robbins & M. Aydede (Eds.), *The Cambridge handbook of situated cognition* (pp. 35–51). Cambridge University Press.

Glenberg, A. (2010). Embodiment as a unifying perspective for psychology. *Wiley Interdisciplinary Reviews: Cognitive Science, 1*(4), 586–596. https://doi.org/10.1002/wcs.55

Gomez, A. F., Barthel, A. L., & Hofmann, S. G. (2018). Comparing the efficacy of benzodiazepines and serotonergic anti-depressants for adults with generalized anxiety disorder: A meta-analytic review. *Expert Opinion on Pharmacotherapy, 19*, 883–894.

Gotlib, I. H., & Joormann, J. (2010). Cognition and depression: Current status and future directions. *Annual Review of Clinical Psychology, 6*, 285–312. https://doi.org/10.1146/annurev.clinpsy.121208.131305

Hales, C. A., Stuart, S. A., Anderson, M. H., & Robinson, E. S. (2014). Modelling cognitive affective biases in major depressive disorder using rodents. *British Journal of Pharmacology, 171*(20), 4524–4538.

Haller, S. P. W., Cohen Kadosh, K., & Lau, J. Y. F. (2014). A developmental angle to understanding the mechanisms of biased cognitions in social anxiety. *Frontiers in Human Neuroscience, 7*, 846. https://doi.org/10.3389/fnhum.2013.00846

Hammen, C., Henry, R., & Daley, S. (2000). Depression and sensitization to stressors among young women as a function of childhood adversity. *Journal of Consulting and Clinical Psychology, 68*, 782–787.

Harmer, C. J., & Cowen, P. J. (2013). It's the way that you look at it'—A cognitive neuropsychological account of SSRI action in depression. *Philosophical Transactions of the Royal Society of London. Series B, Biological Sciences, 368*(1615), 20120407. https://doi.org/10.1098/rstb.2012.0407

Harmer, C. J., O'Sullivan, U., Favaron, E., Massey-Chase, R., Ayres, R., Reinecke, A., … Cowen, P. J. (2009). Effect of acute antidepressant administration on negative affective bias in depressed patients. *American Journal of Psychiatry, 166*, 1178–1184.

Jazaieri, H., Urry, H. L., & Gross, J. J. (2013). Affective disturbance and psychopathology: An emotion regulation perspective. *Journal of Experimental Psychopathology, 4*(584), 599.

Kever, A., Grynberg, D., Bayot, M., & Vermeulen, N. (2016). Embodying emotions: The role of bodily changes in emotional processing: Evidence from normal and psychopathological populations. In Y. Coello & M. H. Fischer (Eds.), *Foundations of embodied cognition: Perceptual and emotional embodiment* (pp. 246–261). Routledge/Taylor & Francis Group.

Kuppens, P., Champagne, D., & Tuerlinckx, F. (2012). The dynamic interplay between appraisal and Core affect in daily life. *Frontiers in Psychology, 3*, 380. https://doi.org/10.3389/fpsyg.2012.00380

Leichsenring, F., Steinert, C., & Ioannidis, J. P. A. (2019). Toward a paradigm shift in treatment and research of mental disorders. *Psychological Medicine, 49*(13), 2111–2117. https://doi.org/10.1017/S0033291719002265

Lieder, F., & Griffiths, T. L. (2019). Resource-rational analysis: Understanding human cognition as the optimal use of limited computational resources. *Behavior Brain Science, 4*, 43:e1. https://doi.org/10.1017/S0140525X1900061X

Liu, H., Li, X., Han, B., & Liu, X. (2017). Effects of cognitive bias modification on social anxiety: A meta-analysis. *PLoS One, 12*, e0175107.

Matheson, H. E., & Barsalou, L. W. (2018). Embodiment and grounding in cognitive neuroscience. In J. Wixted, E. Phelps, L. Davachi, J. Serences, S. Ghetti, S. Thompson-Schill, & E. J. Wagenmakers (Eds.), *The Stevens' handbook of experimental psychology and cognitive neuroscience* (Vol. 3, 4th ed., pp. 1–32). Wiley.

Mathews, A., & MacLeod, C. (2005). Cognitive vulnerability to emotional disorders. *Annual Review of Clinical Psychology, 1*, 167–195.

Meteyard, L., Cuadrado, S. R., Bahrami, B., & Vigliocco, G. (2012). Coming of age: A review of embodiment and the neuroscience of semantics. *Cortex, 48*(7), 788–804. https://doi.org/10.1016/j.cortex.2010.11.002

Monroe, S. M., & Harkness, K. L. (2005). Life stress, the "kindling" hypothesis, and the recurrence of depression: Considerations from a life stress perspective. *Psychological Review, 112*, 417–445.

Morris, M. C., Ciesla, J. A., & Garber, J. (2010). A prospective study of stress autonomy versus stress sensitization in adolescents at varied risk for depression. *Journal of Abnormal Psychology, 119*(2), 341–354. https://doi.org/10.1037/a0019036

Niedenthal, P. M. (2007). Embodying emotion. *Science, 316*, 1002–1005.

Ouimet, A. J., Gawronski, B., & Dozois, D. J. A. (2009). Cognitive vulnerability to anxiety: A review and an integrative model. *Clinical Psychology Review, 29*, 459–470.

Patel, V., Saxena, S., Lund, C., Thornicroft, G., Baingana, F., Bolton, P., … UnÜtzer, J. (2018). The lancet commission on global mintal health and sustainable development. *Lancet, 392*, 1553–1598.

Post, R. M. (1992). Transduction of psychosocial stress into the neurobiology of recurrent affective disorder. *American Journal of Psychiatry, 149*, 999–1010.

Roiser, J. P., Elliott, R., & Sahakian, B. J. (2012). Cognitive mechanisms of treatment in depression. *Neuropsychopharmacology, 37*, 117–136.

Swartz, J. R., Knodt, A. R., Radtke, S. R., & Hariri, A. R. (2015). A neural biomarker of psychological vulnerability to future life stress. *Neuron, 85*(3), 505–511. https://doi.org/10.1016/j.neuron.2014.12.055

Tiba, A. I. (2018). Feelings-as-embodied information: Studying the role of feelings as images in emotional disorders. *Frontiers in Psychology, 9*, 186. https://doi.org/10.3389/fpsyg.2018.00186

Varela, F., Thompson, E., & Rosch, E. (1991). *The embodied mind: Cognitive science and human experience*. MIT Press.

Wartman, S. A. (2008). Toward a virtuous cycle: The changing face of academic health centers. *Academic Medicine, 83*(9), 797–799. https://doi.org/10.1097/ACM.0b013e318181cf8c

Watkins, E. R. (2008). Constructive and unconstructive repetitive thought. *Psychological Bulletin, 134*(2), 163–206. https://doi.org/10.1037/0033-2909.134.2.163

Winkielman, P., Niedenthal, P., Wielgosz, J., Eelen, J., & Kavanagh, L. C. (2015). Embodiment of cognition and emotion. In M. Mikulincer, P. R. Shaver, E. Borgida, & J. A. Bargh (Eds.), *APA handbooks in psychology®. APA handbook of personality and social psychology, Vol. 1. Attitudes and social cognition* (pp. 151–175). American Psychological Association. https://doi.org/10.1037/14341-004

World Health Organization [WHO]. (2012). *Depression: A global public health concern*. World Health Organization. Retrieved from http://www.who.int/mental_health/management/depression/who_paper_depression_wfmh_2012.pdf

Wyer, R. S., Clore, G. L., & Isbell, L. (1999). Affect and information processing. In M. Zanna (Ed.), *Advances in experimental social psychology* (pp. 1–77). Academic Press.

Chapter 2
Embodying Hot Cognition

2.1 What Is Hot Cognition?

In 1958, Abelson and Rosenberg proposed the term *hot cognition* to refer to cognition influenced by emotion (Abelson and Rosenberg 1958). Although there are many conceptualizations of this distinction (e.g., Roiser and Sahakian 2013), the most influential understanding of hot cognition conceptualizes hot cognition as cognition related to emotions (David and David 2017). According to this distinction, hot cognition refers to cognitive processes that result in emotion (e.g., appraising something as being bad for me). Cold cognition refers to knowing, cognitive processes, or knowledge that do not result directly in emotion (e.g., *I lost money*) (Ellis et al. 2010; David et al. 2010; David and David 2017; David and Matu 2017; David and Szentagotai 2006). There are many types of cognition that result in emotion (from perception to learning and understanding). In this book, I focus on cognition relevant to psychotherapy. Much effort in psychotherapy is directed at verbally changing how individuals think or interpret external and internal negative situations relevant to their personal goals. Thus, I will discuss emotional knowledge in terms of thinking of emotional situations and personal significance of encounters. In this chapter, I begin by defining hot cognition. Second, I contrast the embodied simulation theory with theories that are based on a propositional nature of emotional knowledge. Third, I move on to a detailed description of research on embodied simulation in emotional thinking, emotional language comprehension, and the interaction between language and embodied simulation. Finally, I discuss the implications of embodied simulation for hot thinking.

A. Tiba, *Embodied Hot Cognitive Vulnerability to Emotional Disorders*,
https://doi.org/10.1007/978-3-030-53989-4_2

2.2 Why Is Hot Cognition Important for Psychotherapy?

Psychotherapy is known as "talk therapy." A person in need (the client) talks to a therapist. The therapist talks back to the client to help him sort out and solve his psychological problems. For "gold standard" psychotherapies (cognitive behavior psychotherapies/CBT), self-talk is a fundamental pillar. Most of the CBT treatment is about helping clients change their negative self-talk, which is the self-talk that results in exaggerated negative emotions. Verbal disputation methods of rigid and exaggerated hot thinking are the core methods used in CBT (Ellis et al. 2010). Given this, if we want to optimize existing psychological treatments, then insights about (a) how hot negative thinking or self-talk results in emotions and (b) how using language shapes our emotional thinking and emotional consequences (verbal disputation) are important. Traditional theories of cognition-emotion interaction applied to psychological treatment consider that emotional cognition automatically determines emotion (Winkielman et al. 2015). There is little space between emotional cognition and emotion. Yet the embodied theories suggest that there are important processes that intervene in the interaction between verbal emotional cognition and emotion (e.g., situated simulations). Because many psychotherapies aim to verbally change hot self-talk, a better understanding of cognition-emotion interaction would help extant treatments of emotional disorders.

2.3 Disembodied and Embodied Theories of Hot Cognition

2.3.1 Disembodied Theories of Hot Cognition

In the traditional approach to cognition, emotional cognition is represented by amodal symbols (Niedenthal 2007; Winkielman et al. 2015; Wyer et al. 1999). Emotional experiences (sensations, actions, physiological responses, and so forth) are described in the cognitive system by using symbolic language independent from the underlying experience (i.e., described amodally). Then, they are stored in the semantic system (e.g., network models; Bower 1981) in this new representational format. When a negative situation is encountered (including negative mood), those representations are activated from semantic memory either as emotional schemas (Bower 1981; Lang 1979) or appraisals (e.g., Lazarus 1991). Emotional schemas and appraisals interact with affective, autonomic, somatic, and/or behavioral systems and generate the corresponding emotional responses (Barsalou 2008). Traditional theories of cognition generally assume that knowledge resides in a modular semantic system separate from modality-specific systems for perception, action, and emotion (Barsalou 2008). These theories further assume that conceptual representations are amodal (unlike representations in modality-specific systems) and operate according to different principles (Barsalou 2008). Although amodal theories differ widely in form, they share a common underlying assumption: the transduction principle

(Barsalou 2008). The transduction principle underlies the theories of knowledge that have dominated cognitive science since the cognitive revolution, including semantic networks, feature lists, frames, schemata, and predicate calculus (Barsalou and Hale 1993). The transduction principle refers to the idea that life experiences emerge into internal cognitive structures that further impact on behaviors independently from the processes of the experiences involved in their formation.

For example, the experience of encountering an aggressive person produces a neural pattern in the brain modal processing areas such as visual, auditory, somatic, and interoceptive areas. It produces visual representations in the brain's visual systems for perceived face and body gestures. The voice produces auditory representations in the brain's auditory areas. Internal sensations to the voice produce representations in the brain's affective systems, such as insula. Other internal states might also arise while facing the aggressive person, which similarly utilize representations in the respective modality-specific systems, such as avoidance being represented in the systems that process motivation. As this example illustrates, a given experience produces a complex multimodal representation distributed across the brain's modality-specific systems. As this example further illustrates, some of these states represent the external world (vision, movement, touch, audition), whereas others represent the agent's internal states (emotion, motivation) (Barsalou et al. 2003). Once states in the brain's modality-specific systems are produced by experience, amodal symbols are transduced from this experience to describe it in knowledge. In other words, we develop internal cognitive structures or knowledge such as beliefs about aggressive individuals and our reactions to aggressive individuals that are stored in a semantic memory system. Later, when activated, they guide our inferences, behavior, and emotions. In all of these standard theories, amodal symbols transduced from modality-specific representations are assumed to represent the properties, relations, and concepts that constitute knowledge. Even more recent, relatively radical approaches, such as exemplar and connectionism theories, often assume the transduction principle as well (Barsalou et al. 2003). From a disembodied view, hot cognition and appraisals are represented by propositions (a thought-like language; Fodor 1975) that describe their content and which are stored in a semantic memory system.

2.3.2 *Embodied Theories of Hot Cognition*

Embodied theories of cognition refer to a group of theories centered on the idea that our cognition is body-based and reflects the way our bodies are built and used (Wilson 2002). Embodied cognition theories are very divergent, ranging from functionalism models such as the radical embodiment in which the term cognition dissipates (e.g., Chemero 2009) to structuralist symbolic approaches such as the perceptual symbol theory (i.e., grounded cognition; Barsalou 1999). However, many of the embodied accounts converge on the very basic idea that partial re-enactments or simulations of body and brain states (embodied simulations) and body-environment interactions corresponding to the modal referents have the power to realize the cognitive computations of those referents. In this book, I focus on the "re-enactment or simulation" principle of embodied theories. I choose the concept of embodied simulations (Kavanagh et al. 2012; Vermeulen et al. 2007; Winkielman et al. 2008, 2015) because I analyze (1) how distorted emotional cognition predisposes people to emotional disorders being embodied in altered affective brain systems and (2) how simulations of altered brain states bring alterations in the construction of our emotional experiences. I argue that differences or alterations in our brain are of special importance for distorted types of emotional cognition acting as vulnerabilities for disturbed emotions. Moreover, I focus on central neural mechanisms of embodied simulations such as simulations of neural states corresponding to emotional experiences represented in emotional cognition. I highlight distorted neural embodiments as of importance for the mechanisms of vulnerability to disturbed emotions (i.e., central embodiment). Nonetheless, the embodied simulation account of distorted emotional cognition may have a different focus. It may focus on how differences in peripheral states of the body involved in cognition (peripheral embodiment processes such as facial expressions, cardiac rate, macrocytes release, and so forth) may contribute to emotional disorders. Also it may deal with how differences in specific modal experiences (e.g., intense negative emotions; metaphoric use of basic sensorimotor experiences, physical disgust or pain) or actions (approach-avoidance) that constitute embodiments result in disturbed emotions. Instead, I focus on neural states of negative emotional experiences used for representational purposes and I refer to them as neural embodiments of emotional cognition. By doing so, we can underline important processes revealed during disturbances of emotional experiences (stress sensitization) into concepts of cognitive vulnerability. Moreover, we can bridge data from affective science research to the field of cognitive vulnerability to emotional disorders. Other types of representations, besides embodied simulations, may be required to cover extensively all the forms of linguistic and cognitive processing (Andrews et al. 2014). Similarly, other types of simulation grounding (e.g., environment) may be important for cognition (e.g., Barsalou 2008). Yet I suggest that emotional embodied simulations are essentially required for representing emotional meanings in the context of the meaning-directed generation of emotional experiences (near-experience meanings).

The embodied simulation account tells a different story about cognition than the disembodied account. In the embodied simulation approach to cognition, emotional cognition is represented by modal symbols (Niedenthal et al. 2009, 2005b; Vermeulen et al. 2007; Winkielman et al. 2008, 2015). Embodied cognition is not transduced from experience. It is represented by partial re-instantiations of the neural states that were active during the experience reflected in the cognitive content (i.e., embodied simulations; Niedenthal 2007). Emotional cognition is a partial re-instantiation of the neural states that were active during emotional experiences. Thus, emotional cognition is part emotion (Niedenthal 2007). Motivational cognition is part motivation (Papies and Barsalou 2015). From a developmental stance, neural states (repeated or the subject of selective attention) that were active during emotional experiences in sensorial, interoceptive, motor areas, introspection, regulatory and defense circuits are captured into simulators (perceptual symbols) and stored in memory (Barsalou 2008). When we experience the (inside and outside) world, states in modal processing systems are captured during the experience, stored in memory in forms of interconnected perceptual (i.e., modal) symbols, and later are re-enacted to represent that experience (Barsalou 1999). Repeated experience or focus of attention in different modalities leads to the formation of perceptual symbols such as visual, auditory, affective, introspective, and motor symbols. A perceptual symbol is the memory of the neural states that arise in a modality during the perception of a part of a complex situation (Barsalou 2008). Multiple perceptual symbols, for all the modalities involved in an experience, became integrated into an interconnected pattern of modal symbols in the form of a simulator. Simulators are interconnected perceptual symbols (i.e., visual, auditory, introspective, motor) that represent complex experiences (Barsalou 1999). They are a kind of modal schema. Representation of complex multimodal experiences requires the activation of a simulator. Although modal theories differ widely (Barsalou 2008), they share a common underlying assumption: the simulation principle. The reactivation of perceptual simulators (linked to other simulations such as entrenched and situated conceptualizations) results in partial simulations of neural states from the circuits directly involved in experience (Barsalou 2003, 2008).

Suppose you have an abusive parent who hits you. When you see or hear her/him, various neural patterns change in different parts of your brain: in the visual areas, as you see your parent and their facial expressions; in temporal areas, as you hear the sound of their voice; in the motor areas, as you act; in the anterior insula, the sensations of your body at that moment; in the limbic circuits, such as the amygdala centered circuits, as you assess it is important; in the striatum circuits, as you assess how important it is to avoid being hit; in the hippocampus, as you perceive the context details and the relations between objects; in the periaqueductal nucleus' circuits as your brain activates defense reactions; and in different parts of the prefrontal cortex as you evaluate its importance for your goals, label your states or regulate your emotions and you start to label your states and so forth. A situated neural pattern of activation emerges. Unique fear experiences may arise in other situations not related to your abusive parent. Specific neural patterns repeated across emotional experiences from the fear category or in the focus of attention are captured in memory in the form of emotional simulators for fear. Such simulators exist for different emotions such as fear, anger, sadness, and happiness but also for "within" emotional categories such as depression, anxiety, worry, irritation, guilt, and remorse depending on their composition (i.e., defense circuits, behavioral adaptations, language and knowledge, regulatory recruitment, and so forth) (Barrett et al. 2014). Later, when thinking of the emotional situation (i.e., remembering the parent, evaluating how bad was being hit and so forth) the relevant components of the emotional simulator are partially reactivated in the same circuits as those were experienced (depending on the context such as the task or the concomitant processing) and fuse with ongoing core sensations. What a person feels in that situation is the internal sensations shaped by the partial re-instantiation of past feelings in similar situations constrained by context. For example, recognizing internal sensations in a situation as fear (by activating a fear simulator), a fear experience will emerge into consciousness, or recognizing internal sensations as anger will cause anger experience by re-instantiation of the states in the neural circuits involved in the corresponding experience. The embodied simulation account highlights a basic ground of our experience: meanings are central for the embodied construction of experience (e.g., situated conceptualizations, Barrett et al. 2014) and at least the experience-near meanings are in the form of embodied situated simulations. Moreover, the focus on meanings in the construction of our experience is the common ground that makes the embodied perspective of importance for cognitive behavior therapies.

2.4 From Theories of Cognition to Types of Cognition

Although disembodied and embodied views of cognition have been followed by a long-lasting debate about cognition, they revealed that cognition can be based on multiple representational formats (or codes) and that the use of these codes is dynamic and context-dependent. Both traditional (Leventhal and Scherer 1987; Moors et al. 2013) and embodied theories (Barsalou 2013) agree that multiple representational codes can be used in the representation. They also agree that these codes are used in a context-dependent fashion (Niedenthal et al. 2009). In some contexts, different codes can come in the forefront and influence the expression and experience of cognition and emotion. One of these contexts, as I propose, is emotional sensitivity. Some individuals are characterized by biological makeups (e.g., general biological vulnerabilities) that favor quickly triggered, intense, and long-lasting negative emotions (e.g., neuroticism; Barlow et al. 2014). These individual differences may predispose vulnerable individuals to use more often embodied codes for appraisals and emotional sources for thinking than individuals without these vulnerabilities. In special conditions, these vulnerabilities may transform in pathologies. From this standpoint, embodied appraisal, in the context of vulnerability to emotional disorders, is a type of appraisal (embodied appraisal) which can characterize cognition in individuals with general biological vulnerabilities to emotional disorders. When these cognitions are targets of cognitive restructuring, the mechanisms that underlie cognition are again of importance. Embodied appraisals point to mechanisms that underlie cognition and suggest pathways for change. We can make elegant integration of this idea by using David Marr's computational model. According to David Marr's (1982) model, cognition can be understood at three distinct and complementary levels: (a) a computational level, which comprises the task and the goals; (b) an algorithmic level, which carries out the computation and involves the representation of the input, the output, and the transformation of the input into output; and (c) an implementation level, which realize the representation and algorithms. Theoretical developments have proposed embodiment as a context that may specify the interconnection between levels (Marshall 2014; Overton and Lerner 2012). Thus, the embodiment may be analyzed as a code at the algorithmic levels. Moreover, the embodied view suggests (different from Marr) that the levels are not independent. Changes at the implementation level can result in changes at the algorithmic level. In emotional regulation, the integration of biological and learning methods for regulating emotions based on Marr's multilevel model can provide clues about mechanisms of cognition and emotion.

2.5 Empirical Support for Embodied Hot Cognition

In the following section, I review studies that support the idea that thinking affects emotions depending on the context-related embodied simulations recruited by the appraisal of situations. Moreover, several studies showed that our thinking can recruit particular neural embodiments in the understanding of emotional situations depending on the external or internal context. In some situations, thinking recruits emotion generation neural resources in representation. In other situations, the same thinking recruits nonemotional-related brain resources such as visual resources for representation (Oosterwijk et al. 2010, 2017; Oosterwijk and Barrett 2014; Niedenthal et al. 2009). In the context of the treatment of disturbed emotions, finding individual and contextual differences that selectively recruit in representation neural resources of affective or non-affective brain is of importance. When thinking about the possibility of *being fired*, focusing on the emotional features of the situation (e.g., how I will feel) may direct the recruitment of brain resources related to emotion generation in thinking and maintain a prolonged emotional response. This may be counterproductive and is a process that maintains emotional disorders (sustained activation of emotional simulations in thinking). Thinking of the same situation in a different context (from a third perspective) may direct the simulations in nonemotional brain regions. Concerning the maintenance of an emotional response, the problem becomes not the content of thinking but the embodied simulations recruited to understand the situations during thinking. Not a specific context of thinking, but a context of thinking that promotes unhelpful embodied simulations in understanding. In the traditional amodal perspective, the implementation basis of cognition is fixed in a semantic or episodic memory system. In the embodied simulation account of cognition, the implementation of cognition by our brain is dynamic, flexible, and context-dependent. We cannot find a unique implementation basis of thinking. Yet we can find different ways of implementation of thinking, some of which are detrimental for emotional control and can contribute to emotional disorders.

2.5.1 Emotional Thinking Affects Emotions Depending on Emotional Embodiments

To test the idea that emotional embodiments are considered responsible for the impact of thinking on emotion, Oosterwijk and colleagues investigated whether threat thinking is represented by simulations of negative emotions and whether these simulations explain the effect of threat thinking on subsequent fear reactions to negative stimuli. They asked participants to unscramble fear sentences in a scrambled sentence task by determining which word does not belong to the presented sentence (e.g., "*Bite poisonous is the death*") and monitored the electrodermal and corrugator muscle activity as embodiments of the presented sentences (Oosterwijk et al. 2010). They found a higher electrodermal response and corrugator muscle activity for the fear sentences which occurred in the absence of subjective fear experience. After concept activation, they presented participants with negative and neutral pictures in combination with startling sounds and measured electrodermal and startle response. The results showed that the level of emotional embodiment during the fear concepts task mediates the magnitude of emotional response when viewing negative pictures later. In other words, fear sentences are embodied by partial emotional activations responsible for their effect on negative emotions (Oosterwijk et al. 2010). While the replication of this study in different emotional domains and types of thinking is required, other sources of evidence reinforce the idea that the meaning of both emotional words and emotional linguistic expressions is represented by emotional embodiments (Havas et al. 2007, 2010; Oosterwijk et al. 2010; Niedenthal et al. 2009; for a review, see Niedenthal 2007).

2.5.2 Embodied Emotional Simulations Are Recruited in Emotion Understanding

Emotional simulations may be used in our understanding, but they are not necessarily required to our emotional understanding. Previous studies showed that emotional simulations are recruited only when the task requires so.

In a series of four experiments, Niedenthal et al. (2009) found direct support that emotional knowledge is represented by simulations in sensory-motor and affective systems, that simulations are causal in representations, and that simulations are situated. In the fourth experiment presented by Niedenthal et al. (2009), participants performed a property generation task in which they listed the features of joy, anger, and other abstract mental concepts. Participants were to convey this conceptual content either to a "hot" audience that was informal and more interested in bodily aspects of emotion or to a "cold" audience that was formal and more interested in the lexical aspects of emotion. They recorded activity of muscles related to smiling and frowning as an indicator of embodied simulation. Niedenthal et al. observed that those participants who considered the "hot" audience engaged in more facial activity and embodied positive emotions (i.e., smiled) when generating positively valenced properties of concepts, as compared with individuals who considered the "cold" audience. The same result was observed when participants were asked to judge emotional concepts in an emotional decision task (to decide whether an emotional word—ANGER—is emotional or not) compared to the condition when the participants were asked to judge the emotional concepts in a lexical decision task (to decide whether an emotional word—ANGER—is a word or not) (Niedenthal et al. 2009).

Taken together, these demonstrations support a situated simulation view of cognition in which the current (social or other) context influences how a concept is represented in a conceptual task and the extent of which individuals recruit embodied information to solve it (Niedenthal et al. 2009). Subsequent studies have supported these findings by different research methodology. For instance, Wilson-Mendenhall et al. (2014), using functional magnetic resonance imaging (fMRI), measured the pattern of brain response of fear during unique situations. They found that the neural pattern for the same emotion is situation-specific, supporting a situated conceptualization for emotional cognition. The results suggest that emotional knowledge is represented by situated conceptualizations.

Oosterwijk et al. (2011) used a switch cost paradigm to test the embodied hypothesis of emotional cognition. They presented participants sentences describing emotional and nonemotional mental states while manipulating their "internal" (including sensations and introspection) or "external" (including expressions and action). Participants were asked to judge sentence sensibility by pressing (m) for "sensible" sentences or the (z) key for "nonsensible" sentences. The sentences were presented in pairs so that an internal focus sentence can be presented after an external focus sentence or an internal focus sentence. Results showed that participants require longer reaction times when they shift between emotional sentences with an internal and with an external focus. Yet, this study says nothing about whether the brain resources required for representation can differ between the internal and external conditions.

To investigate this problem, Oosterwijk et al. (2015) used an fMRI design during the emotional switch cost paradigm. In this study, Oosterwijk et al. (2015) used a neuroimaging method to investigate whether processing concepts about our emotional and nonemotional mental states recruits neural regions associated with different aspects of experience depending on the context in which people understand a concept. Again, they presented participants sentences describing emotional and nonemotional mental states with an internal and external focus and asked them to judge whether or not the sentence described a mental state. The results showed that the ventromedial prefrontal cortex, a region associated with the generation of internal states, was engaged more by internal emotion sentences than external sentence categories. This study suggests that emotional cognition is represented using context-dependent interoceptive and sensorimotor resources (Oosterwijk et al. 2015).

In another fMRI study, Oosterwijk et al. (2017) presented participants images of emotional scenes (a woman shouting at a man) and asked them to identify actions that tell the person's emotional state (i.e., "How does this person express his/her emotions?"), the interoceptive sensations that the person could experience (i.e.,

"What does this person feel in his/her body"), and the reasons for the person's emotional state (i.e., "Why does this person feel an emotion?"). At a week distance they instructed the subjects to imagine performing or experiencing actions (e.g., pushing someone away), interoceptive sensations (e.g., "being out of breath"; "an increased heart rate"), or situations (e.g., "alone in a park at night"). Results showed that thinking of specific experiences recruits neural resources involved in those experiences. Moreover, the authors could decode based on the activated brain pattern during the self-focused task whether subjects were focused on emotional actions, interoceptive sensations, or situations of others in other focused tasks.

2.5.3 Embodied Simulations Direct Our Understanding of Emotional Situations

The idea that language directs our simulations during the understanding of ongoing situations is backed up by consistent support (Carr et al. 2018). Yet the link is bidirectional. The characteristics of our embodiments also influence our understanding of the situations. I will discuss this reciprocity of interaction. Although several studies show the effect of manipulating peripheral embodiments on understanding (Carr et al. 2018), in this book I focus on the central embodiment of emotional knowledge.

To test whether emotional cognition requires simulations of bodily emotional states relevant to the cognition, Kever and her collaborators used an attentional blink task. Participants were asked to detect and report high arousal and low arousal target words among a series of nonword distracters in two conditions: after a cycling session (increased arousal) and after a relaxation session (reduced arousal). Results showed that increased physiological arousal improved the reports of high arousal words, whereas reduced physiological arousal improved the reports of low arousal words (Kever et al. 2016). These findings point to a grounding of emotional cognition in our bodily systems of arousal. In other words, changes in the affective embodiment influence our emotional thinking and our interaction with the environment.

Other studies have investigated whether interfering with the emotional embodiment also interferes with our emotional understanding. These studies are of importance for cognitive restructuring. When simulations are assumed as a cause of emotional responses and they include emotional brain resources, the necessity of controlling emotional responses accentuates the importance of evidencing methods that direct simulations in nonemotional areas. Different methods of controlling simulations can be delineated. Yet behavioral-based methods are the most accessible ones in psychotherapy.

Havas and his colleagues carried out a series of experiments in which they interfered with peripheral embodiments (facial muscles) during language comprehension of emotional situations. These studies did not look at how blocking emotional simulations by interventions targeting peripheral simulation controls changes the emotional effect of emotional thinking. However, they are important in showing that simulation-targeted interventions can impact emotional understanding (Havas et al. 2007, 2010).

Havas et al. (2007) have investigated whether blocking emotional simulations by targeting peripheral controls (blocking facial expression for positive or negative emotions) interferes with emotional cognition. In a seminal study, the authors instructed participants to hold a pen in the mouth using just the teeth or just the lips and asked to judge the valence of various sentences by indicating whether they are "pleasant" or "unpleasant." Results showed that participants judged sentences faster when facial posture and sentence valence match than when they mismatch. The authors replicated the results using a different method for blocking the emotional simulations: temporarily paralyzing the facial muscles used in frowning by the administration of subcutaneous injections of botulinum toxin-A (BTX) (Havas et al. 2010). Similarly to their 2007 study (Havas et al. 2007), emotional sentences were presented (for angry sentences "The workload from your pompous professor is unreasonable."). Instead of judging the pleasantness of each sentence, participants were instructed to read the sentence and then they were asked whether they comprehended the sentence. They found that reading of sentences that described situations that recruit the paralyzed muscle for expressing the emotions evoked by the sentences was slowed (Havas et al. 2010).

To investigate how blocking peripheral facial expressions affects the brain's real-time response to emotional cognition, Davis et al. (2015) used an event-related potential (ERP) methodology. Participants were asked to read sentences about positive and negative events (e.g., "She reached inside the pocket of her coat from last winter and found some (cash/bugs) inside it.") while ERPs were recorded and smile-specific facial expressions were blocked (participants in the study held chopsticks in their mouths using a position that either allowed or blocked smiling). Results showed that the embodiment affects especially the aspects of high-level comprehension of the last words of sentences.

These studies suggest that emotional cognition (most often linguistic) impacts emotion when it recruits simulations that include emotional brain resources (e.g., interoception). Changing embodied simulations in a direction that does not recruit neural resources involved in emotional experiences results in reduced emotional impact of linguistic cognition. There are many methods to control simulations such as peripheral (body-based methods), brain-based methods (medication, activity-dependent hormonal release), memory-based, behavioral, experience-based, and so on. Probably the most relevant methods to control simulations are based on linguistic symbols. Psychological treatments, specifically cognitive behavior therapies (CBT), are based on changing the "inner voice" during a challenging situation. In the following section, I discuss evidence that supports the linguistic control over embodied simulations.

2.6 Language Is Essential in Controlling the Embodied Emotional Simulations

There are several excellent reviews of the role of language in constituting emotional embodied simulations. In a recent review, Lindquist et al. (2015) layout two main roles of language concerning embodied simulations: (a) it drives the storage and the composition of embodied simulations in memories (simulators and situated conceptualizations) and (b) it directs the composition of online emotional simulations. Language determines how we acquire, organize, and use embodied simulations to conceptualize situations and build our experiences. Because language is intrinsically linked with concepts, language has a special role in determining our understanding of emotional experiences.

Recent experiments show that using linguistic instructions describing different aspects of emotional experiences results in the unique recruitment of embodied simulation of visual experiences or interoceptive experiences (imagining your heart pounding during a roller coaster ride) (Wilson-Mendenhall et al. 2013a, b, 2011, 2019). When participants were instructed by very detailed verbal descriptions of what to imagine, the corresponding simulation in visual, auditory, or interoceptive neural systems was engaged. These experiments conclude that changing the linguistic description of the situation we encounter and of our experiences may change which neural systems are engaged in the understanding of our experience in the situation.

This idea is supported also by research showing that simulations induced by verbal labels of emotions influence more than emotions. They influence perception and memory of emotional faces (Halberstadt et al. 2009; Roberson et al. 2007; for review, see Barrett et al. 2007). Direct experimental evidence for the language-as-context hypothesis comes from studies that manipulate language and look at the effects on emotion perception (for a review see Barrett et al. 2007; Lindquist and Gendron 2013). Gendron et al. (2012) demonstrated that perceptual priming of emotional faces (e.g., a scowling face) was disrupted when the accessibility of a relevant emotion word (e.g., "anger") was temporarily reduced. Thus, they showed that the same face was encoded differently when a word was accessible versus when it was not (Gendron et al. 2012). Roberson and Davidoff (2000) found that verbalizing words disrupts the ability to make correct perceptual judgments about faces, presumably because it interferes with access to judgment necessary language. Furthermore, Lindquist et al. (2006) showed that a temporary reduction in the accessibility of an emotion word's meaning using semantic satiation procedure leads to slower and less accurate perceptions of emotion, even when participants are not required to verbally label the target faces (Lindquist et al. 2006).

2.6.1 Emotional Embodied Simulations Are Shaped by Verbal Processes

The importance of verbal processes refers to the idea that cognition is the result of the interaction between verbal symbols and partial re-enactments of experience. In the modal model of cognition, verbal processes are determining cognition by compositional control over underlying simulations. Specifically, the online verbal processes activate, determine, and compose partial simulations of multimodal experiences corresponding to verbal symbols. For example, when saying "*love is awful*" the verbal processes determine partial activations of love-related experiences and awful-related experiences. These partial activations bias the current processing of experience.

The proposal that verbal beliefs shape simulations of prior emotional states in emotional brain circuits is supported by several lines of research. An important line of support comes from neuroscience and emotional regulation research (i.e., research lines in emotional regulation and top-down generation of emotional reactions; Ochsner and Gross 2007) that investigate the effect of verbal instructions and beliefs on emotional brain response. Another line of support comes from social and cognitive psychology research reviewed by Niedenthal et al. (2005a, b). For example, studies have shown modulation of "affective brain" by verbal beliefs or expectations of the cortical systems involved in sensory and affective responses regarding pain (Porro et al. 2002); by looking at aversive images or thinking about neutral images in negative ways (Ochsner and Gross 2004); or by expectations of electrical shocks (Phelps et al. 2001). Moreover, understanding emotional verbal sentences were faster when participants had to simulate a congruent emotional state during reading compared with the situation when they had to simulate an incongruent emotional state (Havas et al. 2007). These studies have shown that during verbal instructions about emotional experiences, partial activations are engaged differentially in the same affective brain areas that are involved during the generation of emotions.

2.6.2 Verbal Beliefs Determine the Partial Simulations: Specificity

The idea that generated simulations are specified by the content of verbal beliefs is supported by neuroscience research that has investigated the selective effect of verbal labels and instructions on different brain activations during the processing of primary reinforcers such as odors, flavor, taste, and touch (de Araujo et al. 2005; Grabenhorst et al. 2008; Grabenhorst and Rolls 2008; McCabe et al. 2008; Rolls et al. 2008).

As I discussed in the beginning of the chapter, psychotherapy is known as "talk therapy." Thus, most therapy efforts focus mainly on altering the content of verbal statements used by people when they encounter activating events. Showing that the specific content of verbal statements used by people uniquely alters their brain response involved in processing experiences referred to by those verbal statements is one of the most powerful arguments for the idea that meaning is represented in specific modalities. This is true even for activating events in forms of primary reinforcers like taste or olfaction. Moreover, modality-specific processing depends on the simulations directed by the specific content of verbal statements. Also, it provides ideas about how different verbal beliefs affect brain response dependent on their content. Considering the distinction between interpretative and evaluative beliefs, one conclusion is that the meaning of interpretative beliefs is represented by simulations in sensorimotor systems and affects perceptual and motor brain processing and that the meaning of evaluative beliefs is represented by simulations in brain's affective and introspection-related systems and affects emotional processing in response to activating events. What you say or what you pay attention to when you smell or taste is decisive for what your brain actually smells, tastes, and feels. More exactly, it is decisive for what your brain is letting you know what you smell, taste, and feel while doing that.

Original studies have shown directly (Grabenhorst and Rolls 2008; Rolls et al. 2008) or indirectly (de Araujo et al. 2005; Grabenhorst et al. 2008) that linguistic context of processing, as verbal labels or instructions, biases the activation of the brain regions engaged in processing different types of sensory stimuli in a content-specific fashion. These findings are consistent with the proposal that specific simulations produced in brain circuits (as observed by the increase in fMRI activations) are dependent on specific verbal instructions or contents. Also, in support of this idea, it has been observed that content-specific top-down attentional effects in vision bias the processing of particular locations or particular objects (Rolls 2008). The dependency of the bias of brain regions engaged in processing a sensory stimulus on whether the cognitive demand is for affect-related or for more sensory-related processing may apply to several sensory modalities (Grabenhorst and Rolls 2008).

2.6.3 The Effect of Verbal Beliefs on Emotions Depends on Simulations

The idea that simulations directed by verbal beliefs influence ongoing activation of emotional processing circuits and emotional reactions during emotional encounters is supported by the following lines of research. The first line of support comes from studies that investigated the effect of verbal labels on primary reinforcers (de Araujo et al. 2005; Grabenhorst et al. 2008; Grabenhorst and Rolls 2008; McCabe et al. 2008; Rolls et al. 2008). In all these studies, the magnitude of the embodied neural response to verbal labels, as shown by fMRI activations, correlated with a subjective rating of pleasantness. The second line of support comes from studies that investigated the effect of expectations of negative stimuli at the moment of encountering expected stimuli (Ochsner and Gross 2007). For example, Nitschke et al. (2006), in their fMRI investigation of expectancy influence on taste processing, found that expectancy modulates the neural responses in the primary taste cortex. When participants were led to believe that a highly aversive bitter taste was more distasteful than it actually was, the primary taste cortex was less strongly activated and they reported it to be less aversive than when they had accurate information about the taste (Nitschke et al. 2006). In their study, Sawamoto et al. (2000) found that expectations of painful stimuli amplified the perceived unpleasantness of innocuous stimulus and the brain responses to somatosensory stimulation which may play certain roles in regulating pain-dependent behavior. The third line of support for the effect of verbal beliefs on neural embodiments comes from studies that investigated the effect of cognitive reappraisal strategies on increasing and decreasing emotional reactions (e.g., emotional regulation). It was observed that when subjects used cognitive reappraisals to interpret the situation as less aversive, affective areas involved in emotional generation like amygdala were less activated and the emotional responses diminished; when subjects were instructed to think of the worst negative outcome of the situation, the activations in the amygdala and other emotional-related areas were increased (Beauregard et al. 2001; Jackson et al. 2000; Ochsner et al. 2002). To summarize, the proposal that simulations directed by verbal instructions or beliefs affect modal or affective brain activations during the processing of ongoing stimuli and that the magnitude of this effect is reflected in increased or decreased emotional reactions is supported by multiple lines of evidence.

2.7 Summary

Hot cognition is defined according to its ability to produce emotions. Hot cognition is cognition that results in emotion. Cold cognition is cognition that results in no emotion. Embodied theories of cognition suggest that cognition results in emotion when it recruits in context-dependent manner simulations of affective experiences (Niedenthal et al. 2009). According to the embodied simulation view, the hot-cold distinction of cognition is more dynamic. Cold cognition is a cognition that recruits non-affective simulations (e.g., in visual or linguistic systems) in the representation of its meaning while hot cognition is cognition that recruits affective simulations and in the representation of its meaning. The same cognition can be "heated" or "cooled down" depending on whether emotional simulations are recruited in the representation of its meaning. Directing simulations used in thinking in other modalities (affect is considered as a modality like visual, auditory, tactile, gustatory, olfactory modalities; Vermeulen et al. 2007) will result in a reduction of the emotional impact. For instance, when a person is asked to count the letters in the statement (counting letters in the affirmation "getting this interview will result in getting me the job I wanted"), then no emotion will result. The type of emotional experiences simulated in thinking will determine the type of experienced emotions. When a person understands how badly it is a situation by simulating aversive uncontrolled past emotions (or a situation associated with these emotions), a disturbed emotional experience will be set off. Language is a core mechanism that organizes, recruits, and compositionally structures embodied simulations (Barrett et al. 2014; Barsalou et al. 2008; Lindquist et al. 2015). When our interest is to regulate emotions to help individuals strained by intense and disruptive negative emotions, revealing core mechanisms that underlie the regulation of emotional experiences is of importance. On one hand, we have many processes that have extensive empirical support for their involvement in the determination of emotion. On the other hand, we need to understand how we can use the process in our control to change emotions. Embodied emotional cognition brings both together.

References

Abelson, R. P., & Rosenberg, M. J. (1958). Symbolic psycho-logic: A model of attitudinal cognition. *Behavioral Science, 3*(1), 1–13.

Andrews, M., Frank, S. L., & Vigliocco, G. (2014). Reconciling embodied and distributional accounts of meaning in language. *Topics in Cognitive Science, 6*, 359–370.

Barlow, D. H., Sauer-Zavala, S., Carl, J. R., Bullis, J. R., & Ellard, K. K. (2014). The nature, diagnosis, and treatment of neuroticism: Back to the future. *Clinical Psychological Science, 2*(3), 344–365.

Barrett, L. F., Lindquist, K. A., & Gendron, M. (2007). Language as context in the perception of emotion. *Trends in Cognitive Sciences, 11*, 327–332.

Barrett, L. F., Wilson-Mendenhall, C. D., & Barsalou, L. W. (2014). A psychological construction account of emotion regulation and dysregulation: The role of situated conceptualizations. In J. J. Gross (Ed.), *The handbook of emotion regulation* (2nd ed., pp. 447–465). Guilford.

Barsalou, L. W. (1999). Perceptual symbol systems. *Behavioral and Brain Sciences, 22*(577), 609.

Barsalou, L. W. (2003). Situated simulation in the human conceptual system. *Language and Cognitive Processes, 18*, 513–562. [Reprinted in H. Moss and J. Hampton, Conceptual representation (p. 513-566). Psychology Press.].

Barsalou, L. W. (2008). Grounding symbolic operations in the brain's modal systems. In G. R. Semin & E. R. Smith (Eds.), *Embodied grounding: Social, cognitive, affective, and neuroscientific approaches* (pp. 9–42). Cambridge University Press.

Barsalou, L. W. (2013). Mirroring as pattern completion inferences within situated conceptualizations. *Cortex, 49*, 2951–2953.

Barsalou, L. W., & Hale, C. R. (1993). Components of conceptual representation: From feature lists to recursive frames. In I. Van Mechelen, J. Hampton, R. Michalski, & P. Theuns (Eds.), *Categories and concepts: Theoretical views and inductive data analysis* (pp. 97–144). Academic Press.

Barsalou, L. W., Santos, A., Simmons, W. K., & Wilson, C. D. (2008). Language and simulation in conceptual processing. In M. De Vega, A. M. Glenberg, A. C. Graesser, & A. (Eds.), *Symbols, embodiment, and meaning* (pp. 245–283). Oxford University Press.

Barsalou, L. W., Simmons, W. K., Barbey, A. K., & Wilson, C. D. (2003). Grounding conceptual knowledge in modality-specific systems. *Trends in Cognitive Sciences, 7*, 84–91.

Beauregard, M., Levesque, J., & Bourgouin, P. (2001). Neural correlates of conscious self-regulation of emotion. *Journal of Neuroscience, 21*(18), RC165. 1-6.

Bower, G. H. (1981). Mood and memory. *American Psychologist, 36*, 129–148.

Carr, E. W., Kever, A., & Winkielman, P. (2018). Embodiment of emotion and its situated nature. In A. Newen, L. de Bruin, & S. Gallagher (Eds.), *The Oxford handbook of 4E cognition* (pp. 529–551). Oxford University Press.

Chemero, A. (2009). *Radical embodied science*. MIT Press.

David, D., & David, O. (2017). Hot cognitions. In V. Zeigler-Hill & T. Shackelford (Eds.), *Encyclopedia of personality and individual differences*. Cham: Springer.

David, D., Lynn, S. J., & Ellis, A. (2010). *Rational and irrational beliefs: Research, theory, and clinical practice*. Oxford University Press.

David, D., & Matu, S. (2017). Cold cognition. In V. Zeigler-Hill & T. Shackelford (Eds.), *Encyclopedia of personality and individual differences*. Cham: Springer.

David, D., & Szentagotai, A. (2006). Cognition in cognitive behavior psychotherapies. *Clinical Psychology Review, 26*, 284–298.

Davis, J. D., Winkielman, P., & Coulson, S. (2015). Facial action and emotional language: ERP evidence that blocking facial feedback selectively impairs sentence comprehension. *Journal of Cognitive Neuroscience, 27*, 2269–2280.

de Araujo, I. E. T., Rolls, E. T., Velazco, M. I., Margot, C., & Cayeux, I. (2005). Cognitive modulation of olfactory processing. *Neuron, 46*, 671–679.

Ellis, A., David, D., & Lynn, S. J. (2010). Rational and irrational beliefs: A historical and conceptual perspective. In D. David, S. J. Lynn, & A. Ellis (Eds.), *Rational and irrational beliefs: Research, theory, and clinical practice* (pp. 3–22). Oxford University Press.

Fodor, J. A. (1975). *The language of thought*. Harvard University Press.

Gendron, M., Lindquist, K. A., Barsalou, L., & Barrett, L. F. (2012). Emotion words shape emotion percepts. *Emotion, 12*(2), 314–325. https://doi.org/10.1037/a0026007

Grabenhorst, F., & Rolls, E. T. (2008). Selective attention to affective value alters how the brain processes taste stimuli. *European Journal of Neuroscience, 27*, 723–729.

Grabenhorst, F., Rolls, E. T., & Bilderbeck, A. (2008). How cognition modulates affective responses to taste and flavor: Top-down influences on the orbitofrontal and pregenual cingulate cortices. *Cerebral Cortex, 18*, 1549–1559.

Halberstadt, J., Winkielman, P., Niedenthal, P. M., & Dalle, N. (2009). Emotional conception: How embodied emotion concepts guide perception and facial action. *Psychological Science, 20*, 1254–1261.

Havas, D. A., Glenberg, A. M., Gutowski, K. A., Lucarelli, M. J., & Davidson, R. J. (2010). Cosmetic use of botulin toxin-a affects processing of emotional language. *Psychological Science, 21*, 895–900.

Havas, D. A., Glenberg, A. M., & Rinck, M. (2007). Emotion simulation during language comprehension. *Psychonomic Society Bullentin and Review, 14*, 436–441.

Jackson, D. C., Malmstadt, J. R., Larson, C. L., & Davidson, R. J. (2000). Suppression and enhancement of emotional responses to unpleasant pictures. *Psychophysiology, 37*, 515–522.

Kavanagh, L., Niedenthal, P., & Winkielman, P. (2012). Embodied simulation as grounds for emotion concepts. In P. Wilson (Ed.), *Lodz studies in language* (Vol. 27, pp. 139–155). Peter Lang.

Kever, A., Grynberg, D., Bayot, M., & Vermeulen, N. (2016). Embodying emotions: The role of bodily changes in emotional processing: Evidence from normal and psychopathological populations. In Y. Coello & M. H. Fischer (Eds.), *Foundations of embodied cognition: Perceptual and emotional embodiment* (pp. 246–261) Routledge/Taylor & Francis Group.

Lang, P. J. (1979). A bio-informational theory of emotional imagery. *Psychophysiology, 16*, 495–512. https://doi.org/10.1111/j.1469-8986.1979.tb01511.x

Lazarus, R. S. (1991). *Emotion and adaptation*. Oxford University Press.

Leventhal, H., & Scherer, K. R. (1987). The relationship of emotion to cognition: A functional approach to a semantic controversy. *Cognition and Emotion, 1*, 3–28.

Lindquist, K. A., Barrett, L. F., Bliss-Moreau, E., & Russell, J. A. (2006). Language and the perception of emotion. *Emotion, 6*, 125–138.

Lindquist, K. A., & Gendron, M. (2013). What's in a word? Language constructs emotion perception. *Emotion Review, 5*, 66–71.

Lindquist, K. A., MacCormack, J. K., & Shablack, H. (2015). The role of language in emotion: Predictions from psychological constructionism. *Frontiers in Psychology, 6*, 444. https://doi.org/10.3389/fpsyg.2015.00444

Marr, D. (1982). *Vision: A computational approach*. MIT Press.

Marshall, P. J. (2014). Beyond different levels: Embodiment and the developmental system. *Frontiers in Psychology, 5*, 929. https://doi.org/10.3389/fpsyg.2014.00929

McCabe, C., Rolls, E. T., Bilderbeck, A., & McGlone, F. (2008). Cognitive influences on the affective representation of touch and the sight of touch in the human brain. *Social, Cognitive and Affective Neuroscience, 3*, 97–108.

Moors, A., Ellsworth, P. C., Scherer, K. R., & Frijda, N. H. (2013). Appraisal theories of emotion: State of the art and future development. *Emotion Review, 5*(2), 119–124. https://doi.org/10.1177/1754073912468165

Niedenthal, P. M. (2007). Embodying emotion. *Science, 316*, 1002–1005.

Niedenthal, P. M., Barsalou, L. W., Ric, F., & Krauth-Gruber, S. (2005b) Embodiment in the acquisition and use of emotion knowledge. In L. Feldman Barrett, P. M. Niedenthal, & P. Winkielman (Eds.), Emotion and consciousness (pp. 21-50). Guilford.

Niedenthal, P. M., Barsalou, L. W., Winkielman, P., Krauth-Gruber, S., & Ric, F. (2005a). Embodiment in attitudes, social perception, and emotion. *Personality and Social Psychology Review, 9*, 184–211.

Niedenthal, P. M., Winkielman, P., Mondillon, L., & Vermeulen, N. (2009). Embodiment of emotional concepts: Evidence from EMG measures. *Journal of Personality and Social Psychology, 96*, 1120–1136.

Nitschke, J. B., Dixon, G. E., Sarinopoulos, I., Short, S. J., Cohen, J. D., Smith, E. E., ... Davidson, R. J. (2006). Altering expectancy dampens neural response to aversive taste in primary taste cortex. *Nature Neuroscience, 9*, 435–442.

Ochsner, K. N., Bunge, S. A., Gross, J. J., & Gabrieli, J. D. (2002). Rethinking feelings: An FMRI study of the cognitive regulation of emotion. *Journal of Cognitive Neuroscience, 14*, 1215–1229.

Ochsner, K. N., & Gross, J. J. (2004). Thinking makes it so: A social cognitive neuroscience approach to emotion regulation. In R. Baumeister & K. Vohs (Eds.), *The handbook of self-regulation* (pp. 221–255). Guilford Press.

Ochsner, K. N., & Gross, J. J. (2007). The neural architecture of emotion regulation. In J. J. Gross (Ed.), *Handbook of emotion regulation* (pp. 87–109). New York: Guilford Press.

Oosterwijk, S., & Barrett, L. F. (2014). Embodiment in the construction of emotion experience and emotion understanding. In L. Shapiro (Ed.), *Routledge handbook of embodied cognition* (pp. 250–260). Routledge.

Oosterwijk, S., Mackey, S., Wilson-Mendenhall, C., Winkielman, P., & Paulus, M. P. (2015). Concepts in context: Processing mental state concepts with internal or external focus involves different neural systems. *Social Neuroscience, 10*, 294–307.

Oosterwijk, S., Snoek, L., Rotteveel, M., Barrett, L. F., & Scholte, H. S. (2017). Shared states: Using MVPA to test neural overlap between self-focused emotion imagery and other-focused emotion understanding. *Social Cognitive Affective Neuroscience, 12*, 1025–1035. https://doi.org/10.1093/scan/nsx037

Oosterwijk, S., Topper, M., Rotteveel, M., & Fischer, A. H. (2010). When the mind forms fear: Embodied fear knowledge potentiates bodily reactions to fearful stimuli. *Social Psychological and Personality Science, 1*, 65–72.

Oosterwijk, S., Winkielman, P., Pecher, D., Zeelenberg, R., Rotteveel, M., & Fischer, A. H. (2011). Mental states inside out: Switching costs for emotional and non-emotional sentences that differ in internal and external focus. *Memory and Cognition, 40*, 93–100. https://doi.org/10.3758/s13421-011-0134-8

Overton, W. F., & Lerner, R. M. (2012). Relational developmental systems: A paradigm for developmental science in the postgenomic era. *Behavioral Brain Science, 35*, 375–376. https://doi.org/10.1017/S0140525X12001082

Papies, E. K., & Barsalou, L. W. (2015). Grounding desire and motivated behavior: A theoretical framework and review of empirical evidence. In W. Hofmann & L. F. Nordgren (Eds.), *The psychology of desire*. Guilford Press.

Phelps, E. A., O'Connor, K. J., Gatenby, J. C., Grillon, C., Gore, J. C., & Davis, M. (2001). Activation of the human amygdala to a cognitive representation of fear. *Nature Neuroscience, 4*, 437–441.

Porro, C. A., Baraldi, P., Pagnoni, G., Serafini, M., Facchin, P., Maieron, M., & Nichelli, P. (2002). Does anticipation of pain affect cortical nociceptive systems? *The Journal of Neuroscience: The Official Journal of the Society for Neuroscience, 22*(8), 3206–3214. https://doi.org/10.1523/JNEUROSCI.22-08-03206.2002

Roberson, D., Damjanovic, L., & Pilling, M. (2007). Categorical perception of facial expressions: Evidence for a "category adjustment" model. *Memory & Cognition, 35*, 1814–1829.

Roberson, D., & Davidoff, J. (2000). The categorical perception of colors and facial expressions: The effect of verbal interference. *Memory and Cognition, 28*, 977–986.

Roiser, J. P., & Sahakian, B. J. (2013). Hot and cold cognition in depression. *CNS Spectrums, 18*(03), 139–149.

Rolls, E. T. (2008). Top-down control of visual perception: Attention in natural vision. *Perception, 37*, 333–354.

Rolls, E. T., Grabenhorst, F., Margot, C., da Silva, M., & Velazco, M. I. (2008). Selective attention to affective value alters how the brain processes olfactory stimuli. *Journal of Cognitive Neuroscience, 20*, 1815–1826.

Sawamoto, N., Honda, M., Okada, T., Hanakawa, T., Kanda, M., Fukuyama, H., … Shibasaki, H. (2000). Expectation of pain enhances responses to nonpainful somatosensory stimulation in the anterior cingulate cortex and parietal operculum/posterior insula: An event-related functional magnetic resonance imaging study. *The Journal of Neuroscience, 20*(19), 7438–7445. https://doi.org/10.1523/JNEUROSCI.20-19-07438.2000

Vermeulen, N., Niedenthal, P. M., & Luminet, O. (2007). Switching between sensory and affective systems incurs processing costs. *Cognitive Science, 31*, 183–192.

Wilson, M. (2002). Six views of embodied cognition. *Psychonomic Bulletin and Review, 9*(4), 625–636. https://doi.org/10.3758/BF03196322

Wilson-Mendenhall, C., Barrett, L. F., & Barsalou, L. W. (2013a). Neural evidence that human emotions share core affective properties. *Psychological Science, 24*, 947–956.

Wilson-Mendenhall, C., Barrett, L. F., & Barsalou, L. W. (2013b). Situating emotional experience. *Frontiers in Human Neuroscience, 7*, 1–16.

Wilson-Mendenhall, C. D., Barrett, L. F., & Barsalou, L. W. (2014). Variety in emotional life: Within-category typicality of emotional experiences is associated with neural activity in large-scale brain networks. *Social Cognitive and Affective Neuroscience, 10*, 62–71.

Wilson-Mendenhall, C. D., Barrett, L. F., Simmons, W. K., & Barsalou, L. W. (2011). Grounding emotion in situated conceptualization. *Neuropsychologia, 49*, 1105–1127.

Wilson-Mendenhall, C. D., Henriques, A., Barsalou, L. W., & Barrett, L. F. (2019). Primary interoceptive cortex activity during simulated experiences of the body. *Journal of Cognitive Neuroscience, 31*(2), 221–235. https://doi.org/10.1162/jocn_a_01346

Winkielman, P., Niedenthal, P., Wielgosz, J., Eelen, J., & Kavanagh, L. C. (2015). Embodiment of cognition and emotion. In M. Mikulincer, P. R. Shaver, E. Borgida, & J. A. Bargh (Eds.), *APA handbooks in psychology®. APA handbook of personality and social psychology, Vol. 1. Attitudes and social cognition* (pp. 151–175). American Psychological Association. https://doi.org/10.1037/14341-004

Winkielman, P., Niedenthal, P. M., & Oberman, L. (2008). The embodied emotional mind. In G. R. Semin & E. M. Smith (Eds.), *Embodied grounding: Social, cognitive, affective, and neuroscientific approaches*. Cambridge University Press.

Wyer, R. S., Clore, G. L., & Isbell, L. (1999). Affect and information processing. In M. Zanna (Ed.), *Advances in experimental social psychology* (Vol. 31, pp. 1–77). Academic Press.

Chapter 3
Embodying Distorted Hot Cognition

3.1 Introduction

Convergent research from many fields has shown that individuals may use both embodied and disembodied types of cognition in guiding their behavior (Barsalou 2013). Embodied cognition comprises those representations based on experience-related body and brain resources. Disembodied cognition does not use experience-related body and brain resources in representation. Recently, increasing research points to the fact that individuals show differences in their ability to use their body in representations (Fuchs and Schlimme 2009; Fuchs and Koch 2014; Kever et al. 2016; Zatti and Zarbo 2015) across many psychopathologies. Thus, the embodiment of representations (embodied cognition) seems to be affected in depressive disorders (Eggart et al. 2019; Harshaw 2015), eating disorders (Klabunde et al. 2017; Zatti and Zarbo 2015), autism spectrum disorders (Eigsti 2013), schizophrenia (Zatti and Zarbo 2015), or emotional disorders associated with motor disorders (Mermillod et al. 2011). Furthermore, it is suggested that these distortions in embodied cognition are not epiphenomena but may act as maintenance processes (Compare et al. 2014; Füstös et al. 2013; Mermillod et al. 2011; Paley 2004), determinants of additional emotional or behavioral symptoms (e.g., deficits in expressive movements can cause emotional experience deficits; Mermillod et al. 2011), or as early signs of disorders (action embodiment of language as early signs in neuropsychological disorders; Cardona 2017). Psychotherapy interventions based on changing the recruitment of body processes in cognition have been proposed (Leitan and Murray 2014; Pietrzak et al. 2018; Tiba 2010). Furthermore, theoretical analyses have suggested that distorted embodied representations may underlie several cognitive vulnerabilities such as exaggerated motor incapacity underlying hopelessness (Lindeman and Abramson 2008), failed simulations underlying generalized thinking (Gjelsvik et al. 2018), sensorimotor and affective simulations underlying negative memory bias (Ianì 2019; Michalak et al. 2014, 2015), exaggerated emotional experiences underlying emotional appraisals (Tiba 2010), and interoceptive

A. Tiba, *Embodied Hot Cognitive Vulnerability to Emotional Disorders*,
https://doi.org/10.1007/978-3-030-53989-4_3

experiences (Füstös et al. 2013) and posture (Veenstra et al. 2017) underlying emotional regulation. Thus, distortions of embodied cognition may be important in disorders that are characterized by disturbed emotions such as emotional disorders (e.g., Barlow et al. 2014). However, a systematic analysis related to the embodiment of cognitive vulnerabilities to disturbed emotions is lacking.

Research of the embodiment of cognition has shown that non-distorted cognition is often embodied in partial activations of the neural patterns in the modal brain (i.e., visual, auditory, motor, gustatory) corresponding to its content (Barsalou 1999). Moreover, the embodied cognition research on emotional cognition has demonstrated that non-distorted emotional cognition is often embodied in the partial activation of the neural patterns in the affective brain, parts active during emotional experiences (i.e., neural emotional embodiments) (Niedenthal 2007; Niedenthal et al. 2009; Vermeulen et al. 2007). Thus, in order to describe the emotional embodied simulations underlying distorted embodied emotional cognition that predispose to disturbed negative emotions, one should describe disturbed negative emotional experiences and the characteristics of the neural patterns in the affective systems that are involved in disturbed negative emotions.[1]

3.2 What Is Distorted or Exaggerated Hot Cognition?

Hot cognition is emotional cognition. Although there are many definitions of hot cognition, a widely accepted view defines hot cognition as appraisals of personal significance (Abelson 1963; David and David 2017). During various encounters that contradict individuals' goals and desires, individuals describe, represent, and interpret their reality (e.g., "not getting a promotion means that I failed and it is my fault"). This is cold cognition (e.g., a schema about events, other or self; inferences and attributions). Then, this reality is appraised in terms of personal significance. This appraisal is hot cognition (e.g., "Getting a promotion and not failing is important for me; I do not know what to do to get the promotion; I can manage my feelings"). Ellis suggests that *hot cognition* can be *warm* or non-distorted appraisal (e.g., "I like or prefer to get a vacation") or (really hot) or distorted and exaggerated

[1] Although I focus here on the central processes involved in the embodiment, I recognize that embodiment is a situated process involving peripheral mechanisms, other body processes influencing the neural emotional embodiments as well. For example, using an animal model of stress, Wohleb and his colleagues (2015) showed that after single-stress exposure the mice become sensitized and at the presentation of a new stressor the re-establishment of anxiety in stress-sensitized mice is dependent on monocytes trafficking from the spleen to the brain circuits. If replicated in humans, this result may point to a role of monocytes trafficking from the spleen in the distorted emotional embodiments and distorted cognition. Other peripheral processes in the embodiment of cognition may be represented by heart activity, breathing, postures, facial expressions, movements, and so forth. For example, facial expression may participate in *biases of attention* such as disgust-facial muscle movements in gating sensory input and fear-facial movements in increasing sensory input (Vermeulen et al. 2009).

appraisals (e.g., irrational beliefs, "I must get a vacation") (Ellis 1994, 2001). Although several cognitive theories of emotion focus on the role of cold cognition in emotion (schema, interpretations, attributions), appraisal theories suggest that cold cognition results in emotion only when cold cognition is appraised through hot cognition (David et al. 2002; Lazarus 1991; Smith and Lazarus 1993).

According to the appraisal theory, only hot cognition results in emotion (Lazarus 1991; David et al. 2002). Smith and Lazarus (1993) suggested two types of hot cognitions: "primary appraisals" (motivational congruence and relevance) and "secondary appraisals" (appraisals of emotion-focused coping potential, problem-focused coping potential, self or other accountability and future expectancy). Combinations of these appraisals result in a theme related to emotions. For instance, the situation of not getting a promotion interacts with a person's specific goals such as the goal of advancing a job (a transaction). This transaction is appraised as important and incongruent with his goals. Only then an emotion is triggered. Furthermore, the individual appraises how he can cope with this situation (can deal with not advancing right now), with associated emotions (appraises whether he can control his feelings), who is responsible (self or other accountability), and what to expect in the future (that situation will change). If the person will appraise "not getting the promotion" as something important, incongruent with his goal of advancing professionally and that he will not be able to cope with the emotions, he will experience negative emotions such as anxiety. Negative emotions are not a problem per se. They have a highly adaptive value stimulating the organism to solve problems. When we feel anxious, we take the necessary measures to protect ourselves. When we feel fear, we are more efficient to escape eventual dangers. Negative emotions become a problem only when they become disturbed or unhealthy. They are too intense and individuals become distressed because of them resulting in unhealthy behaviors (e.g., being aggressive instead of discussing social problems).

Emotion research focuses on finding how appraisals result in disturbed emotions. Although many cognitive theories of emotional disorders have focused on deficits of cold cognition (Beck 1976), A. Ellis's cognitive theory of emotions focused on appraisals or evaluative cognition. According to A. Ellis, disturbed negative emotions (or unhealthy negative emotions) result from an exaggerated evaluation of significance of adverse events. Thus, it is not the adversity (or the transaction) that determines the experience of disturbed emotion but the Irrational Beliefs (IB) (the rigid and exaggerated evaluation or appraisal of the situation) (Ellis 1994). There are four types of distorted hot cognitions involved in disturbed emotions (unhealthy emotions): (1) demandingness (e.g., the rigid evaluative belief referring to the demand that things should be as a person desire them to be; "I should get that promotion"), (2) awfulizing (e.g., an extreme evaluative belief referring to the appraisal of a situation as 100% bad; "Is awful if I do not get that job promotion"), (3) frustration intolerance (FI) (e.g., "I cannot stand getting a job promotion"), and (4) global evaluation of human worth or depreciation (other, life, or self-downing; "I am a failure if I do not get that promotion") (Ellis 1994; Ellis et al. 2010; DiGiuseppe et al. 2014).

A. Ellis' theory of appraisals is an influential theory. It resulted in a widely used evidence-based treatment of emotional disorders such as Rational Emotive Behavior Therapy (REBT; David et al. 2010), being the first major school of cognitive-oriented cognitive behavior therapies. However, because REBT uses terms that do not overlap with terms used in psychological and related sciences (e.g., irrational beliefs), the scientific impact of A. Ellis theory was limited (in contrast with the impact of cognitive therapy based on concepts of schema). David and his collaborators solved this problem by showing that irrational beliefs are forms of exaggerated appraisals (David et al. 2002).

In 2002, David and his collaborators investigated whether IBs can be conceptually understood as exaggerated appraisals. Specifically, they hypothesized that demandingness is a rigid form of appraisal linked with motivational congruence. Moreover, they investigated whether awfulizing and frustration intolerance are extreme forms of appraisal linked with low emotion coping potential, and self-depreciation is an extreme form of appraisal linked with low potential coping potential (David et al. 2002). The authors asked 120 participants to focus on a particular past incident and to write an open-ended description of the incident: "(a) you felt a need to question whether your career plan was right for you; (b) you received a low grade on an exam in a course that mattered to you; (c) your parent(s) would not let you do something you really wanted; and (d) the person you were dating criticized you about something you cared about" (David et al. 2002, p. 109). The participants completed a form regarding appraisals, emotions, and irrational beliefs. Results showed that demandingness (DEM) was associated more with primary appraisals (motivational congruence and relevance), and awfulizing, low frustration tolerance, and global evaluation of human worth were associated more with secondary appraisals (David et al. 2002). Furthermore, irrational beliefs were associated with dysfunctional negative emotions beyond primary and secondary appraisals. Thus, distorted primary and secondary appraisals are involved in disturbed negative emotions. Distorted primary appraisals are demandingness or absolutistic evaluation of desirability while secondary distorted appraisals of low emotion-focused potential are awfulizing and frustration intolerance. As presented in Chap. 2, often, and when cognition results in emotion, emotional cognition is based on embodied representations consisting of simulation of emotional experiences. Similarly, individuals may use an embodied type of distorted emotional cognition grounded in disturbed or dysfunctional negative emotional experiences. Below, I discuss the embodied types of distorted emotional cognition as targets of evidence-based psychological treatments, and I discuss the characteristics of central embodiments involved in distorted emotional cognition.

3.3 The Revised ABC Model

Over thirty years ago, A. Ellis proposed a revised ABC model. In his revised ABC model, Ellis suggested that Beliefs are in fact composite states of believing-emoting-behaving (Ellis 2001). According to Ellis, believing is the same with feeling and with behaving. When we believe that "we must get appreciation," at the same time we feel we should get appreciation and we behave to get appreciation. When a therapist has to change Irrational Beliefs, in order to change dysfunctional emotions, they have to change their *believing-emoting-behaving* rather than just their beliefs (Ellis 2001). Yet for brevity, Ellis referred to these composites of believing-emoting-behaving as Beliefs (Ellis 2001). To illustrate this, in his book *Feeling Better, Getting Better, Staying Better: Profound Self-help Therapy*, A. Ellis presents IBs from the view of his revised ABC model of REBT in the case of Joyce (Ellis 2001). In this case, Joyce meets adversity and by her IBs (believing-emoting-behaving) developed an unhealthy negative emotion (being depressed).

> "Joyce met an A that is Bob, her husband announced to her that he was leaving her after having an affair and getting his secretary pregnant (Ellis 2001, p. 17). At C Joyce felt depressed. At B Joyce has strong thinking "A is bad for me. It is not what I want. In fact, it is so undesirable that it must not occur! It is terrible and proves I am a poor wife and an inadequate person…" Second, at B, Joyce has understandably negative feelings that go with her negative thinking-feelings of loos, regret, shock, and horror-feelings that, again, help lead her to experience C, depressing herself (actually, B (belief) also includes strong emotional and behavioral elements. Therefore we can call it Believing-Emoting-Behaving.) Third, at B, Joyce has action tendencies-such as to argue, flight, and escape-that accompany her thinking and feeling and probably augment them. Again they help her to depressing herself" (Ellis 2001, p. 17).

In Ellis` revised ABC model, exaggerated appraisals are very similar to embodied exaggerated appraisals. An embodied simulation model of cognition suggests that thinking of a situation involves a re-enactment or a partial simulation of the experience of that situation including feelings, behaviors, and perceptions (Barsalou 1999; Barrett 2017). Salient and repeated experiences of situations are captured in memory as they were experienced. When a part of the situation is encountered (either a situational context or as a thought), a pattern completion inference mechanism triggers simulations of the other parts of the involved experiences as active inferences (Barsalou 2003, 2008). When the partial simulations of some experiences (e.g., fear) are powerful enough, conscious experience may result (Barrett 2017). For instance, when thinking of a dog after an aggressive encounter (being attacked by a dog and experiencing intense fear and strong escape reactions), a partial simulation of the encounter is triggered involving the feeling of fear, avoidance tendencies, and so on. Usually, simulations are unconscious, only thinking being a focus of our conscious attention. In certain conditions, when our emotions are hyper-reactive (e.g., sensitized, disturbed emotions), emotional simulations are strong enough to be felt (almost felt emotions) or even enter consciousness. The same happens with behavior (sensitized behavior) and motivation (sensitized motivation). In this example of activated emotional simulations, thinking that the dog is dangerous is at the same time felt (unconscious feelings of fear) and behaved upon (experiences the urge to avoid). When fully activated (which probably happens when people have disturbed, very intense emotions and sensitized affective brain) simulated feelings and behaviors become conscious, the person can have a full experience of thinking, feeling, and behaving in response to danger. Depending on the focus of attention and the intensity of sensations, an individual may experience the simulation underlying the conceptualization process as a thought, a feeling, or a behavior. In this example, when the focus of attention will be on cognitively assessing the situation, the person will experience the thought *"the dog is frightening"* and will believe he/she must avoid it; when the focus of attention will be on internal sensations, the person will feel fear and the need to avoid (feelings); and when the focus is on behaviors, the person will experience the urge to avoid the dog (action tendencies).

Fully activated embodied beliefs are psychological states that involve loosely coupled and interacting thinking, feeling, and behavioral reactions. They are a kind of affect. The embodiment of primary appraisals in disturbed motivation is discussed in Chaps. 5 and 6. Here, I will focus on secondary appraisals of awfulizing and frustration intolerance as beliefs embodied in disturbed emotions. Thus, when people think something bad is awful and intolerable, they understand the situation based on simulation or partial reactivation of disturbed and aversive negative emotions. When affective simulations are partially activated, they will experience the thinking of awful also as a feeling and tendency to act (I also feel it is awful). When affective simulations of disturbed emotions are fully activated, the individuals will also have full feelings and behavioral reactions as part of their beliefs.

3.4 What Is Disturbed Emotion?

An emotion is a dynamic psychological state with loosely coupled experiential, behavioral, and physiological components (Gross 2015). D. H. Barlow's group (Barlow et al. 2014; Bullis et al. 2019) suggests the following criteria for an emotional disorder: "(a) the experience of frequent and intense negative emotions; (b) there is an aversive reaction to the emotional experience itself that is driven by the individual's diminished sense of control and negative appraisal of the emotion; and (c) the individual engages in efforts to dampen, escape, or avoid the emotional experience, either preemptively or in reaction to the onset of a negative emotional state" (Bullis et al. 2019, p. 3). Other significant works accentuated different features of disturbed emotions such as exaggerated dynamic dimensions and emotional dysregulation (Gross and Jazaieri 2014; Jazaieri et al. 2013). Disturbed emotions are the core of emotional disorders. They can be defined as negative emotions, which are: (a) exaggerated (are quickly triggered, have rapid onset and accumulation into high intensities, slow return to base rate); (b) aversive for the individual (i.e., aversive); and (c) associated with efforts to dampen, escape, or avoid the experience (i.e., uncontrollable or dysregulated) (Bullis et al. 2019). When disturbed emotion impairs the life of a person, we can refer to it as an emotional disorder. Although emotional deficits are important as well, I focus here on emotional excesses.

3.4.1 Exaggerated Negative Affect

Individuals with emotional disorders have long been characterized as having negative emotions more often (easily triggered) and more intense than healthy individuals (Barlow et al. 2014). Recently, studies showed that other (dynamic) dimensions of negative affect are exaggerated in psychopathologies (Aldao et al. 2010; Houben et al. 2015). For instance, depressive symptoms are associated with the experience of negative emotions as accumulating in higher intensity (Résibois et al. 2018), lasting longer (Siegle et al. 2002), and having higher inertia (Brose et al. 2015; Houben et al. 2015; Koval et al. 2013, 2016). Although the evidence is scarce, the explosiveness of negative emotion has not been found to be associated with depressive symptoms (Résibois et al. 2018). Moreover, a pattern of low reactivity of negative emotion in depressed individuals was found (Bylsma et al. 2008). Common dynamic dimensions of affective experiences are: (a) emotional variability or the tendency of the individuals to reach with more extreme levels and show larger emotional deviations from their average emotional level (measured in terms of within-person standard deviation of emotions across time) (Houben et al. 2015; Koval et al. 2016); (b) emotional instability or the tendency to experience larger emotional shifts from one moment to the next (measured in terms of the magnitude of consecutive emotional changes) (Houben et al. 2015; Koval et al. 2016); and (c) emotional inertia of emotions over time or the tendency of having self-perpetuating emotions over time (measured in terms of autocorrelation) (Houben et al. 2015; Koval et al. 2016). Across many psychopathologies, low psychological well-being is associated with more variable, unstable but also more inert negative but also positive emotions (Houben et al. 2015), emotional variability and instability most probably being a nonspecific characteristic of both mood and anxiety disorders (Lamers et al. 2018).

3.4.2 Negative Reactivity to Emotions and Aversiveness

People do more than just feel. They react to their feelings. Consistent research shows that people with emotional disorders have aversive reactions to negative emotion (Campbell-Sills et al. 2006; Ford and Gross 2019; McLaughlin et al. 2007) and often develop secondary negative emotions or meta-emotions (Predatu et al. 2019). In 1991, D. Barlow suggested that the only thing that differentiates disordered from non-disordered negative emotions is the aversiveness for negative emotions (Barlow 1991).

Recently, a study conducted in the laboratory of Professor D. David by Predatu et al. (2019) validated the initial claims of D. H. Barlow. Predatu et al. (2019) asked

36 participants with an emotional disorder and 50 controls to remember an emotional event in an emotion-provoking autobiographical recall task. Then, they assessed cardiac activity, beliefs about emotions, subjective experiences of negative emotions, negative meta-emotions, and perceived emotional control. Results showed that individuals with emotional disorders showed more negative emotions, a higher increase in negative emotions from baseline to episodic recall, and slow recovery from negative emotions after the recall task. They also had higher levels of irrational beliefs about emotions (aversive appraisal of emotions), more negative meta-emotions, and poorer perceived control of emotions (Predatu et al. 2019). This study suggests that disturbed negative emotions are exaggerated emotions, which include aversive reactions to negative emotions and control difficulties.

3.4.3 Behavioral Reactions to Aversion: Avoidance as a Meta-Emotion Behavior

A common finding in individuals with emotional disorders (anxiety and depressive disorders) is that these individuals consistently show high levels of emotional escape and avoidance behaviors (Aldao et al. 2010; Campbell-Sills et al. 2006; Ottenbreit et al. 2014). These behaviors are in turn associated with increases in negative emotion and poorer recovery from negative emotion (Cisler and Olatunji 2012). Avoidance behavior can be seen in overt behaviors such as avoidance of emotion-arousing situations (avoiding getting in a car when having a phobia, isolated spaces in panic disorder) or cognitive behaviors (rumination, worry and thought suppression) (Barlow et al. 2014).

3.4.4 Disturbed Emotions: Hyper-Reactive States of the Affective Brain

Considerable evidence from the research of intense normal emotional experiences (Waugh et al. 2010) and pathological emotional states (e.g., Bishop 2007; Rauch et al. 2000) identified exaggerated neural response of affective (i.e., amygdala centered; Johnstone et al. 2007; Liu et al. 2014; Rauch et al. 2000; Ressler 2010; Shin et al. 2005), motivational (accumbens centered; Berridge and Robinson 2003), and cortical (anterior insula; Seth 2013; Silvers et al. 2014) brain regions (both in intensity and duration; Hazlett et al. 2012; Siegle et al. 2002) in conjunction with a failure of efficient recruitment of prefrontal regulatory regions (the dorsal, lateral, and ventromedial prefrontal cortex) (Bishop 2007; Forster et al. 2014; Johnstone et al. 2007; Kim et al. 2003; Peters et al. 2009; Urry et al. 2006) in response to negative stimuli. Furthermore, exaggerated neural response in emotional circuits along with prefrontal under-recruitment have been considered characteristic for pathological affective disturbances (Bishop 2007; Drevets 2000), related to symptom severity (Demenescu et al. 2013), and identified as a predisposition in individuals with personality (i.e., neuroticism; Servaas et al. 2013) and biological vulnerabilities (Ma et al. 2013) to develop emotional disorders (EDs).

Exaggerated neural responses in limbic emotion generation areas after stress exposure probably occur because of several mechanisms such as loss in local inhibition networks (Quirk and Gehlert 2003; Liu et al. 2014), dendritic hyper-arborization (Vyas et al. 2002), or intrinsic excitability due to altered calcium-activated potassium channels (Rosenkranz et al. 2010). In general, emotional over-activation has been linked to a deterioration of limbic connectivity to prefrontal regions controlling inhibitory networks of limbic structures (Motzkin et al. 2014a, b; Wagner and Heatherton 2013).

Although prefrontal-limbic relations are complex (Myers-Schulz and Koenigs 2012), the over-activation of the neural states in emotional circuits underlying intense negative emotions because of a faulty interplay between circuits involved in affect generation and affect regulation have been also consistently supported by the emotional regulation framework (Ochsner and Gross 2008; Ochsner et al. 2012; Silvers et al. 2014). Accordingly, intense negative emotions reflect the over-activation of emotional generation brain regions resulting from both increased excitability in emotion generation regions (Liu et al. 2014) and/or under-recruitment of prefrontal regulation brain regions (Arnsten 2009; Buhle et al. 2014; Forster et al. 2014; Motzkin et al. 2014a, b; Silvers et al. 2014) while an increased coupling between amygdala and prefrontal regions predicts emotional regulatory success over time (Lee et al. 2012). Thus, a specific neural pattern corresponding to dysregulated emotional experiences emerges as a characteristic of both normal intense emotions (Silvers et al. 2014) and affective disturbances (Bishop 2007; Jazaieri et al. 2013).

3.5 The Embodiment of Hot Cognition into Disturbed Emotions

Embodied simulation perspective suggests that our cognition is represented by the re-enactment of referenced experiences (Barrett et al. 2014; Barsalou 2008) through the recruitment of neural resources involved in those experiences. When embodied cognition determines emotions, it recruits referenced emotional experience and brain systems involved in emotional experiences (Carr et al. 2018; Winkielman et al. 2015). When embodied cognition determines disturbed negative emotions, it recruits (1) disturbed negative emotions and (2) the neural systems that implement disturbed emotions.

There are two types of emotional appraisals important for disturbed emotions: catastrophizing (e.g., awfulizing; *It is awful*) and frustration intolerance (e.g., *I cannot stand the situation*). These appraisals are core processes both in the REBT theory and cognitive theories of emotional disorders (catastrophizing and emotional intolerance; Barlow et al. (2014) and are considered as exaggerated forms of secondary appraisals, specifically of low emotion-focused coping potential (David et al. 2002). Thus, if we think the experience is awful, our embodied understanding of *awful* will be based on simulation of disturbed aversive emotions. When the emotional embodiment of awful is powerful and activated, the appraisals will be felt as aversive negative feelings and as an urge to avoid. If we think we cannot stand the experiences, our embodied understanding of *I cannot stand it* will be based on simulations of craving for relief and compulsive avoidance of negative states. As positive emotions are a currency for the positive value of situations, negative aversive emotions are a currency for the negative value.

3.6 The Experience of Disturbed Emotions as Simulation Basis

As mentioned above, there are two ways by which we can look at the central embodiments of distorted emotional appraisals. First, we can look at the characteristics of the emotional experiences used as resources for representation. Second, we can look at the characteristics of the neural patterns that implement disturbed emotions and are re-enacted during cognition. Above, I described the experience of disturbed emotions. It involves exaggerated negative emotions that are experienced aversively and uncontrolled, and are accompanied by avoidance behaviors. Because of various factors and conditions, individuals develop disturbed emotions. These experiences are captured in memory. Later on, they are reactivated to understand the personal significance of emotional encounters. Individuals simulate the negative emotions appropriate for understanding the valence of the situation. When situations are considered very negative, the situated conceptualizations that are reactivated include intense distorted negative emotions. When these simulations are powerful, but not complete, an individual not only thinks the situation is awful but also feels it is awful and has the urge to avoid it. When the simulations are fully activated, a fully conscious experience of disturbed emotions and behaviors are accompanying the appraisal of the situation as awful. For instance, let us consider the example of *being left by a partner*. When a person appraises this situation as awful, the meaning of awful is created by simulation of how he feels in a situation that had the biggest emotional impact on him: past disturbed negative emotions. If the emotional systems are also sensitized because of concurrent stress states, thinking "is awful" determines a fully activated feeling of disturbed emotion. Being left is not only awful, it feels this way, and the individuals tend to act as if in a disturbed situation. Following this logic, the evaluation of a situation as awful carries in it the elements of disturbed emotions. As composite IB (Ellis 2001), the meaning of awful is very intense negative emotions accompanied by intolerance, uncontrollability, and behaviorally by avoidance and escape behaviors. Using linguistic labels as "*It is awful*" may recruit (by simulations) disturbed emotions. Then, a fully activated composite belief of "It is awful" is triggered, which has thinking (It is awful), feeling (exaggerated emotions), and behavior (avoidance) dimensions.

3.7 Looking at the Brain

According to the embodied simulation principle, disturbed emotional experiences are generated by emotional knowledge when underlying simulations re-enact dysfunctional neural patterns in affective networks. Then, they fuse with ongoing states of the body (Barrett et al. 2014).

Thus, emotional embodied simulations become dysfunctional when they re-enact, in our understanding of the world (as activated situated conceptualizations), hyper-reactive neural states of affective networks (Pichon et al. 2014; Seth 2013) either by direct activation of over-reactive affective networks (Buhle et al. 2014; Liu et al. 2014) or by under-recruitment of their frontal control (Motzkin et al. 2014a, b). Furthermore, dysfunctional recruitment of executive control may derive either from deficient control such as decoupling of limbic regions from inhibitory prefrontal regions (decreased connectivity between ventromedial prefrontal and amygdala, Arnsten 2009; Bishop 2009; Buhle et al. 2014; Heatherton and Wagner 2011; Indovina et al. 2011; Motzkin et al. 2014a; Wagner and Heatherton 2013) or from inappropriate control, such as shifting the prefrontal-limbic coupling to an amplification mode (increased connectivity between dorsomedial prefrontal cortex and amygdala; Vytal et al. 2014). Besides this facilitated recruitment of bottom-up driven and uncontrolled over-reactive emotional simulations, regulatory difficulties set another mechanism that may maintain disturbed emotions. Emotional situations are under constant change, as it is our relationship with them. Thus, emotions result from sequential changes from one situated conceptualization to the other (Barrett et al. 2014). Updating new conceptualizations and the underlying re-enactment of neural patterns to reflect situational changes require the integrity of the same frontoparietal network. If the frontoparietal network is deficient, the new conceptualizations will lose their power to engage re-enactments of the corresponding neural states in affective, sensory, and motor brain regions and to change the competing emotional activation (Barrett et al. 2014). In other words, they lose the power to produce embodied responses to non-emotional meanings. Moreover, they will engage general simulations that will not have the power to override an overactive emotional activation, promoting inappropriate emotional reactions. Embodied cognition suggests that brain systems involved in disturbed emotions are reused to implement cognition which labels those experiences. Although these proposals have not been yet directly investigated, several types of dysfunctional knowledge have been shown to reflect such a pattern.

3.7.1 Catastrophizing

Catastrophizing has been extensively studied in the domain of pain and panic disorder. Neuroimaging studies show that catastrophizing related to pain involves over-active pain experience-related brain regions such as somatosensory cortex, insula, anterior cingulate, and amygdala (Cottam et al. 2016; Gracely et al. 2004; Seminowicz and Davis 2006) and under-reactive regulatory prefrontal cortex (PFC) recruitment (Bell et al. 2018). Similar findings showed that in panic disorder, catastrophizing about somatic sensations (difficulty of breathing) similarly involves over-reactive regions of anterior cingulate cortex (ACC) (Stoeckel et al. 2018). Thus, these studies suggest that catastrophizing beliefs are implemented by neural systems that implement disturbed experiences.

3.7.2 Frustration and Emotional Intolerance

REBT theory suggests that frustration intolerance (FI) is a core secondary appraisal (Ellis 1994). Although several general IBs scales measure FI (e.g., ABS scale), Harrington developed a Frustration Discomfort Scale (FDS) based on REBT appraisal theory. FDS scale has four factors: Discomfort Intolerance, Entitlement, Emotional Intolerance, and Achievement/Frustration (Harrington 2005). Both emotional (e.g., "I can't bear disturbing feelings", "I must be free of disturbing feelings as soon as possible", "I can't bear if they continue.") and discomfort intolerance (e.g., "I can't stand having to persist at unpleasant tasks", "I can't stand doing tasks when I'm not in the mood") are included in FI concepts. While FI beliefs are seen separate from demandingness, FDS includes both demandingness and frustration intolerance beliefs into the same concept of emotional (beliefs regarding uncertainty, controllability, and aversiveness of emotion) or frustration (life should be easy, and free of a hassle) intolerance (Leyro et al. 2010).

Studies using FDS showed that FI is related to emotional problems and self-control difficulties (Harrington 2005). Frustration intolerance is considered a type of distress intolerance (Leyro et al. 2010). Although little is known about the neural underpinnings of frustration intolerance, the concept of distress intolerance can provide ideas about the central embodiments recruited in FI. Distress intolerance is the inability to withstand aversive affective states and situations (Leyro et al. 2010). Distress intolerance has been associated with different psychopathologies such as major depression and anxiety disorders (Allan et al. 2014; Macatee et al. 2015, 2013), substance use disorders (Brown et al. 2009; Daughters et al. 2005; Strong et al. 2012), attention deficit and hyperactivity disorder symptoms (Cummings et al. 2013; Seymour et al. 2016), and personality disorders (Daughters et al. 2005).

Insights about the recruitment of hyper-reactive neural responses during distress intolerance come from the study of Daughters et al. (2017). Daugherts et al. modified a working memory task (participants were presented a number every 3 s and were asked to add the number they just heard with the number they heard before) to measure distress tolerance in healthy controls and substance use participants. They found greater activation in the cortico-limbic network involved in emotional regulation, the connectivity between the right medial frontal gyrus and ventromedial prefrontal cortex/subgenual anterior cingulate cortex predicting distress tolerance. These findings are related to conceptualizations of distress intolerance as a form of emotional dysregulation (Leyro et al. 2010).

Theories that analyze the biological basis of distress intolerance suggest that distress intolerance is linked with the inability to inhibit the behavioral option that could relieve distress immediately (i.e., responding to immediate negative reinforcement (NR) opportunity) during stressful states (Trafton and Gifford 2011). According to this conceptualization, the appraisal of escaping a distressing stimulus is analogous to an estimation of an immediate reward. As individuals may crave for a reward, similarly they may crave for escaping from a distressing stimulus. Animal studies show that brain regions activated during reward processing (ventral striatum, nucleus accumbens, OFC, PFC) also serve as neurobiological implementation for distress intolerance (Rodriguez et al. 2006). Furthermore, the excitability of inhibitory neurons in the mesocorticolimbic system moderates the association between the value of the reward and the pursuit of reward or relief (Zvolensky et al. 2011). Based on these ideas, FI overlaps with the concept of demandingness, but in the case of FI, individuals demand for relief not for obtaining the omitted reward or controlling the threat.

3.7.3 Other Types of Cognitions Involve Hot Simulations

In their study on perceived criticism, Hooley and colleagues asked participants to rate the criticism they perceive in the comments made by their mothers (Hooley et al. 2012). Functional magnetic resonance imaging scans showed that perceiving comments as very critical engaged a neural pattern characterized by over-activation of amygdala and anterior insula and decoupling from prefrontal regulatory regions across healthy, depressed, and formerly depressed individuals (Hooley et al. 2012). A similar pattern has been observed in other studies investigating negative self-referential statements (e.g., “I’m bad”) in vulnerable participants (Ma et al. 2013), social cognition in mood disorders (Cusi et al. 2012), or threat interpretation biases (Bishop 2007; Kim et al. 2003). Besides the high limbic-low inhibitory prefrontal pattern of connectivity engaged by negative self-knowledge, studies also revealed a high limbic-high prefrontal pattern of emotional over-reactivity. For instance, Doll et al. evidenced that implicit perseveration knowledge in reward learning and perseverative reactions recruit a prefrontal-hippocampal amplification of limbic dopaminergic activity (Doll et al. 2009). There are several implications of these findings for distorted embodied hot cognition.

During their developmental trajectories, some people may experience large amounts of intense and disinhibited emotional experiences. For example, they may experience fear during prolonged periods with no regulatory effort, anger or sadness in which they do not downregulate emotions or, worse, they upregulate negative emotions. People with innate biological emotional hyper-reactivity, increased autonomic activity, and parental misguidance for emotional reactions in early childhood are probably more predisposed to disinhibited emotional experiences. As a consequence, they acquire in memory disinhibited emotional situated conceptualizations and simulators. Building emotional simulators with disinhibited (deficient synaptic connections with inhibitory frontoparietal networks) and amplifying (increased synaptic connections with dorsomedial prefrontal brain regions) components and engaging them in the process of online situated conceptualization of negative emotional situations will cause an experience of disinhibited intense negative emotions such as anger, depression, panic, or anxiety. Moreover, the use of linguistic expressions such as those used for emotional or motivational upregulation ("I must be approved", "It is awful") may preferentially recruit disinhibited emotional simulations and constrain situated conceptualizations to include dysregulated activation of emotional simulators. When this process overlaps with sensitized emotional and motivational brain regions, the activation of disinhibited emotional simulators may constantly promote disturbed emotions. But stress exposure also induces a state (that can add to the trait vulnerability) vulnerability both in the generation and in the regulation of emotional networks. Prolonged stress exposure results in active states of overactive limbic structures and reduced engagement of frontoparietal systems. These state-like changes will be recruited in the conceptualization process by the underlying embodied simulations, thus favoring emotionally loaded situated conceptualizations. Frontoparietal deficiencies may result in impaired top-down re-enactments of brain and body states in affective, motor, visual, and mentalizing systems corresponding to alternative conceptualizations and thus in the perseveration of emotional simulations (Barrett et al. 2014).

For example, when approaching from a distance a barking, agitated dog that turns out to be on a leash (or someone tells you that is on a leash), the impairments of the re-enacting the brain states (in affective, motor, visual, mentalizing systems, and so forth) corresponding to dogs in a safe context will result in perseverative negative emotional simulations and inappropriate and dysregulated emotions.

Furthermore, individuals may be more vulnerable or more affected by the stress-induced damage on regulatory frontoparietal and hippocampal systems when they have untrained emotional inhibition networks or biological vulnerabilities. State and trait vulnerabilities may interact. For example, early life stress may result in long-term discrete prefrontal deficiency, later alteration of regulatory function becoming evident only in situations of high regulatory demands or regulatory depletion condition (stress, excessive or prolonged regulation, dietary reasons, glucose depletion, sleep deprivation, and so forth).

Other individuals may experience higher amounts of downregulated emotions either because they are biologically predisposed to and have initial low-intensity emotional reactions or they are supported to downregulate their emotions (i.e., by parental control, other induced regulation, rules, increased prefrontal efficacy, and so forth). Thus, they are prone to form inhibited emotional simulators (emotional memories including increased inhibitory synaptic plasticity) that will determine attenuated emotional experiences in terms of duration or intensity. Having strengthened emotional inhibition in brain regions, they may be less affected by the stress-induced damage on the regulatory prefrontal-hippocampus system.

3.8 Summary

Hot cognition is cognition that results in emotions. In order to result in emotions, embodied hot cognition should be based on embodied simulations of emotional experiences. The characteristics of emotional simulations determine the characteristics of resulting emotional experiences. Disturbed emotions are characterized by high intensity, averseness to emotional experience, lack of control, and attempts to control the emotional experience. Furthermore, brain activity during disturbed emotions is characterized by hyper-reactive emotional generation neural systems, hypoactive regulatory brain, and deficient coupling between affective and regulatory systems. Although studies did not investigate features of disturbed emotional experiences into distorted secondary appraisals, several studies suggest that a similar brain pattern of emotional dysregulation observed during disturbed emotional experiences can be observed during distorted secondary appraisals. Exaggerated secondary appraisals (catastrophizing and frustration intolerance) and other types of cognition involved in disturbed negative emotions seem to recruit hyper-reactive affective generation areas and hypoactive regulatory brain areas. All these lines of evidence suggest that embodied distorted cognition is a type of cognition involved in emotional psychopathologies. By considering hyper-reactive emotional embodied simulations as central to embodied distorted emotional cognition, differences that confer distorted quality of emotional simulations depend on whether they engage (besides the other multimodal components) hyper-reactive generative affective brain regions usually associated to deficient recruitment of regulatory brain regions or a shift from an inhibitory mode to an emotional amplification mode.

References

Abelson, R. P. (1963). Computer simulation of "hot" cognition. In S. Tomkins & S. Messick (Eds.), *Computer simulation of personality*. Wiley.

Aldao, A., Nolen-Hoeksema, S., & Schweizer, S. (2010). Emotion regulation strategies across psychopathology: A meta-analytic review. *Clinical Psychology Review, 30*, 217–237. https://doi.org/10.1016/j.cpr.2009.11.004

Allan, N. P., Macatee, R. J., Norr, A. M., & Schmidt, N. B. (2014). Direct and interactive effects of distress tolerance and anxiety sensitivity on generalized anxiety and depression. *Cognitive Therapy and Research, 38*(5), 530–540. https://doi.org/10.1007/s10608-014-9623-y

Arnsten, A. F. (2009). Stress signalling pathways that impair prefrontal cortex structure and function. *Nature Review Neuroscience, 10*(6), 410–422.

Barlow, D. H. (1991). Disorders of emotion. *Psychological Inquiry, 2*(1), 58–71. https://doi.org/10.1207/s15327965pli0201_15s

Barlow, D. H., Sauer-Zavala, S., Carl, J. R., Bullis, J. R., & Ellard, K. K. (2014). The nature, diagnosis, and treatment of neuroticism: Back to the future. *Clinical Psychological Science, 2*(3), 344–365.

Barrett, L. F. (2017). *How emotions are made: The secret life of the brain*. Houghton Mifflin Harcourt.

Barrett, L. F., Wilson-Mendenhall, C. D., & Barsalou, L. W. (2014). A psychological construction account of emotion regulation and dysregulation: The role of situated conceptualizations. In J. J. Gross (Ed.), *The handbook of emotion regulation* (2nd ed., pp. 447–465). Guilford.

Barsalou, L. W. (1999). Perceptual symbol systems. *Behavioral and Brain Sciences, 22*, 577–609.

Barsalou, L. W. (2003). Situated simulation in the human conceptual system. *Language and Cognitive Processes, 18*, 513–562.

Barsalou, L. W. (2008). Grounded cognition. *Annual Review of Psychology, 59*(1), 617–645.

Barsalou, L. W. (2013). Mirroring as pattern completion inferences within situated conceptualizations. *Cortex, 49*, 2951–2953.

Beck, A. T. (1976). *Cognitive therapy and the emotional disorders*. International Universities Press.

Bell, T., Mirman, J. H., & Stavrinos, D. (2018). Pain, pain Catastrophizing, and individual differences in executive function in adolescence. *Children's Health Care, 48*(1), 18–37. https://doi.org/10.1080/02739615.2018.1441028

Berridge, K. C., & Robinson, T. E. (2003). Parsing reward. *Trends in Neurosciences, 26*(9), 507–513.

Bishop, S. J. (2007). Neurocognitive mechanisms of anxiety: An integrative account. *Trends in Cognitive Sciences, 11*, 307–316.

Bishop, S. J. (2009). Trait anxiety and impoverished prefrontal control of attention. *Nature Neuroscience, 12*, 92–98.

Brose, A., Schmiedek, F., Koval, P., & Kuppens, P. (2015). Emotional inertia contributes to depressive symptoms beyond perseverative thinking. *Cognition and Emotion, 29*, 527–538. https://doi.org/10.1080/02699931.2014.916252

Brown, R. A., Lejuez, C. W., Strong, D. R., Kahler, C. W., Zvolensky, M. J., Carpenter, L. L., & Price, L. H. (2009). A prospective examination of distress tolerance and early smoking lapse in adult self-quitters. *Nicotine & Tobacco Research, 11*(5), 493–502.

Buhle, J. T., Silvers, J. A., Wager, T. D., Lopez, R., Onyemekwu, C., Kober, H., … Ochsner, K. N. (2014). Cognitive reappraisal of emotion: A meta-analysis of human neuroimaging studies. *Cerebral Cortex, 24*, 2981–2990.

Bullis, J. R., Boettcher, H., Sauer-Zavala, S., & Barlow, D. H. (2019). What is an emotional disorder? A transdiagnostic mechanistic definition with implications for assessment, treatment, and prevention. *Clinical Psychology: Science and Practice*, e12278. https://doi.org/10.1111/cpsp.12278.

Bylsma, L., Morris, B., & Rottenberg, J. (2008). A meta-analysis of emotional reactivity in major depressive disorder. *Clinical Psychology Review, 28*, 676–691. https://doi.org/10.1016/j.cpr.2007.10.001

Campbell-Sills, L., Barlow, D. H., Brown, T. A., & Hofmann, S. G. (2006). Acceptability and suppression of negative emotion in anxiety and mood disorders. *Emotion, 6*(4), 587–595. https://doi.org/10.1037/1528-3542.6.4.587

Cardona, J. F. (2017). Embodied cognition: A challenging road for clinical neuropsychology. *Frontiers in Aging Neuroscience, 9*, 388. https://doi.org/10.3389/fnagi.2017.00388

Carr, E. W., Kever, A., & Winkielman, P. (2018). Embodiment of emotion and its situated nature. In A. Newen, L. de Bruin, & S. Gallagher (Eds.), *The Oxford handbook of 4E cognition* (pp. 529–551). Oxford University Press.

Cisler, J. M., & Olatunji, B. O. (2012). Emotion regulation and anxiety disorders. *Current Psychiatry Reports, 14*(3), 182–187. https://doi.org/10.1007/s11920-012-0262-2

Compare, A., Zarbo, C., Shonin, E., Van Gordon, W., & Marconi, C. (2014). Emotional regulation and depression: A potential mediator between heart and mind. *Cardiovascular Psychiatry and Neurology*, 324374. https://doi.org/10.1155/2014/324374

Cottam, W. J., Condon, L., Alshuft, H., Reckziegel, D., & Auer, D. P. (2016). Associations of limbic-affective brain activity and severity of ongoing chronic arthritis pain are explained by trait anxiety. *NeuroImage. Clinical, 12*, 269–276. https://doi.org/10.1016/j.nicl.2016.06.022

Cummings, J. R., Bornovalova, M. A., Ojanen, T., Hunt, E., MacPherson, L., & Lejuez, C. (2013). Time doesn't change everything: The longitudinal course of distress tolerance and its relationship with externalizing and internalizing symptoms during early adolescence. *Journal of Abnormal Child Psychology, 41*(5), 735–748.

Cusi, A. M., Nazarov, A., Holshausen, K., Macqueen, G. M., & McKinnon, M. C. (2012). Systematic review of the neural basis of social cognition in patients with mood disorders. *Journal of Psychiatry Neuroscience, 37*(3), 154–169.

Daughters, S. B., Lejuez, C. W., Bornovalova, M. A., Kahler, C. W., Strong, D. R., & Brown, R. A. (2005). Distress tolerance as a predictor of early treatment dropout in a residential substance abuse treatment facility. *Journal of Abnormal Psychology, 114*(4), 729–734.

Daughters, S. B., Ross, T. J., Bell, R. P., Yi, J. Y., Ryan, J., & Stein, E. A. (2017). Distress tolerance among substance users is associated with functional connectivity between prefrontal regions during a distress tolerance task. *Addiction Biology, 22*(5), 1378–1390. https://doi.org/10.1111/adb.12396

David, D., & David, O. (2017). Hot cognitions. In V. Zeigler-Hill & T. Shackelford (Eds.), *Encyclopedia of personality and individual differences*. Springer.

David, D., Lynn, S. J., & Ellis, A. (2010). *Rational and irrational beliefs: Research, theory, and clinical practice*. Oxford University Press.

David, D., Schnur, J., & Belloiu, A. (2002). Another search for the "hot" cognition: Appraisal irrational beliefs, attribution, and their relation to emotion. *Journal of Rational-Emotive and Cognitive-Behavior Therapy, 20*, 93–131.

Demenescu, L. R., Kortekaas, R., Cremers, H. R., Renken, R. J., van Tol, M. J., van der Wee, N. J. A., … Aleman, A. (2013). Amygdala activation and its functional connectivity during perception of emotional faces in social phobia and panic disorder. *Journal of Psychiatric Research, 47*, 1024–1031.

DiGiuseppe, R., Doyle, K. A., Dryden, W., & Bacx, W. (2014). *A practioner's guide to rational emotive behavior therapy*. Oxford University Press.

Doll, B. B., Jacobs, W. J., Sanfey, A. G., & Frank, M. J. (2009). Instructional control of reinforcement learning: A behavioral and neurocomputational investigation. *Brain Research, 1299*, 74–94.

Drevets, W. C. (2000). Neuroimaging studies of mood disorders. *Biological Psychiatry, 48*, 813–829.

Eggart, M., Lange, A., Binser, M. J., Queri, S., & Müller-Oerlinghausen, B. (2019). Major depressive disorder is associated with impaired interoceptive accuracy: A systematic review. *Brain Sciences, 9*(6), 131. https://doi.org/10.3390/brainsci9060131

Eigsti, I. M. (2013). A review of embodiment in autism spectrum disorders. *Frontiers in Psychology, 4*, 224. https://doi.org/10.3389/fpsyg.2013.00224

Ellis, A. (1994). *Reason and emotion is psychotherapy*. Citadel Press.

Ellis, A. (2001). *Feeling better, getting better, staying better: Profound self-help therapy for your emotions*. Impact Publishers.

Ellis, A., David, D., & Lynn, S. J. (2010). Rational and irrational beliefs: A historical and conceptual perspective. In D. David, S. J. Lynn, & A. Ellis (Eds.), *Rational and irrational beliefs: Research, theory, and clinical practice* (pp. 3–22). Oxford University Press.

Ford, B. Q., & Gross, J. J. (2019). Why beliefs about emotion matter: An emotion-regulation perspective. *Current Directions in Psychological Science, 28*(1), 74–81. https://doi.org/10.1177/0963721418806697

Forster, S., Castle, E., Nunez-elizalde, A. O., & Bishop, S. J. (2014). Moderate threat causes longer lasting disruption to processing in anxious individuals. *Frontiers in Human Neuroscience, 8*, 626. https://doi.org/10.3389/fnhum.2014.00626

Fuchs, T., & Koch, S. (2014). Embodied affectivity: On moving and being moved. *Frontiers in Psychology. Psychology for Clinical Settings, 5*, 1–12. https://doi.org/10.3389/fpsyg.2014.00508

Fuchs, T., & Schlimme, J. (2009). Embodiment and psychopathology: A phenomenological perspective. *Current Opinion in Psychiatry, 22*, 570–575.

Füstös, J., Gramann, K., Herbert, B. M., & Pollatos, O. (2013). On the embodiment of emotion regulation: Interoceptive awareness facilitates reappraisal. *Social Cognitive and Affective Neuroscience, 8*(8), 911–917. https://doi.org/10.1093/scan/nss089

Gjelsvik, B., Lovric, D., & Williams, J. M. G. (2018). Embodied cognition and emotional disorders. Embodiment and abstraction in understanding depression. *Journal of Experimental Psychopathology*, 1–41. https://doi.org/10.5127/pr.035714

Gracely, R. H., Geisser, M. E., Giesecke, T., Grant, M. A. B., Petzke, F., Williams, D. A., & Clauw, D. J. (2004). Pain catastrophizing and neural responses to pain among persons with fibromyalgia. *Brain, 127*, 835–843.

Gross, J. J. (2015). The extended process model of emotion regulation: Elaborations, applications, and future directions. *Psychological Inquiry, 26*, 130–137. https://doi.org/10.1080/1047840X.2015.989751

Gross, J. J., & Jazaieri, H. (2014). Emotion, emotion regulation, and psychopathology: An affective science perspective. *Clinical Pyschological Science, 2*(4), 387–401. https://doi.org/10.1177/2167702614536164

Harrington, N. (2005). The frustration discomfort scale: Development and psychometric properties. *Clinical Psychology and Psychotherapy, 12*, 374–387. https://doi.org/10.1002/cpp.465

Harshaw, C. (2015). Interoceptive dysfunction: Toward an integrated framework for understanding somatic and affective disturbance in depression. *Psychological Bulletin, 141*(2), 311–363. https://doi.org/10.1037/a0038101

Hazlett, E. A., Zhang, J., New, A. S., Zelmanova, Y., Goldstein, K. E., Haznedar, M. M., & Chu, K. W. (2012). Potentiated amygdala response to repeated emotional pictures in borderline personality disorder. *Biological Psychiatry, 72*, 448–456.

Heatherton, T. F., & Wagner, D. D. (2011). Cognitive neuroscience of self-regulation failure. *Trends in Cognitive Sciences, 15*(3), 132–139.

Hooley, J. M., Siegle, G., & Gruber, S. A. (2012). Affective and neural reactivity to criticism in individuals high and low on perceived criticism. *PLoS One, 7*(9), e44412.

Houben, M., Van Den Noortgate, W., & Kuppens, P. (2015). The relation between short-term emotion dynamics and psychological Well-being: A meta-analysis. *Psychological Bulletin, 141*(4), 901–930. https://doi.org/10.1037/a0038822

Ianì, F. (2019). Embodied memories: Reviewing the role of the body in memory processes. *Psychonomic Bulletin & Review, 26*(6), 1747–1766. https://doi.org/10.3758/s13423-019-01674-x

Indovina, I., Robbins, T. W., Núñez-Elizalde, A. O., Dunn, B. D., & Bishop, S. J. (2011). Fear conditioning mechanisms associated with trait vulnerability to anxiety in humans. *Neuron, 69*, 563–571. https://doi.org/10.1016/j.neuron.2010.12.034

Jazaieri, H., Urry, H. L., & Gross, J. J. (2013). Affective disturbance and psychopathology: An emotion regulation perspective. *Journal of Experimental Psychopathology, 4*(584), 599.

Johnstone, T., van Reekum, C. M., Urry, H. L., Kalin, N. H., & Davidson, R. J. (2007). Failure to regulate: Counterproductive recruitment of top-down prefrontal-subcortical circuitry in major depression. *The Journal of Neuroscience, 27*(33), 8877–8884.

Kever, A., Grynberg, D., Bayot, M., & Vermeulen, N. (2016). Embodying emotions: The role of bodily changes in emotional processing: Evidence from normal and psychopathological populations. In Y. Coello & M. H. Fischer (Eds.), *Foundations of embodied cognition: Perceptual and emotional embodiment* (pp. 246–261). Routledge/Taylor & Francis Group.

Kim, H., Somerville, L. H., Johnstone, T., Alexander, A. L., & Whalen, P. J. (2003). Inverse amygdala and medial prefrontal cortex responses to surprised faces. *Neuroreport, 14*, 2317–2322.

Klabunde, M., Collado, D., & Bohon, C. (2017). An interoceptive model of bulimia nervosa: A neurobiological systematic review. *Journal of Psychiatric Research, 94*, 36–46. https://doi.org/10.1016/j.jpsychires.2017.06.009

Koval, P., Pe, M. L., Meers, K., & Kuppens, P. (2013). Affect dynamics in relation to depressive symptoms: Variable, unstable or inert? *Emotion, 13*, 1132–1141.

Koval, P., Sütterlin, S., & Kuppens, P. (2016). Emotional inertia is associated with lower Well-being when controlling for differences in emotional context. *Frontiers in Psychology, 6*, 1–11.

Lamers, L., Swendsen, J., Cui, L., Husky, M., Johns, J., Zipunnikov, V., & Merikangas, K. R. (2018). Mood reactivity and affective dynamics in mood and anxiety disorders. *Journal of Abnormal Psychology, 127*, 659–669. https://doi.org/10.1037/abn0000378

Lazarus, R. S. (1991). *Emotion and adaptation*. New York: Oxford University Press.

Lee, H., Heller, A. S., van Reekum, C. M., Nelson, B., & Davidson, R. J. (2012). Amygdala-prefrontal coupling underlies individual differences in emotion regulation. *NeuroImage, 62*(3), 1575–1581.

Leitan, N. D., & Murray, G. (2014). The mind-body relationship in psychotherapy: Grounded cognition as an explanatory framework. *Frontiers in Psychology, 5*, 472. https://doi.org/10.3389/fpsyg.2014.00472

Leyro, T. M., Zvolensky, M. J., & Bernstein, A. (2010). Distress tolerance and psychopathological symptoms and disorders: A review of the empirical literature among adults. *Psychological Bulletin, 136*(4), 576–600. https://doi.org/10.1037/a0019712

Lindeman, L. M., & Abramson, L. Y. (2008). The mental simulation of motor incapacity in depression. *Journal of Cognitive Psychotherapy, 22*(3), 228–249.

Liu, Z. P., Song, C., Wang, M., He, Y., Xu, X. B., Pan, H. Q., … Pan, B. X. (2014). Chronic stress impairs GABAergic control of amygdala through suppressing the tonic GABAA receptor currents. *Molecular Brain, 7*, 32. https://doi.org/10.1186/1756-6606-7-32

Ma, Y., Li, B., Wang, C., Shi, Z., Sun, Y., Sheng, F., … Han, S. (2013). 5-HTTLPR polymorphism modulates neural mechanisms of negative self-reflection. *Cerebral Cortex, 24*(9), 2421–2429. https://doi.org/10.1093/cercor/bht099

Macatee, R. J., Capron, D. W., Guthrie, W., Schmidt, N. B., & Cougle, J. R. (2015). Distress tolerance and pathological worry: Tests of incremental and prospective relationships. *Behavior Therapy, 46*(4), 449–462.

Macatee, R. J., Capron, D. W., Schmidt, N. B., & Cougle, J. R. (2013). An examination of low distress tolerance and life stressors as factors underlying obsessions. *Journal of Psychiatric Research, 47*(10), 1462–1468.

McLaughlin, K. A., Mennin, D. S., & Farach, F. J. (2007). The contributory role of worry in emotion generation and dysregulation in generalized anxiety disorder. *Behaviour Research and Therapy, 45*, 1735–1752.

Mermillod, M., Vermeulen, N., Droit-Volet, S., Jalenques, I., Durif, F., & Niedenthal, P. M. (2011). Embodying emotional disorders: New hypotheses about possible emotional consequences of motor disorders in Parkinson's disease and Tourette's syndrome. *ISRN Neurology*, 306918. https://doi.org/10.5402/2011/306918

Michalak, J., Mischnat, J., & Teismann, T. (2014). Sitting posture makes a difference-embodiment effects on depressive memory bias. *Clinical Psychology & Psychotherapy, 21*, 519–524.

Michalak, J., Rohde, K., & Troje, N. F. (2015). How we walk affects what we remember: Gait modifications through biofeedback change negative affective memory bias. *Journal of Behavior Therapy and Experimental Psychiatry, 46*, 121–125.

Motzkin, J. C., Baskin-Sommers, A., Newman, J. P., Kiehl, K., & Koenigs, M. (2014b). Neural correlates of substance abuse: Reduced functional connectivity between areas underlying reward and cognitive control. *Human Brain Mapping, 35*, 4282–4292.

Motzkin, J. C., Philippi, C. L., Wolf, R. C., Baskaya, M. K., & Koenigs, M. (2014a). Ventromedial prefrontal cortex is critical for the regulation of amygdala activity in humans. *Biological Psychiatry*. https://doi.org/10.1016/j.biopsych.2014.02.014

Myers-Schulz, B., & Koenigs, M. (2012). Functional anatomy of ventromedial prefrontal cortex: Implications for mood and anxiety disorders. *Molecular Psychiatry, 17*, 132–141.

Niedenthal, P. M. (2007). Embodying emotion. *Science, 316*, 1002–1005.

Niedenthal, P. M., Winkielman, P., Mondillon, L., & Vermeulen, N. (2009). Embodiment of emotional concepts: Evidence from EMG measures. *Journal of Personality and Social Psychology, 96*, 1120–1136.

Ochsner, K. N., & Gross, J. J. (2008). Cognitive emotion regulation: Insights from social cognitive and affective neuroscience. *Current Directions in Psychological Science, 17*, 153–158.

Ochsner, K. N., Silvers, J. A., & Buhle, J. T. (2012). Functional imaging studies of emotion regulation: A synthetic review and evolving model of the cognitive control of emotion. *Annals of the New York Academy of Sciences, 1251*, E1–E24.

Ottenbreit, N. D., Dobson, K. S., & Quigley, L. (2014). A psychometric evaluation of the cognitive-Behavioral avoidance scale in women with major depressive disorder. *Journal of Psychopathology and Behavioral Assessment, 36*(4), 591–599. https://doi.org/10.1007/s10862-014-9416-3

Paley, J. (2004). Clinical cognition and embodiment. *International Journal of Nursing Studies, 41*, 1–13.

Peters, J., Kalivas, P. W., & Quirk, G. J. (2009). Extinction circuits for fear and addiction overlap in prefrontal cortex. *Learning and Memory, 16*, 279–288.

Pichon, S., Miendlarzewska, E., Eryilmaz, H., & Vuilleumier, P. (2014). Cumulative activation during positive or negative emotional events predicts inertia of future amygdala reactivity. *Social Cognitive & Affective Neuroscience*. https://doi.org/10.1093/scan/nsu044

Pietrzak, T., Lohr, C., Jahn, B., & Hauke, G. (2018). Embodied cognition and the direct induction of affect as a compliment to cognitive behavioural therapy. *Behavioral Sciences (Basel, Switzerland), 8*(3), 29. https://doi.org/10.3390/bs8030029

Predatu, R., David, D. O., & Maffei, A. (2019). Beliefs about emotions, negative meta-emotions, and perceived emotional control during an emotionally salient situation in individuals with emotional disorders. *Cognitive Therapy and Research*. https://doi.org/10.1007/s10608-019-10064-5

Quirk, G. J., & Gehlert, D. R. (2003). Inhibition of the amygdala: Key to pathological states? *Annals of New York Academy of Sciences, 985*, 263–272.

Rauch, S. L., Whalen, P. J., Shin, L. M., Mcinerney, S. C., Macklin, M. L., Lasko, N. B., … Pitman, R. K. (2000). Exaggerated amygdala response to masked facial stimuli in posttraumatic stress disorder: A functional MRI study. *Biological Psychiatry, 47*, 769–776.

Résibois, M., Kuppens, P., Van Mechelen, I., Fossati, P., & Verduyn, P. (2018). Depression severity moderates the relation between self-distancing and features of emotion unfolding. *Personality and Individual Differences, 123*, 119–124.

Ressler, K. J. (2010). Amygdala activity, fear, and anxiety: Modulation by stress. *Biological Psychiatry, 67*, 1117–1119. https://doi.org/10.1016/j.biopsych.2010.04.027

Rodriguez, P. F., Aron, A. R., & Poldrack, R. A. (2006). Ventral–striatal/nucleus–accumbens sensitivity to prediction errors during classification learning. *Human Brain Mapping, 27*(4), 306–313. https://doi.org/10.1002/hbm.20186

Rosenkranz, J. A., Venheim, E. R., & Padival, M. (2010). Chronic stress causes amygdala hyperexcitability in rodents. *Biological Psychiatry, 67*, 1128–1136. https://doi.org/10.1016/j.biopsych.2010.02.008

Seminowicz, D. A., & Davis, K. D. (2006). Cortical responses to pain in healthy individuals depend on pain catastrophizing. *Pain, 120*(3), 297–306.

Servaas, M. N., van der Velde, J., Costafreda, S. G., Horton, P., Ormel, J., Riese, H., & Aleman, A. (2013). Neuroticism and the brain: A quantitative meta-analysis of neuroimaging studies investigating emotion processing. *Neuroscience and Biobehavioral Reviews, 37*(8), 1518–1529.

Seth, A. K. (2013). Interoceptive inference, emotion, and the embodied self. *Trends in Cognitive Sciences, 17*(11), 656–663.

Seymour, K. E., Macatee, R., & Chronis-Tuscano, A. (2016). Frustration tolerance in youth with ADHD. *Journal of Attention Disorders, 23*(11), 1229–1239. https://doi.org/10.1177/1087054716653216.

Shin, L. M., Wright, C. I., Cannistraro, P. A., Wedig, M. M., Mcmullin, K., Martis, B., ... Rauch, S. L. (2005). A functional magnetic resonance imaging study of amygdala and medial prefrontal cortex responses to overtly presented fearful faces in posttraumatic stress disorder. *Archives of General Psychiatry, 62*, 273–281.

Siegle, G. J., Steinhauer, S. R., Thase, M. E., Stenger, V. A., & Carter, C. S. (2002). Can't shake that feeling: Event-related fMRI assessment of sustained amygdala activity in response to emotional information in depressed individuals. *Biological Psychiatry, 51*, 693–707.

Silvers, J. A., Buhle, J. T., & Ochsner, K. N. (2014). The neuroscience of emotion regulation: Basic mechanisms and their role in development, aging and psychopathology. In K. N. Ochsner & S. M. Kosslyn (Eds.), *The Oxford handbook of cognitive neuroscience, Vol. 2: The cutting edges* (pp. 53–78). Oxford University Press.

Smith, C. A., & Lazarus, R. S. (1993). Appraisal components, core relational themes, and the emotions. *Cognition & Emotion, 7*(3–4), 233–269.

Stoeckel, M. C., Esser, R. W., Gamer, M., Buchel, C., & Leupoldt, A. (2018). Dyspnea catastrophizing and neural activations during the anticipation and perception of dyspnea. *Psychophysiology, 55*(4). https://doi.org/10.1111/psyp.13004

Strong, D. R., Brown, R. A., Sims, M., Herman, D. S., Anderson, B. J., & Stein, M. D. (2012). Persistence during stress-challenge associated with lapse to opioid use during buprenorphine treatment. *Journal of Addiction Medicine, 6*(3), 219–225.

Tiba, A. I. (2010). Grounded cognition perspective on irrational beliefs in rational emotive behaviour therapy. *Journal of Cognitive and Behavioral Psychotherapies, 10*, 87–99.

Trafton, J. A., & Gifford, E. V. (2011). Biological bases of distress tolerance. In M. J. Zvolensky, A. Bernstein, & A. A. Vujanovic (Eds.), *Distress tolerance: Theory, research, and clinical applications* (pp. 80–102). The Guilford Press.

Urry, H. L., van Reekum, C. M., Johnstone, T., Kalin, N. H., Thurow, M. E., Schaefer, H. S., ... Davidson, R. J. (2006). Amygdala and ventromedial prefrontal cortex are inversely coupled during regulation of negative affect and predict the diurnal pattern of cortisol secretion among older adults. *Journal of Neuroscience, 26*, 4415–4425.

Veenstra, L., Schneider, I. K., & Koole, S. L. (2017). Embodied mood regulation: The impact of body posture on mood recovery, negative thoughts, and mood-congruent recall. *Cognition and Emotion, 7*, 1361–1376. https://doi.org/10.1080/02699931.2016.1225003

Vermeulen, N., Godefroid, J., & Mermillod, M. (2009). Emotional modulation of attention: fear increases but disgust reduces the attentional blink. *PloS one, 4*(11), e7924. https://doi.org/10.1371/journal.pone.0007924

Vermeulen, N., Niedenthal, P. M., & Luminet, O. (2007). Switching between sensory and affective systems incurs processing costs. *Cognitive Science, 31*, 183–192.

Vyas, A., Mitra, R., Shankaranarayana Rao, B. S., & Chattarji, S. (2002). Chronic stress induces contrasting patterns of dendritic remodeling in hippocampal and amygdaloid neurons. *Journal of Neuroscience, 22*, 6810–6818.

Vytal, K. E., Overstreet, C., Charney, D. R., Robinson, O. J., & Grillon, C. (2014). Sustained anxiety increases amygdala-dorsomedial prefrontal coupling: A mechanism for maintaining an anxious state in healthy adults. *Journal of Psychiatry & Neuroscience, 39*(4), 321–329. https://doi.org/10.1503/jpn.130145

Wagner, D. D., & Heatherton, T. F. (2013). Self-regulatory depletion increases emotional reactivity in the amygdale. *Social Cognitive and Affective Neuroscience, 8*, 410–417. https://doi.org/10.1093/scan/nss082

Waugh, C. E., Hamilton, J. P., & Gotlib, I. H. (2010). The neural temporal dynamics of the intensity of emotional experience. *NeuroImage, 49*, 1699–1707.

Winkielman, P., Niedenthal, P., Wielgosz, J., Eelen, J., & Kavanagh, L. C. (2015). Embodiment of cognition and emotion. In M. Mikulincer, P. R. Shaver, E. Borgida, & J. A. Bargh (Eds.), *APA handbooks in psychology®. APA handbook of personality and social psychology, Vol. 1. Attitudes and social cognition* (pp. 151–175). American Psychological Association. https://doi.org/10.1037/14341-004

Wohleb, E. S., McKim, D. B., Sheridan, J. F., & Godbout, J. P. (2015). Monocyte trafficking to the brain with stress and inflammation: a novel axis of immune-to-brain communication that influences mood and behavior. *Frontiers in neuroscience, 8*, 447. https://doi.org/10.3389/fnins.2014.00447

Zatti, A., & Zarbo, C. (2015). Embodied and exbodied mind in clinical psychology. A proposal for a psycho-social interpretation of mental disorders. *Frontiers in Psychology, 6*, 236. https://doi.org/10.3389/fpsyg.2015.00236

Zvolensky, M. J., Leyro, T., Bernstein, A., & Vujanovic, A. A. (2011). Distress tolerance: Historical perspectives, theory, and measurement. In M. J. Zvolensky, A. Bernstein, & A. A. Vujanovic (Eds.), *Distress tolerance* (pp. 3–20). Guildford.

Chapter 4
Embodying Hot Cognition in Stress-Related Neuroadaptations

The embodied simulation account posits that "partial re-enactment" of modal brain states is at the core of cognition (Barsalou 1999). When the brain is altered, those altered brain states may be selectively "re-enacted" (by embodied simulations) for carrying on the requirements of various tasks and result in biased performance. For example, when the auditory areas are damaged, recruiting the damaged auditory brain circuits in processing results in selectively impaired performance for sound relevant concepts (Trumpp et al. 2013). On the contrary, when the visual areas (right inferior temporo-occipital lobes) are damaged, recruiting the damaged visual brain circuits in processing results in selectively impaired performance for visual-related nouns, whereas patients with right frontal lobe lesions showed most severe deficits in processing action verbs (Neininger and Pulvermüller 2003). Furthermore, damage to the motor cortex impairs the comprehension of action-related concepts (Gainotti 2006).

Other types of "transient" brain alterations besides lesions have been revealed to be recruited by embodied simulations. Pulvermüller and colleagues used transcranial magnetic stimulation (TMS) to induce alterations of different parts of the motor cortex. They showed that induced alterations of the hand area of motor cortex bias the recognition of hand-related concepts. In turn, alterations of leg motor cortex bias the recognition of foot-related words (Pulvermüller et al. 2005).

Furthermore, studies have provided evidence that induced motor alterations (facilitation) are recruited and bias conceptual processing, especially when the conceptual task is designed to rely heavily on motor simulations (recruit motor resources). For example, Tomasino and colleagues used TMS to stimulate hand motor cortex after word presentation. They asked participants to indicate whether they finished reading, judge whether the action involved a rotation of the hand, or whether the word occurred frequently in a newspaper. The results revealed that when the level of action simulation required in word processing is manipulated (silent reading, action simulation judgment, or frequency judgment), different levels of biasing in conceptual tasks can be observed. TMS induced alterations on hand motor cortex bias conceptual processing when participants use action simulation

A. Tiba, *Embodied Hot Cognitive Vulnerability to Emotional Disorders*,
https://doi.org/10.1007/978-3-030-53989-4_4

(imagery) in processing (Tomasino et al. 2008). These results suggest that those specific embodied simulations that are recruited for conceptual processing may differ depending on the contextual conditions (task requirements) (Tomasino et al. 2008). These studies suggest that recruiting specific embodied simulations that tag altered brain areas determines whether altered or non-altered brain states are recruited in situated conceptualizations. This is of importance when cognition is more than just a lab designed task. Situated conceptualizations based on embodied simulations are considered the very foundation on which our moment-by-moment conscious experience is built (Barrett et al. 2014). When embodied simulations recruit altered brain states in the construction of our experience, they contribute also to disturbances of our experience. The disturbance of emotional experiences is one of the most common problems for modern humans and is the core of emotional disorders.

Altered brain states are not exceptional conditions of our emotional life. Although aforementioned studies have shown the effect of recruiting damaged or artificial alterations (inhibition or excitation) in laboratory tasks, a wide variety of brain alterations, especially in our emotional brain, occurs during quite common life conditions. One of these life conditions is prolonged or intense exposure to stress.

Considerable animal and human research demonstrates that early negative life events (Lupien et al. 2009) and chronic stress (Arnsten 2009) determine the hyper-reactivity and sensitization of hypothalamic-pituitary-adrenal (HPA) axis and limbic circuits (Heim and Nemeroff 2001; McEwen et al. 2015) involved in bottom-up affective processes. Additionally, chronic stress determines the deterioration of prefrontal (Arnsten 2009; Datta and Arnsten 2019; Davidson and McEwen 2012), hippocampal (McEwen 1999), and habenula (Hikosaka 2010) systems involved in top-down emotion processes. These stress-induced changes determine long-term hyper-reactivity of affective circuits (i.e., named here hyper-reactive emotional embodied simulations when engaged for representational purpose) and subsequent vulnerability to stress and stress-related emotional disorders (SEDs) (Cabib et al. 2020; Douma and de Kloet 2020; Flinn et al. 2011; McEwen et al. 2015).

Although many other unique conditions may result in sensitized emotional and motivational systems (drugs, hormones, homeostatic changes, chemicals), I will focus on stress and stress-related glucocorticoid release by HPA activation. It is important to mention that early or prolonged exposure to stressful events does not determine sensitization by default. Sensitization of emotional and motivational states most likely occurs in genetically susceptible people (e.g., Val allele of the brain-derived neurotrophic factor (BNDF) and short allele of the reuptake by the serotonin transporter (5-HTT) polymorphism; Vergne and Nemeroff 2006; or in other genetic polymorphisms; Gillespie et al. 2009).

4.1 Hot Embodied Simulations Carry Stress-Related Neuroadaptations

As with other types of brain alterations, stress-related brain alterations (neuroadaptations) may be recruited for the construction of our experience, resulting in disturbed emotions. According to the embodied simulation view, this is one of the main mechanisms of cognitive vulnerability to SEDs.

The fact that people become more sensitive to stress stimuli after stress exposure is one of the most recognized phenomena related to stress. There are two main views that explain how sensitization contributes to SEDs. On one hand, there is the biological view which posits that stress or mood episodes result in a wide variety of brain changes, including the sensitization of emotional circuits to negative stimuli. Because of sensitization, in future encounters, small amounts of stressors will be enough to activate the stress responses or negative mood (Morris et al. 2010; Post 1992; Stroud et al. 2008).

On the other hand, there is the cognitive view. The cognitive view posits that stress or mood episodes result in increased accessibility of negative thoughts and this is how they contribute to later vulnerability (Segal et al. 1996). During the first stress or depression episode, negative cognition (stored as amodal nodes along with nodes for mood in associative networks) becomes strengthened by frequent use and repetition. In the subsequent periods of stress, because of repetition and strengthened association with negative mood, dysfunctional knowledge becomes more accessible (Segal et al. 1996). As a consequence, in the future, small amounts of stressors (or negative mood) will be enough to result in increased response by negative cognition (increase in cognitive reactivity).

The embodied simulation view links both cognitive and biological views of sensitization. According to the embodied simulation account, the following sequence occurs. Exposure to early negative events results in the sensitization of emotional and other modal systems along with deterioration of regulatory brain systems. Later on, during periods of stress (encountering activating events), sensitized responses are reactivated along with low (or dysfunctional) recruitment of brain systems involved in their regulation (prefrontal and hippocampal systems). In these conditions, distorted emotional cognition recruits hyper-reactive states of sensitized affective systems for conceptualization or other cognitive processes to build our moment-by-moment experience. Thus, intense, prolonged, and dysregulated negative emotions are generated. Furthermore, hyper-reactive states of affective systems will favor the frequent use of emotional simulations as a basis for situated conceptualization of core sensations (from perception to memory and planning) resulting in emotional biases of cognition and experience. Thus, overactive emotional simulations will pervade the situated conceptualization process. Moreover, deficiencies in prefrontal regulatory systems will also impair the multimodal re-enactments required to implement new non-emotional conceptualizations (Barrett et al. 2014), either as the situation naturally unfolds in a non-emotional resolution (e.g., automatic regulation; "I receive the news that there is no more danger") or when emotional regulation reappraisals are used (deliberate regulation; "I see the situation as unemotional"). Consequently, these deficiencies will determine the loss of the power of new situated conceptualizations to change the modal and peripheral emotional pattern of activation. Thus, inappropriate negative emotions are maintained.

At the same time, the recurrent use of distorted negative emotional cognition in conceptualization will consistently reactivate states of hyper-reactivity of affective brain systems and of under-recruitment of inhibitory brain systems. This may further maintain the hyper-reactivity of affective systems. From an embodied simulation perspective, early stress (even prenatal) contains a confounding effect besides dysfunctional negative knowledge that results in disturbed negative emotions: the sensitization (i.e., hyper-reactivity) of the affective brain systems. When states in sensitized circuits are used for representational purposes, they act as hyper-reactive emotional embodied simulations (i.e., emotional embodiments). Dysfunctional negative knowledge represents emotional vulnerability if it engages hyper-reactive motivational and emotional embodiments for conceptualization and maintains the affective systems in a sensitized state. Although other types of dysfunctional simulations (overgeneralized, rigid, or content-inappropriate simulations) may also be important for emotional disturbances (Barrett et al. 2014), I highlight the dysfunctional aspect of simulations in relation to recruiting stress-induced neuroadaptations of affective systems in the construction of emotional experiences.

Nonetheless, distorted emotional knowledge (i.e., demandingness, awfulizing) preferentially activates sensitized and/or disinhibited affective systems over other types of cognition (preferences) and results in intense negative emotions. People are not emotionally disturbed by irrational beliefs, but by the disturbed emotional embodiments they use for understanding irrational beliefs. Yet irrational linguistic statements preferentially activate disturbed dysregulated embodiments. Changing the embodiments by directing them in other non-sensitized systems or tailoring them to recruit inhibitory control will change the emotional experience (e.g., the instruction to find rhymes for *I need love* will recruit linguistic embodiments and will block associated emotional reactions). The power of distorted emotional knowledge to determine disturbed emotional reactions does not result from the type of knowledge per se but from its core embodied simulations of hyper-reactive neural states in affective (emotional-motivational) systems. The embodied simulation account puts distorted emotional cognition and underlying hyper-reactive emotional embodied simulations at the center of vulnerability to SEDs.

In the following part of the chapter, I discuss human and nonhuman animal evidence for the idea that distorted hot cognition, as vulnerability for disturbed emotions, is embodied in stress-related brain neuroadaptations. To this end, I discuss sources of evidence that support each part of this idea. Specifically, I illustrate research supporting that (1) stress hormones induce plastic brain alterations of affective systems and their regulatory counterparts, (2) plasticity-related alterations in our modal and affective brain are recruited in cognition resulting in differences in cognition, (3) stress-induced plasticity interacts with learning-induced plasticity in the brain and results in distorted affective representations, (4) stress-related brain plastic alterations are recruited to represent cognition in SEDs, (5) stress-related brain plastic alterations predispose people to develop SEDs, and (6) specific genotypes predict distorted thinking in response to stress.

4.2 Exposure to Stress Hormones and the Affective Brain

Stressful life events and threats activate specialized neurohormonal systems (e.g., sympatho-adrenomedullary, hypothalamic-pituitary-adrenal/HPA) that result in large plastic reconfigurations of brain networks supporting optimal responses to threats (Belda et al. 2015; Callaghan et al. 2013; Garcia 2002; McEwen and Gianaros 2011). It is thought that these systems first reconfigure the brain into a threat mode, mobilizing the organisms to face threat and then work to restore it to "non-threat" functioning. This is called adaptive or functional neuroadaptation or plasticity (Cabib et al. 2020). Often, the exposure to stress is prolonged, too frequent, or intense and this may cause the dysregulation of the stress HPA axis and excessive levels of stress hormones (McEwen and Gianaros 2011). Depending on the specific genetic susceptibility of brain networks (Pechtel and Pizzagalli 2011), when the level of stress hormones is too high, long-lasting alterations may develop (dysfunctional neuroadaptations) in both the connectivity and the structure of the brain (Gunnar and Quevedo 2007; Lupien et al. 2009; Soares et al. 2014). For instance, stress-related changes have been described across various affect-related brain areas such as amygdala (Admon et al. 2009; Tottenham and Sheridan 2009), striatum (Bogdan et al. 2013; de Kloet et al. 2019; Douma and de Kloet 2020; Pizzagalli 2014), hippocampus (Gourley et al. 2013; Kim and Diamond 2002; McEwen 1999; McEwen and Gianaros 2011), habenula (Hikosaka 2010), and prefrontal cortex (Arnsten 2009, 2015; Datta and Arnsten 2019) but also in primary sensory cortex (e.g., olfactory cortex, Li 2014; auditory cortex, Apergis-Schoute et al. 2014; Kluge et al. 2011, and visual cortex, Krusemark and Li 2011). Furthermore, stress-related effects have been described at the level of brain networks (measured at rest) such as greater activation and impairments in the deactivation of the default mode, dorsal attention, ventral attention, sensorimotor, and primary visual networks (Soares et al. 2013a), some being reversible (Soares et al. 2013b). This is called maladaptive or dysfunctional neuroadaptation/plasticity or brain alterations (Cabib et al. 2020).

This line of evidence concludes that significant or chronic exposure to stress hormones results in dysfunctional neuroplastic brain alterations (some being reversible) underlying a general pattern of affective hyper-reactivity and regulatory deficiency involved in SEDs (Davidson and McEwen 2012; McEwen et al. 2015).

By embodying cognition, changes (stable or reactive) in modal brain states result in disturbed affective and behavioral responses and are recruited for representational proposes being reflected in distortions of cognition.

As I described in the beginning of the chapter, this hypothesis has received direct support from several studies of patients with lesions in sensory and motor brain areas. For instance, Trumpp and colleagues asked J.R., a patient with left auditory cortex damage, to undergo visual word recognition, category fluency, sound recognition, and voice classification task for different types of auditory-related or non-related words. They found that J. R. had impaired conceptual processing of sound-related everyday objects (e.g., bell) while his performance for other types of words remained intact (Trumpp et al. 2013). Similarly to J. R., patients with lesions of the right frontal lobe showed most severe deficits in processing action verbs, whereas those with lesions in their right temporo-occipital area in processing visually related nouns (Neininger and Pulvermüller 2003). Patients with lesions of insula showed disrupted "gambling" cognitive biases (Clark et al. 2014). Patients with lesions of amygdala showed deficits in fear cognition (Adolphs et al. 1995). Moreover, other types of selective modal brain alteration (e.g., excitation) result in selective effects on concepts. Pulvermüller and colleagues showed that stimulation by TMS of foot areas of the motor cortex selectively improves recognition of leg-related words while stimulation of hand area improved recognition of arm-related words (Pulvermüller et al. 2005). Similarly, stress-induced plastic neuroadaptations of the affective brain (and its regulatory counterparts) regions may be recruited for the representation of emotional cognition (Niedenthal 2007).

4.3 Plasticity-Related Brain Differences Are Recruited in Cognition

Glenberg and colleagues tested this idea by a use-induced plasticity model to demonstrate that cognition recruits plastic changes in motor circuits that later result in biases of motor cognition. They asked participants to move 600 beans from a wide-mouthed container to a narrow-mouthed container and manipulated the direction of the movement either toward or away from the body. Results showed that movements result in plastic changes in the motor cortex, which further lead to differences in deciding if sentences involve "away or toward" actions (Glenberg et al. 2008). Thus, plastic changes in the motor cortex can cause biases or distortions of motor cognition. Furthermore, similar results have been observed for object categories (Kiefer et al. 2007) and processing of emotional faces. For instance, Taylor and colleagues investigated the effects of computerized training to attend "toward or away" emotional facial expressions (i.e., disgust expressions) in individuals with high social anxiety. Results showed that attention training resulted in attenuation of activation in the bilateral amygdala, bilateral insula, and subgenual anterior cingulate cortex and increased activation in several regions of the prefrontal cortex. Moreover, individuals with greater enhancement of ventromedial prefrontal (vmPFC) activation after training showed diminished attentional biases for threat and attenuated anxiety reactivity to stressors (Taylor et al. 2013). Thus, the plasticity-related differences in emotional regulation systems because of attention training result in differences in attention to emotional information. These results are strengthened by those of studies that show that complex learning-based interventions such as cognitive behavior therapy (CBT) induce neuroplastic changes underlying symptom reduction and alleviation of negative cognition counteracting maladaptive stress-induced plasticity (Davidson and McEwen 2012). For example, studies using functional magnetic resonance imagining (fMRI) found that after the administration of CBT treatment, patients show more than stable neural changes (e.g., decreased limbic activity and/or increased prefrontal activity) associated with improvement in symptomatology (Clark and Beck 2010; Dichter et al. 2012; Frewen et al. 2008; Goldapple et al. 2004; Linden 2006; Klumpp et al. 2013). They also display changes in neural states underlying biased threat processing (Klumpp et al. 2013) that may represent a mechanism by which CBT ameliorates disturbed emotions (e.g., Goldin et al. 2014).

These studies show that, similar with changes because of lesions, TMS procedures or typical neurodevelopmental differences (Haller et al. 2014), learning-induced plastic changes in modal brain regions (motor, sensory, affective, and regulatory systems) result in differences in cognition suggesting the embodiment of these forms of cognition in corresponding motor and affective brain regions. Additionally, they emphasize the importance of circuit-level plastic changes for psychological treatments of SEDs. Although the studies reviewed above clearly show the embodiment of cognition in circuit-level plastic changes of modal brain and not in a semantic-independent system as assumed by traditional cognitive models, they offer evidence for the effect of learning-induced plasticity and not of stress-induced plasticity. This chapter forwards the role of stress-induced plasticity in making cognition as vulnerability for disturbed emotions. The next section describes studies about the interactions between stress- and learning-induced plasticity.

4.4 Stress-Induced Brain Plasticity Interacts with Learning-Induced Plasticity

The direct manipulation of stress- and learning-induced neuroplastic changes has demonstrated that stress-related neurohormones (i.e., glucocorticoids) have neuroplastic effects on emotional circuits (e.g., lateral amygdala). As a result, they amplify aversive learning-induced synaptic plasticity in the affective brain regions and the formation of exaggerated affective memories for threats (Meyer et al. 2014; Monsey et al. 2014; Suvrathan et al. 2014). For instance, Suvrathan and colleagues exposed rats to chronic immobilization stress for ten consecutive days, 2 h/day. Then, they exposed them to a tone conditioning procedure 1 day after the stress exposure. At the end, they examined the electrophysiological impact of stress on neurons in lateral amygdala. They found that rats exposed to chronic stress compared to controls show amplified synaptic responses in the principal neurons of the lateral amygdala and reduced synaptic inhibition. These changes are accompanied by electrophysiological and morphological effects consistent with the formation of "silent synapses" that further promote experience-dependent plasticity and stronger fear memories (Suvrathan et al. 2014).

Although a direct test of neuroplastic interactions is very limited in humans because of technical difficulties, these studies provide direct evidence that stress-induced plasticity (morphological changes in synaptic receptors, silent synapses, reduced synaptic inhibition) in the affective brain has the power to augment learning-induced synaptic plasticity of affective representations leading to over-reactivity of emotional circuits and to a vulnerability to develop exaggerated affective representations of aversive memories (Conrad et al. 1999; Monsey et al. 2014; Suvrathan et al. 2014). Thus, it is not the dysfunctional learning in terms of high levels of negative knowledge but the underlying stress-related neurohormonal-induced plasticity that sets exaggerated affective representation of aversive memories (Sarabdjitsingh et al. 2012; Zhang et al. 2019). In the same aversive learning environment, individuals susceptible to the effects of stress acquire more than negative knowledge. They develop exaggerated affective representations for aversive cognition and a hyper-reactivity of affective systems set for generating an exaggerated affective "neural load" of negative cognition in the future encounters. This mechanism is likely to promote emotional disturbance and regulation difficulties. When exposed to aversive events, affective resilient individuals may acquire negative knowledge. Yet their affective and regulatory brain areas do not become sensitized and they do not recruit over-reactive affective representations for thinking of negative events. Thus, they probably do not develop disturbed emotions.

It is widely recognized that affective learning (e.g., conditioning) recruits the "affective" brain for representation resulting in biased cognition (e.g., attentional biases; Pischek-Simpson et al. 2009), and these normal learning-induced biases are enhanced in pathology. Enhanced conditioning was evidenced in both vulnerable (Holloway et al. 2012) and diagnosed anxious individuals (Lissek et al. 2005; for a discussion about threat safety discrimination, see Britton et al. 2011). Yet in vulnerable individuals (Meyer et al. 2014; Monsey et al. 2014; Suvrathan et al. 2014) enhanced conditioning most probably results from stress-related neurohormonal-induced neural alterations grounded on genetic susceptibility and not from the accumulation of negative knowledge during early experiences. By taking a traditional amodal position on cognition, plastic changes observed in the amygdala cannot be considered as an index of excessive negative knowledge even when they result from learning rather than stress hormones. They do not occur in brain regions that support the semantic "language-like" amodal representation. They occur in the "affective" brain. Increased conditioning involves increased emotional responses attached to stimuli and cognitive representations. Therefore, they may be considered as an index of changes in affective structures parallel to cognitive structures (e.g., Ingram 2003). Yet often and mistakenly, they are considered as a neural index of dysfunctional knowledge, an idea that implicitly assumes an embodied perspective on affective knowledge.

4.5 Stress-Related Brain Plastic Alterations Represent Cognition in SEDs

Admon and colleagues used fMRI methodology to investigate the neurodynamics of amygdala and hippocampus in relation to processing emotional information and symptoms of posttraumatic stress disorder (PTSD). The participants were Israeli soldiers in two conditions: before and after they engaged in battles. Admon et al. found that after stress exposure, the development of greater amygdala and hippocampus responsiveness when processing stress-related picture stimuli was associated with an increase in stress symptoms. Moreover, they found a selective involvement of both structures. Amygdala's reactivity during cognitive tasks before exposure to battles predicted the increase in stress symptoms. Instead, the hippocampal's change in activation over time correlated with the increase in stress symptoms (Admon et al. 2009). Furthermore, increasing evidence suggests that acute exposure to stress results in proximal brain alterations that support pathogenic distorted cognition taking the form of intrusive sensorial memories. For instance, enhanced sensory (especially visual) representations following traumatic stress are considered diagnostic criteria for PTSD (intrusive perceptual memories), being included in "updated" dual models of PTSD (e.g., Brewin et al. 2010; Brewin 2013). Yet enhanced sensory images are identifiable also in anxiety and affective disorders (Brewin et al. 2010; Holmes and Mathews 2010). They are causally linked to stress-induced plastic alterations in visual and amygdala circuits (Kleim et al. 2012) and manifested in a wide variety of cognitive forms from perceptual identification tasks (Kleim et al. 2012), memory (Brewin et al. 2010), verbal thoughts (Klein and Moritz 2014; Moritz et al. 2014), to thinking about future (Morina et al. 2011).

Re-experiencing/re-enactment or simulation of modal states such as perceptual and sensorial states in thinking is the core of the embodied simulation framework of cognition (Barsalou 1999). Sound evidence is supporting the idea that exaggerated sensory simulations are causally linked to stress-induced plastic alterations in visual and amygdala circuits (Kleim et al. 2012) as determinants for SEDs. Furthermore, the quality of distorted cognition is linked with vulnerability to SEDs and is determined by the recruitment of stress-induced brain alterations in its representation.

Additionally, substantial neurobiological research showing that the pattern of affective over-reactivity and regulatory deficiency (similar to that observed after exposure to chronic stress; Mahan and Ressler 2012; McEwen and Gianaros 2011; Sadeh et al. 2014;) is associated with distorted cognition has been already integrated in the cognitive models of vulnerability to SEDs by important reviews (e.g., Clark and Beck 2010; Disner et al. 2011; Hofmann et al. 2012).

Opposed to neuropsychological models (e.g., Harmer et al. 2009; Roiser et al. 2012), these reviews integrate data about alterations of the brain into the cognitive models of vulnerability to SED. Yet, they fall in a system interaction amodal paradigm: neural embodiments are viewed as "*genetic and neurochemical pathways that interact with or are parallel to cognitive variables*" (Beck 2008, p. 969). Nonetheless, they show a consistent association of a neurobiological pattern in relation to cognitive vulnerabilities to SEDs similar with the neural pattern of changes induced by stress. Thus, their conclusions make intuitively appealing the hypothesis of a stress-related neural embodiment of cognitive vulnerability to SEDs.

4.6 Stress-Related Brain Plastic Alterations Represent Vulnerabilities to SED

Early life stress-related brain alterations (Herzberg and Gunnar 2019; McCrory et al. 2010, 2012), such as the hyper-reactivity of emotional brain (Cohen et al. 2013; Suzuki et al. 2014; Tottenham and Sheridan 2009), have been identified as vulnerabilities to SEDs (Heim and Nemeroff 2001; McCrory et al. 2012; Penza et al. 2003) in both children (Suzuki et al. 2014) and adults (McLaughlin et al. 2014b; McLaughlin 2016). Burghy and colleagues used fMRI to measure amygdala-vmPFC functional connectivity at rest and asked adolescents to complete self-report measures of stress events, anxiety, and depression. They found that in adolescent girls, early life stress was positively associated with later childhood cortisol levels. They also observed that cortisol level predicted reduced connectivity between the amygdala and vmPFC (Burghy et al. 2012). In turn, this connectivity pattern predicted increased symptoms of anxiety and depression (Bogdan and Hariri 2012; Burghy et al. 2012). This conclusion is strengthened by studies showing that preexisting brain neuroadaptations (e.g., amygdala hyper-reactivity) that usually follow early life stress (Suzuki et al. 2014) predict the development of emotional psychopathology after exposure to stress (Admon et al. 2013; Lupien et al. 2009). One study illustrative in the support of this idea is the study of McLaughlin et al. (2014b). McLaughlin and her colleagues used fMRI to study people exposed to the Boston marathon bombing. They found that brain abnormalities similar to those occurring after stress exposure such as hyper-reactivity of amygdala before bombing predicted the later development of PTSD symptoms (McLaughlin et al. 2014b). Swartz and her colleagues used an fMRI longitudinal design to investigate the neurobiological markers of vulnerability to emotional symptoms in 753 healthy participants over 4 years. First, participants were subject to fMRI scanning of brain activity at angry and fearful faces and then, every 3 months, they completed self-report measures of stressful events, anxiety, and depression. The researchers found that the level of the reactivity of the amygdala to emotional faces predicted the severity of anxiety and depression symptoms 4 years later, but not when stress was not present (Swartz et al. 2015). Furthermore, studies showed that distal and proximal exposure to stress may result in distinct vulnerabilities. Distal (early) stress exposure alters brain networks involved in automatic emotion regulation, whereas recent stress exposure alters networks of effortful control (Birn et al. 2014). In sum, stress results in brain neuroadaptations and these neuroadaptations later act as vulnerabilities to SEDs. Furthermore, they confer distorted cognition the power of acting as vulnerability to SEDs. When they are recruited for representation, these neuroadaptations act as embodied cognitive vulnerabilities to SEDs.

4.7 Specific Genotypes Predict Distorted Thinking in Response to Stress

Johnson and colleagues investigated the relation between the serotonin transporter genotype (5-HTTLPR), reports of childhood physical abuse, and attentional biases for angry faces in women. They found that the reported history of physical abuse was associated with attentional biases for angry faces only in women carrying the 5-HTTLPR short (S) allele but no association was found in women carrying 5-HTTLPR long (L) allele (Gibb et al. 2013; Johnson et al. 2010). Similar results were found in studies involving children (Gibb et al. 2011) and with other types of genetic polymorphisms (e.g., interaction between 5-HTTLPR and brain-derived neurotrophic factor (BDNF) polymorphisms, α2B adrenergic receptor deletion polymorphism (ADRA2b) carriers, catechol-O-methyltransferase Val158Met genotype). Furthermore, they were found across unique types of distorted cognition such as dysfunctional attitudes (Wells et al. 2010), rumination (Clasen et al. 2011), trait-worry (Bredemeier et al. 2014), attributional style (Sheikh et al. 2008), negative schematic processing (Hayden et al. 2008), enhanced perception, and memory vividness (ADRA2b deletion carriers; de Quervain et al. 2007; Todd et al. 2013). All these show that specific genotypes predict the amplification of negative thinking in response to stress. Most of these polymorphisms, by their neural effects, determine differences in the sensitivity of the neural systems involved in stress response and negative thinking such as attenuation in cognitive regulation (Markus and De Raedt 2011) or enhanced amygdala neural responses (Markovic et al. 2014; Munafo et al. 2008; Rasch et al. 2009, 2010). Overall, genetic findings suggest that when they encounter stress, genetically susceptible individuals most likely develop and then recruit in processing hyper-reactive affective systems and/or hypo-reactive regulatory systems associated with distorted cognition (Pergamin-Hight et al. 2012). A genetic mediation of cognitive vulnerability to SEDs in response to stress is a strong foundation for the idea that cognitive vulnerability to SEDs is embodied in stress-related neuroadaptations. If the assertion that distorted cognition is based on dysfunctional learning and knowledge-driven processing errors only is correct, then no such mediation would be expected. Instead, the embodied simulation framework predicts that abnormalities of the brain result in distorted cognition if they are recruited for representational purpose. Thus, the genetic differences that result in either abnormal brain development or in susceptibility to develop brain adaptations after exposure to chronic stress are also likely to alter cognition. Hence, the genetic studies investigating the genetic mediation of cognitive vulnerability indirectly support the embodiment of biased cognition in disturbed affective systems of genetically susceptible individuals.

Altogether, these ideas suggest that cognitive vulnerability to SEDs is likely to be embodied in stress-related neurohormonal-induced adaptations or alterations in the neural regions mediating the generation and regulation of emotional and motivational responsiveness (exaggerating the affective and sensory neural representation of negative knowledge) in genetically susceptible individuals. Furthermore, by embodying cognition, cognition may act as a vehicle of carrying those alterations in the construction of new experiences (Barrett et al. 2014). Some of these alterations are adaptive, reversible plastic changes of the affective brain (and its connectivity) resulting in threat-enhanced cognition during acute stress states that assures adaptive experience and behavior (threat mode). Yet alterations may transform in long-lasting and toxic conditions resulting in stable and generalized cognitive biases that disturb emotional experience. Moreover, therapy may recover these effects by learning-induced plastic changes that optimize the regulatory control of affective brain systems (Davidson and McEwen 2012).

This proposal differs from the traditional cognitive vulnerability models. It says that are the differences in the recruitment of dysfunctional stress-related neurohormonal-induced adaptations of affective brain regions and regulatory networks by negative cognition that underlie the cognitive vulnerability to SEDs and not the differences in learning-dependent negative knowledge per se. The current dominant view of cognitive vulnerability posits learning-dependent exaggerated negative knowledge (negative schema, evaluative beliefs; Beck and Haigh 2014) as a foundation for biased cognition in vulnerability to SEDs. Although the traditional cognitive models recognize that differences in these biological sensory, regulatory, and affective systems represent biological vulnerabilities to SEDs, cognitive vulnerability is seen as independent of them or they are seen to represent mere brain correlates (e.g., Beck 2008).

The proposal of exaggerated negative knowledge as a source of cognitive vulnerability has been favored by the predominant use of behavioral and self-report designs in the cognitive vulnerability research (Riskind and Alloy 2006) in which dysfunctional affective embodiments (as a confound) determine the exaggeration of negative knowledge and both result from stressful life events (therefore they are confounds). Furthermore, this position has been strengthened by an amodal perspective in cognitive science (e.g., Fodor 1975), and a strong learning and knowledge-based causation model of non-pathological emotions (Lazarus 1993; Oatley and Johnson-Laird 2014; Schachter and Singer 1962; Siemer et al. 2007; Webb et al. 2012) and non-pathological cognitive biases (Hilbert 2012; Nisbett and Ross 1980; Pischek-Simpson et al. 2009). Moreover, the knowledge foundation of cognitive vulnerability has been successfully defended over decades by a strong system interaction framework in clinical sciences allowing an elegant rejection of the evidence for embodiments to a separate, cognitive independent, but interacting biological/neurobiological system. Undoubtedly, emotional learning and knowledge determine "non-pathological" biases in cognition (e.g., Pischek-Simpson et al. 2009). It also has an important role as distal vulnerability to disturbed emotions. For instance, persistent activation of negative knowledge (Nolen-Hoeksema 1991; Watkins 2008) recruits stress-induced over-reactive affective neural states (and/or attenuated regulatory neural states) in the construction of experiences.

By these means, it may result in exaggerated negative cognition, intense negative emotions, impaired regulation of affect, and physiological reactivity, generating stress (Hammen 1991) and further sensitization (for a review regarding rumination and cortisol reactivity, see Zoccola and Dickerson 2012). However, negative knowledge alone without recruiting simulations of over-reactive affective systems may not have the power to generate "abnormal" biases in cognition (biases that result in disturbed dysregulated negative emotions). Although the hypothesis that exaggeration of negative cognition and its power to produce negative emotions is rooted in dysfunctional affective neural embodiments (and not in early negative knowledge such as negative schema) seems radically different from the traditional cognitive models, substantial evidence for the dysfunction of neural circuits as a source of cognitive biases may be found in both neuropsychological (e.g., Harmer et al. 2009; Harmer and Cowen 2013) and animal (Hales et al. 2014) models of cognitive biases in SEDs. Moreover, evidence of the amelioration of negative cognitive biases after the acute administration of antidepressant medication that modify affective reactivity without changes in subjective ratings of mood or anxiety (Harmer et al. 2009; Harmer and Cowen 2013) strongly support an embodied foundation of distorted cognition.

4.8 Contrasting Learning and Stress-Related Contributions to Distorted Cognition in SED

In this section, I illustrate several "puzzling" phenomena from literature that suggest dysfunctional affective embodiments rather than learning as sources of the effect of distorted cognition on disturbed emotion.

4.8.1 The Mood Dependency of Cognitive Vulnerability

The mood-dependency hypothesis states that in vulnerable individuals, the differences in negative knowledge are demonstrable only under the induction of negative mood. Miranda and Persons (1988) showed that previously depressed and nondepressed individuals differ in negative knowledge (i.e., dysfunctional attitudes) only under the effect of negative mood (i.e., induced by listening to sad music). These results were consistently replicated in original studies (for a review, see Scher et al. 2005). From an embodied clinical cognition perspective, the results of these studies constitute evidence that the differences in negative knowledge that make people vulnerable to depression are rooted in the differences in affective representations of that knowledge (affective embodiments). In other words, people vulnerable to develop depression (compared to non-vulnerable ones) show higher levels of dysfunctional knowledge only when their affective embodiments (i.e., depressed mood, in these studies consciously experienced) are activated by different procedures such as listening sad music or exposing them to negative content (i.e., priming) (for a review, see Scher et al. 2005). Traditionally, these results have been interpreted from a cognitive reactivity position. According to this interpretation, higher levels of dysfunctional knowledge that exist as vulnerability to depression in at-risk individuals can be observed only when negative knowledge is activated by inducing negative mood or other priming methods. Thus, by default, dysfunctional knowledge is "dormant" and we usually do not see differences in dysfunctional knowledge between vulnerable and non-vulnerable persons (e.g., vulnerable individuals do not believe more than non-vulnerable ones that *they or their life is rotten* when they do not experience negative mood, yet when negative mood is activated they display more negative beliefs about themselves, others, or their lives). Mood dependency of cognitive vulnerability is not limited to dysfunctional attitudes but extends to other types of vulnerabilities such as probability estimations and irrational beliefs (Bridges and Harnish 2010). For example, anchoring probability estimations in visual perception and blocking the use of affective information result in elimination of biases in threat estimations in patients with anxiety disorders (Nesse and Klaas 1994).

4.8.2 The Origins of the Cognitive Vulnerability to SED

Adverse childhood life events represent a major risk factor for the development of SED (Heim and Nemeroff 2001). Cognitive models consider that after experiencing negative life events or having negative social interactions, individuals build negative views about others, self, and the world (assimilate exaggerated negative knowledge) becoming vulnerable to SED (Ingram 2003). There is accumulated evidence showing that exposure to negative life events has other consequences besides assimilating negative knowledge. Early life events also result in neurobiological changes such as dysfunctional cortisol reactivity (Luecken and Lemery 2004), altered brain patterns (McLaughlin et al. 2014a) or brain development (Tupler and De Bellis 2006; Whittle et al. 2016), that, at least in part, mediates the development of SEDs (Bick and Nelson 2016). Moreover, genotypes, genotype interactions with early temperament, dysfunctional parenting, environment (Hankin et al. 2009; Hankin 2012), or early brain differences (Hayden et al. 2008) were shown to shape the role of negative life events in the development of cognitive vulnerabilities to SEDs. For instance, research demonstrated that parenting responsiveness predicts cortisol reactivity to stress in children independent of subjective perception of coping (Hackman et al. 2013), that temperament moderates the relationship between negative events and cognitive vulnerability (Mezulis et al. 2006), or that associations between parent depression and cortisol levels becomes significant when children have high levels of cognitive biases (Hayden et al. 2014). Along the same line, behavioral genetic research found that genetic factors accounted for 31% of the variance of early negative knowledge (dysfunctional attitudes) in twin adolescents (11–17 years old) (Chen and Li 2014). Although methodological difficulties make challenging the research of these relations, the abovementioned studies show that stressful life events have other consequences besides negative knowledge (e.g., cortisol reactivity) that co-occur with negative knowledge and may shape distorted cognition and emotional disturbance.

4.8.3 Dissociation of Affective and Knowledge Components in Affective Learning

Having the advantage of using an invasive research methodology, nonhuman animal studies can provide causal evidence that dynamic affective embodiments are responsible for the ability of cognition to act as vulnerability to disturbed emotional reactions. Manipulations of the neural affective embodiment of knowledge were shown to disable the power of affective knowledge and learning to influence behavior and affective reactions. For instance, reversing the affective neural embodiments after learning that a cue is repulsive results in complete changes of both behavioral and affective reactions. Robinson and Berridge (2013) taught rats that a metal lever is repulsive, always predicting the experience of an unpleasant Dead Sea saltiness sensation. After that, rats re-encountered the metal lever in a sodium depletion state that induced hyper-reactivity of their mesocorticolimbic motivational system. "Rats jumped and gnawed on the suddenly attractive Pavlovian lever cue, despite never having tasted intense saltiness as anything other than disgusting" (Robinson and Berridge 2013, p. 282). These results show that our reactions (e.g., desire in this case) do not result only from previous learning history. The value of the stimulus is recomputed integrating previous knowledge with the brain state (Berridge 2018; Robinson and Berridge 2013). In other words, the evaluation of the value of the lever depends on the states of the brain that embody that value. Sometimes, body-driven processes are contradictory and powerful enough to overwrite the learning history. Animal studies also found an opposite shift from "liked" to "disliked values" after using chemical procedures. Rats stop to show positive "liking" reactions and shift toward enhanced "disliking" reactions (fear and disgust) to sucrose after the blockade of glutamatergic receptors by microinjections in the nucleus accumbens shell (Richard and Berridge 2011).

4.8.4 Affective Embodiments Result in the Emotional Effects of Negative Knowledge

Oosterwijk and colleagues have provided direct evidence that the difference in the emotional embodiments of negative knowledge explains the effect of negative knowledge on negative emotions (see Chap. 2). Oosterwijk and colleagues asked participants to unscramble fear sentences in a scramble sentence task by determining which word does not belong to the presented sentence (e.g., "*Bite poisonous is the death*") and monitored the electrodermal and corrugator activity as embodiments of the presented sentences (Oosterwijk et al. 2010). They found a higher electrodermal response and corrugator activity for the fear sentences which occurred in the absence of a subjective fear experience. After concept activation, they presented participants with negative and neutral pictures in combination with startling sounds and measured electrodermal and startle response. The results showed that the level of the embodiment during fear-related knowledge mediates the magnitude of emotional response when viewing negative pictures. In other words, fear sentences are embodied by partial emotional activations responsible for their effect on negative emotions (Oosterwijk et al. 2010). This result provides direct evidence that the differences in affective embodiment are responsible for the effect of differences in negative knowledge on negative emotion, at least for "normal" negative emotions. Further studies should test if the same effect may be replicated for disturbed emotions.

In summary, the results point to the idea that the differences in the affective neural embodiments of negative knowledge are those responsible for the ability of knowledge to predispose to disturbed emotions. Furthermore, the differences in the embodiment of dysfunctional knowledge may also result from the interactions of the neural systems with other peripheral body systems (e.g., immune responses, macrocytes, gut system, gonadal hormones, emotional facial expressions, and so on) which in this way may become cognitive supports (Vermeulen et al. 2009). These peripheral systems may significantly determine differences in the affective embodiments and thus have a potential of distorting affective cognition and conscious experience.

4.9 Summary

This chapter advanced the ideas that: (1) proximal cognitive vulnerabilities to SEDs are likely to be embodied in stress-induced neuroadaptations in the brain regions mediating emotional generation and regulation (exaggerating the affective and sensory neural representation of negative knowledge) in genetically susceptible individuals, (2) the differences in the simulation of affective stress-induced neuroadaptations in negative cognition rather than dysfunctional knowledge underlie "abnormal" (i.e., as vulnerability to disorders) biased cognition, and (3) cognition is an important vehicle of carrying neuroadaptations in the construction and "destruction" of emotional experience. Although I highlight stress-related neuroadaptations as main sources of dysfunctional neural embodiments underlying distorted cognition in SEDs, dysfunctional neural embodiments may arise from other sources such as atypical, age-related (Haller et al. 2014), or gender-specific (Bogdan and Hariri 2012) neurodevelopmental processes, inherited differences, or learning-induced plasticity in modal brain regions. Nonetheless, the actual alterations in the neural embodiments most probably result from the interaction between these multiple mechanisms. In individuals with atypical neurodevelopmental trajectory that leads to increased affective reactivity and regulatory deficiency, these alterations may be further accentuated by age-typical social-affective neurodevelopmental processes (Haller et al. 2014), gender-related differences (Bogdan and Hariri 2012), neurochemical processes (Roiser et al. 2012), or by stress-related plasticity. Learning-induced plasticity may as well add to that by sculpting regulatory and affective regions when life experiences of deficient regulation or intense emotions exceed shifting further the abnormal neural embodiments to an extreme end of emotional reactivity. Persistent and uncorrected use of emotional linguistic cognitions (e.g., ruminations, worries, and rigid appraisals), memories, or perceptions as simulation-control mechanisms may extensively recruit *altered embodiments* in the construction of ongoing experiences disturbing emotions and probably maintaining affective sensitization.

References

Admon, R., Lubin, G., Stern, O., Rosenberg, K., Sela, L., Ben-Ami, H., & Hendler, T. (2009). Human vulnerability to stress depends on amygdala's predisposition and hippocampal plasticity. *Proceedings of the National Academy of Sciences of the United States of America, 106*(33), 14120–14125. https://doi.org/10.1073/pnas.0903183106

Admon, R., Milad, M. R., & Hendler, T. (2013). A casual model of post-traumatic stress disorder: Disentangling predisposed from acquired neural abnormalities. *Trends in Cognitive Sciences, 17*(7), 337–347.

Adolphs, R., Tranel, D., Damasio, H., & Damasio, A. R. (1995). Fear and the human amygdala. *Journal of Neuroscience, 15*, 5879–5891.

Apergis-Schoute, A. M., Schiller, D., LeDoux, J. E., & Phelps, E. A. (2014). Extinction resistant changes in the human auditory association cortex following threat learning. *Neurobiology of Learning and Memory, 113*, 109–114. https://doi.org/10.1016/j.nlm.2014.01.016

Arnsten, A. F. (2009). Stress signalling pathways that impair prefrontal cortex structure and function. *Nature Review Neuroscience, 10*(6), 410–422.

Arnsten, A. F. T. (2015). Stress weakens prefrontal networks: Molecular insults to higher cognition. *Nature Neuroscience, 18*(10), 1376–1385. https://doi.org/10.1038/nn.4087

Barrett, L. F., Wilson-Mendenhall, C. D., & Barsalou, L. W. (2014). A psychological construction account of emotion regulation and dysregulation: The role of situated conceptualizations. In J. J. Gross (Ed.), *The handbook of emotion regulation* (2nd ed., pp. 447–465). Guilford.

Barsalou, L. W. (1999). Perceptual symbol systems. *Behavioral and Brain Sciences, 22*, 577–609.

Beck, A. T. (2008). The evolution of the cognitive model of depression and its neurobiological correlates. *American Journal of Psychiatry, 165*, 969–977.

Beck, A. T., & Haigh, E. A. P. (2014). Advances in cognitive theory and therapy: The generic cognitive model. *Annual Review of Clinical Psychology, 10*, 1–24.

Belda, X., Fuentes, S., Daviu, N., Nadal, R., & Armario, A. (2015). Stress-induced sensitization: The hypothalamic–pituitary–adrenal axis and beyond. *Stress, 18*(3), 269–279. https://doi.org/10.3109/10253890.2015.1067678

Berridge, K. C. (2018). Evolving concepts of emotion and motivation. *Frontiers in Psychology, 9*, 1647. https://doi.org/10.3389/fpsyg.2018.01647

Bick, J., & Nelson, C. A. (2016). Early adverse experiences and the developing brain. *Neuropsychopharmacology, 41*(1), 177–196. https://doi.org/10.1038/npp.2015.252

Birn, R., Shackman, A., Oler, J., Williams, L., McFarlin, D., Rogers, G., … Kalin, N. (2014). Extreme early-life anxiety is associated with an evolutionarily conserved reduction in the strength of intrinsic functional connectivity between the dorsolateral prefrontal cortex and the central nucleus of the amygdala. *Molecular Psychiatry, 19*(8), 853. https://doi.org/10.1038/mp.2014.85

Bogdan, R., & Hariri, A. R. (2012). Neural embedding of stress reactivity. *Nature Neuroscience, 15*, 1605–1607.

Bogdan, R., Nikolova, Y. S., & Pizzagalli, D. A. (2013). Neurogenetics of depression: A focus on reward processing and stress sensitivity. *Neurobiology of Disease, 52*, 12–23.

Bredemeier, K., Beevers, C. G., & McGeary, J. E. (2014). Serotonin transporter and BDNF polymorphisms interact to predict trait worry. *Anxiety, Stress & Coping: An International Journal.* doi:https://doi.org/10.1080/10615806.2014.909928.

Brewin, C. R. (2013). Episodic memory, perceptual memory, and their interaction: Foundations for a theory of posttraumatic stress disorder. *Psychological Bulletin, 140*, 69–97. https://doi.org/10.1037/a0033722

Brewin, C. R., Gregory, J. D., Lipton, M., & Burgess, N. (2010). Intrusive images in psychological disorders: Characteristics, neural mechanisms, and treatment implications. *Psychological Review, 117*(1), 210–232.

Bridges, K., & Harnish, R. (2010). Role of irrational beliefs in depression and anxiety: A review. *Health, 2*, 862–877. https://doi.org/10.4236/health.2010.28130

Britton, J. C., Lissek, S., Grillon, C., Norcross, M. A., & Pine, D. S. (2011). Development of anxiety: The role of threat appraisal and fear learning. *Depression and Anxiety, 28*, 5–17.

Burghy, C. A., Stodola, D. E., Ruttle, P. L., Molloy, E. K., Armstrong, J. M., Oler, J. A., … Birn, R. M. (2012). Developmental pathways to amygdala–prefrontal function and internalizing symptoms in adolescence. *Nature Neuroscience, 15*(12), 1736–1741.

Cabib, S., Campus, P., Conversi, D., Orsini, C., & Puglisi-Allegra, S. (2020). Functional and dysfunctional neuroplasticity in learning to cope with stress. *Brain Sciences, 10*(2), 127. https://doi.org/10.3390/brainsci10020127

Callaghan, B. L., Graham, B. M., Li, S., & Richardson, R. (2013). From resilience to vulnerability: Mechanistic insights into the effects of stress on transitions in critical period plasticity. *Frontiers in Molecular Psychiatry, 4*, 1–15.

Chen, J., & Li, X. (2014). Genetic and environmental etiologies of adolescent dysfunctional attitudes: A twin study. *Twin Research and Human Genetics, 17*(1), 16–22. https://doi.org/10.1017/thg.2013.85

Clark, D. A., & Beck, A. T. (2010). Cognitive theory and therapy of anxiety and depression: Convergence with neurobiological findings. *Trends in Cognitive Science, 14*, 418–424. https://doi.org/10.1016/j.tics.2010.06.007

Clark, L., Studer, B., Bruss, J., Tranel, D., & Bechara, A. (2014). Damage to insula abolishes cognitive distortions during simulated gambling. *Proceedings of the National Academy of Sciences of the United States of America, 111*(16), 6098–6103.

Clasen, P. C., Wells, T. T., Knopik, V. S., McGeary, J. E., & Beevers, C. G. (2011). 5-HTTLPR and BDNF Val66Met polymorphisms moderate effects of stress on rumination. *Genes, Brain, and Behavior, 10*(7), 740–746. https://doi.org/10.1111/j.1601-183X.2011.00715.x

Cohen, M. M., Jing, D., Yang, R. R., Tottenham, N., Lee, F. S., & Casey, B. J. (2013). Early-life stress has persistent effects on amygdala function and development in mice and humans. *Proceedings of the National Academy of Sciences of the United States of America, 110*(45), 18274–18278.

Conrad, C. D., LeDoux, J. E., Magarinos, A. M., & McEwen, B. S. (1999). Repeated restraint stress facilitates fear conditioning independently of causing hippocampal CA3 dendritic atrophy. *Behavioral Neuroscience, 113*, 902–913.

Datta, D., & Arnsten, A. (2019). Loss of prefrontal cortical higher cognition with uncontrollable stress: Molecular mechanisms, changes with age, and relevance to treatment. *Brain Sciences, 9*(5), 113. https://doi.org/10.3390/brainsci9050113

Davidson, R. J., & McEwen, B. S. (2012). Social influences on neuroplasticity: Stress and interventions to promote Well-being. *Nature Neuroscience, 15*(5), 689–695. https://doi.org/10.1038/nn.3093

de Kloet, E. R., de Kloet, S. F., de Kloet, C. S., & de Kloet, A. D. (2019). Top-down and bottom-up control of stress-coping. *Journal of Neuroendocrinology, 31*(3), e12675. https://doi.org/10.1111/jne.12675

de Quervain, D. J., Kolassa, I. T., Ertl, V., Onyut, P. L., Neuner, F., Elbert, T., & Papassotiropoulos, A. (2007). A deletion variant of the alpha2b-adrenoceptor is related to emotional memory in Europeans and Africans. *Nature Neuroscience, 10*(9), 1137–1139.

Dichter, G. S., Sikich, L., Song, A., Voyvodic, J., & Bodfish, J. W. (2012). Functional neuroimaging of treatment effects in psychiatry: Methodological challenges and recommendations. *International Journal of Neuroscience, 122*, 483–493. https://doi.org/10.3109/00207454.2012.678446

Disner, S., Beevers, C. G., Haigh, E. P., & Beck, A. T. (2011). Neural mechanisms of the cognitive model of depression. *Nature Reviews Neuroscience, 12*, 467–477. https://doi.org/10.1016/j.biopsych.2010.07.021

Douma, E. H., & de Kloet, E. R. (2020). Stress-induced plasticity and functioning of ventral tegmental dopamine neurons. *Neuroscience and Biobehavioral Reviews, 108*, 48–77. https://doi.org/10.1016/j.neubiorev.2019.10.015

Flinn, M. V., Nepomnaschy, P. A., Muehlenbein, M. P., & Ponzi, D. (2011). Evolutionary functions of early social modulation of hypothalamic-pituitary-adrenal axis development in humans. *Neuroscience Biobehavioral Review, 35*, 1611–1629.

Fodor, J. A. (1975). *The language of thought*. Cambridge, MA: Harvard University Press.

Frewen, P. A., Dozois, D. J., & Lanius, R. A. (2008). Neuroimaging studies of psychological interventions for mood and anxiety disorders: Empirical and methodological review. *Clinical Psychology Review, 28*, 228–246. https://doi.org/10.1016/j.cpr.2007.05.002

Gainotti, G. (2006). Anatomical functional and cognitive determinants of semantic memory disorders. *Neuroscience and Biobehavioral Reviews, 30*, 577–594. https://doi.org/10.1016/j.neubiorev.2005.11.001

Garcia, R. (2002). Stress, synaptic plasticity, and psychopathology. *Review of Neuroscience, 13*, 195–208. https://doi.org/10.1515/revneuro.2002.13.3.195

Gibb, B. E., Beevers, C. G., & McGeary, J. E. (2013). Toward an integration of cognitive and genetic models of risk for depression. *Cognition & Emotion, 27*(2), 193–216. https://doi.org/10.1080/02699931.2012.712950

Gibb, B. E., Johnson, A. L., Benas, J. S., Uhrlass, D. J., Knopik, V. S., & McGeary, J. E. (2011). Children's *5-HTTLPR* genotype moderates the link between maternal criticism and attentional biases specifically for facial displays of anger. *Cognition & Emotion, 25*(6), 1104–1120. https://doi.org/10.1080/02699931.2010.508267

Gillespie, C. F., Phifer, J., Bradley, B., & Ressler, K. J. (2009). Risk and resilience: Genetic and environmental influences on development of the stress response. *Depression and Anxiety, 26*, 984–992.

Glenberg, A., Sato, M., & Cattaneo, L. (2008). Use-induced motor plasticity affects the processing of abstract and concrete language. *Current Biology, 18*, R1–R2.

Goldapple, K., Segal, Z., Garson, C., Lau, M., Bieling, P., Kennedy, S., & Meyberg, H. (2004). Modulation of cortical-limbic pathways in major depression: Treatment-specific effects of cognitive behavior therapy. *Archives of General Psychiatry, 61*, 34. https://doi.org/10.1001/archpsyc.61.1.34

Goldin, P. R., Ziv, M., Jazaieri, H., Weeks, J., Heimberg, R. G., & Gross, J. J. (2014). Impact of cognitive-behavioral therapy for social anxiety disorder on the neural bases of emotional reactivity to and regulation of social evaluation. *Behaviour Research and Therapy, 62*, 97–106.

Gourley, S. L., Swanson, A. M., & Koleske, A. J. (2013). Corticosteroid-induced neural remodeling predicts behavioral vulnerability and resilience. *Journal of Neuroscience, 33*, 3107–3112. https://doi.org/10.1523/jneurosci.2138-12

Gunnar, M., & Quevedo, K. (2007). The neurobiology of stress and development. *Annual Review of Psychology, 58*, 145–173.

Hackman, D. A., Betancourt, L. M., Brodsky, N. L., Kobrin, L., Hurt, H., & Farah, M. J. (2013). Selective impact of early parental responsivity on adolescent stress reactivity. *PLoS One, 8*(3), e58250. https://doi.org/10.1371/journal.pone.0058250

Hales, C. A., Stuart, S. A., Anderson, M. H., & Robinson, E. S. (2014). Modelling cognitive affective biases in major depressive disorder using rodents. *British Journal of Pharmacology, 171*(20), 4524–4538.

Haller, S. P. W., Cohen, K., Kadosh, K., & Lau, J. Y. F. (2014). A developmental angle to understanding the mechanisms of biased cognitions in social anxiety. *Frontiers in Human Neuroscience, 7*, 846. https://doi.org/10.3389/fnhum.2013.00846

Hammen, C. (1991). The generation of stress in the course of unipolar depression. *Journal of Abnormal Psychology, 100*, 555–561.

Hankin, B. L. (2012). Future directions in vulnerability to depression among youth: Integrating risks across multiple levels of analysis. *Journal of Child and Adolescent Clinical Psychology, 41*, 695–718.

Hankin, B. L., Oppenheimer, C., Jenness, J., Barrocas, A., Shapero, B. G., & Goldband, J. (2009). Developmental origins of cognitive vulnerabilities to depression: Review of processes contributing to stability and change across time. *Journal of Clinical Psychology, 65*, 1327–1338.

Harmer, C. J., & Cowen, P. J. (2013). It's the way that you look at it'—A cognitive neuropsychological account of SSRI action in depression. *Philosophical Transactions of the Royal Society B: Biological Sciences, 368*, 20120407.

Harmer, C. J., O'Sullivan, U., Favaron, E., Massey-Chase, R., Ayres, R., Reinecke, A., … Cowen, P. J. (2009). Effect of acute antidepressant administration on negative affective bias in depressed patients. *American Journal of Psychiatry, 166*, 1178–1184.

Hayden, E. P., Hankin, B. L., Mackrell, S. V., Sheikh, H. I., Jordan, P. L., Dozois, D. J., … Badanes, L. S. (2014). Parental depression and child cognitive vulnerability predict children's cortisol reactivity. *Development and Psychopathology, 26*, 1445–14460. https://doi.org/10.1017/S0954579414001138

Hayden, E. P., Shankman, S. A., Olino, T. M., Durbin, C. E., Tenke, C. E., Bruder, G. E., & Klein, D. N. (2008). Cognitive and temperamental vulnerability to depression: Longitudinal associations with regional cortical activity. *Cognition and Emotion, 22*, 1415–1428.

Heim, C., & Nemeroff, C. B. (2001). The role of childhood trauma in the neurobiology of mood and anxiety disorders: Preclinical and clinical studies. *Biological Psychiatry, 49*(12), 1023–1039.

Herzberg, M. P., & Gunnar, M. R. (2019). Early life stress and brain function: Activity and connectivity associated with processing emotion and reward. *NeuroImage*, 116493. https://doi.org/10.1016/j.neuroimage.2019.116493

Hikosaka, O. (2010). The habenula: From stress evasion to value-based decision making. *Nature Reviews Neuroscience, 11*(7), 503–513. https://doi.org/10.1038/nrn2866

Hilbert, M. (2012). Toward a synthesis of cognitive biases: How noisy information processing can bias human decision making. *Psychological Bulletin, 138*(2), 211–237.

Hofmann, S. G., Ellard, K. K., & Siegle, G. J. (2012). Neurobiological correlates of cognitions in fear and anxiety: A cognitive-neurobiological information-processing model. *Cognition & Emotion, 26*(2), 282–299. https://doi.org/10.1080/02699931.2011.579414

Holloway, J. L., Trivedi, P., Myers, C. E., & Servatius, R. J. (2012). Enhanced conditioned eyeblink response acquisition and proactive interference in anxiety vulnerable individuals. *Frontiers in Behavioral Neuroscience, 6*, 76. https://doi.org/10.3389/fnbeh.2012.00076

Holmes, E. A., & Mathews, A. (2010). Mental imagery in emotion and emotional disorders. *Clinical Psychology Review, 30*(3), 349–362.

Ingram, R. E. (2003). Origins of cognitive vulnerability to depression. *Cognitive Therapy and Research, 27*, 77–88.

Johnson, A. L., Gibb, B. E., & McGeary, J. (2010). Reports of childhood physical abuse, 5-HTTLPR genotype, and women's attentional biases for angry faces. *Cognitive Therapy and Research, 34*(4), 380–387.

Kiefer, M., Sim, E.-J., Liebich, S., Hauk, O., & Tanaka, J. (2007). Experience-dependent plasticity of conceptual representations in human sensory-motor areas. *Journal of Cognitive Neuroscience, 19*, 525–542.

Kim, J. J., & Diamond, D. M. (2002). The stressed hippocampus, synaptic plasticity and lost memories. *Nature Review Neuroscience, 3*, 453–462.

Kleim, B., Ehring, T., & Ehlers, A. (2012). Perceptual processing advantages for trauma-related visual cues in post-traumatic stress disorder. *Psychological Medicine, 42*, 173–181. https://doi.org/10.1017/S0033291711001048

Klein, J. P., & Moritz, S. (2014). On the relevance of mental imagery beyond stress-related psychiatric disorders. *Frontiers in Psychiatry, 5*, 77. https://doi.org/10.3389/fpsyt.2014.00077

Kluge, C., Bauer, M., Leff, A. P., Heinze, H. J., Dolan, R. J., & Driver, J. (2011). Plasticity of human auditory-evoked fields induced by shock conditioning and contingency reversal. *Proceedings of the National Academy of Sciences of the United States of America, 108*, 12545–12550.

Klumpp, H., Fitzgerald, D. A., & Phan, K. L. (2013). Neural predictors and mechanisms of cognitive behavioral therapy on threat processing in social anxiety disorder. *Progress in Neuro-Psychopharmacology & Biological Psychiatry, 45*, 83–91.

Krusemark, E. A., & Li, W. (2011). Do all threats work the same way? Divergent effects of fear and disgust on sensory perception and attention. *Journal of Neuroscience, 31*, 3429–3434.

Lazarus, R. S. (1993). From psychological stress to the emotions: A history of changing outlooks. *Annual Review of Psychology, 44*, 1–21.

Li, W. (2014). Learning to smell danger: Acquired associative representation of threat in the olfactory cortex. *Frontiers in Behavioral Neuroscience, 8*, 98. https://doi.org/10.3389/fnbeh.2014.00098

Linden, D. E. J. (2006). How psychotherapy changes the brain–the contribution of functional neuroimaging. *Molecular Psychiatry, 11*, 528–538. https://doi.org/10.1038/sj.mp.4001816

Lissek, S., Powers, A. S., McClure, E. B., Phelps, E. A., Woldehawariat, G., Grillon, C., & Pine, D. S. (2005). Classical fear-conditioning in the anxiety disorders: A meta-analysis. *Behaviour Research and Therapy, 43*, 1391–1424.

Luecken, L. J., & Lemery, K. S. (2004). Early caregiving and physiological stress responses. *Clinical Psychology Review, 24*, 171–191.

Lupien, S. J., McEwen, B. S., Gunnar, M. R., & Heim, C. (2009). Effects of stress throughout the lifespan on the brain, behaviour and cognition. *Nature Reviews Neuroscience, 6*, 434–445.

Mahan, A. L., & Ressler, K. J. (2012). Fear conditioning, synaptic plasticity and the amygdala: Implications for posttraumatic stress disorder. *Trends Neuroscience, 35*, 24–35.

Markovic, J., Anderson, A. K., & Todd, R. M. (2014). Tuning to the significant: Neural and genetic processes underlying affective enhancement of visual perception and memory. *Behavioural Brain Research, 259*, 229–241.

Markus, R., & De Raedt, R. (2011). Differential effects of 5-HTTLPR genotypes on inhibition of negative emotional information following acute stress exposure and tryptophan challenge. *Neuropsychopharmacology, 36*, 819–826.

McCrory, E., De Brito, S. A., & Viding, E. (2010). The neurobiology and genetics of maltreatment and adversity. *Journal of Child Psychology and Psychiatry, 51*(10), 1079–1095. https://doi.org/10.1111/j.1469-7610.2010.02271.x

McCrory, E., De Brito, S. A., & Viding, E. (2012). The link between child abuse and psychopathology: A review of neurobiological and genetic research. *Journal of the Royal Society of Medicine, 105*(4), 151–156. https://doi.org/10.1258/jrsm.2011.110222

McEwen, B. S. (1999). Stress and hippocampal plasticity. *Annual Review of Neuroscience, 22*, 105–122.

McEwen, B. S., Bowles, N. P., Gray, J. D., Hill, M. N., Hunter, R. G., Karatsoreos, I. N., & Nasca, C. (2015). Mechanisms of stress in the brain. *Nature Neuroscience, 18*(10), 1353–1363. https://doi.org/10.1038/nn.4086

McEwen, B. S., & Gianaros, P. J. (2011). Stress- and allostasis-induced brain plasticity. *Annual Review of Medicine, 62*, 431–445.

McLaughlin, K. A. (2016). Future directions in childhood adversity and youth psychopathology. *Journal of Clinical Child and Adolescent Psychology, 45*, 361–382.

McLaughlin, K. A., Busso, D. S., Duys, A., Green, J. G., Alves, S., Way, M., & Sheridan, M. A. (2014b). Amygdala response to negative stimuli predicts PTSD symptom onset following a terrorist attack. *Depression and Anxiety, 31*(10), 834–842. https://doi.org/10.1002/da.22284

McLaughlin, K. A., Sheridan, M. A., & Lambert, H. K. (2014a). Childhood adversity and neural development: Deprivation and threat as distinct dimensions of early experience. *Neuroscience and Biobehavioral Reviews, 47*, 578–591. https://doi.org/10.1016/j.neubiorev.2014.10.012

Meyer, R. M., Burgos-Robles, A., Liu, E., Correia, S. S., & Goosens, K. A. (2014). A ghrelin–growth hormone axis drives stress-induced vulnerability to enhanced fear. *Molecular Psychiatry, 19*, 1284–1294. https://doi.org/10.1038/mp.2013.135

Mezulis, A., Hyde, J. S., & Abramson, L. Y. (2006). The developmental origins of cognitive vulnerability to depression: Temperament, parenting, and negative life events in childhood as contributors to negative cognitive style. *Developmental Psychology, 42*, 1012–1025.

Miranda, J., & Persons, J. B. (1988). Dysfunctional attitudes are mood-state dependent. *Journal of Abnormal Psychology, 97*, 76–79.

Monsey, M. S., Boyle, L. M., Zhang, M. L., Nguyen, C. P., Kronman, H. G., … Schafe, G. E. (2014). Chronic Corticosterone exposure persistently elevates the expression of memory-related genes in the lateral amygdala and enhances the consolidation of a Pavlovian fear memory. *PLoS One, 9*(3), e91530. https://doi.org/10.1371/journal.pone.0091530

Morina, N., Deeprose, C., Pusowski, C., Schmid, M., & Holmes, E. A. (2011). Prospective mental imagery in patients with major depressive disorder or anxiety disorders. *Journal of Anxiety Disorders, 25*(8), 1032–1037.

Moritz, S., Hörmann, C. C., Schröder, J., Berger, T., Jacob, G. A., Meyer, B., … Klein, J. P. (2014). Beyond words: Sensory properties of depressive thoughts. *Cognition and Emotion, 28*(6), 1047–1056.

Morris, M. C., Ciesla, J. A., & Garber, J. (2010). A prospective study of stress autonomy versus stress sensitization in adolescents at varied risk for depression. *Journal of Abnormal Psychology, 119*(2), 341–354. https://doi.org/10.1037/a0019036

Munafo, M. R., Brown, S. M., & Hariri, A. R. (2008). Serotonin transporter (5-HTTLPR) genotype and amygdala activation: A meta-analysis. *Biological Psychiatry, 63*, 852–857.

Neininger, B., & Pulvermüller, F. (2003). Word category specific deficits after right hemispheric lesions. *Neuropsychologia, 41*, 53–70.

Nesse, R. M., & Klaas, R. (1994). Risk perception by patients with anxiety disorders. *Journal of Nervous and Mental Disease, 182*, 465–470.

Niedenthal, P. M. (2007). Embodying emotion. *Science, 316*, 1002–1005.

Nisbett, R., & Ross, L. (1980). *Human inference: Strategies and short- comings of social judgment.* Englewood Cliffs, NJ: Prentice-Hall.

Nolen-Hoeksema, S. (1991). Responses to depression and their effects on the duration of depressive episodes. *Journal of Abnormal Psychology, 100*, 569–582.

Oatley, K., & Johnson-Laird, P. N. (2014). Cognitive approaches to emotions. *Trends in Cognitive Science, 18*(3), 134–140. https://doi.org/10.1016/j.tics.2013.12.004

Oosterwijk, S., Topper, M., Rotteveel, M., & Fischer, A. H. (2010). When the mind forms fear: Embodied fear knowledge potentiates bodily reactions to fearful stimuli. *Social Psychological and Personality Science, 1*, 65–72.

Pechtel, P., & Pizzagalli, D. A. (2011). Effects of early life stress on cognitive and affective function: An integrated review of human literature. *Psychopharmacology, 214*(1), 55–70. https://doi.org/10.1007/s00213010-2009-2

Penza, K. M., Heim, C., & Nemeroff, C. B. (2003). Neurobiological effects of childhood abuse: Implications for the pathophysiology of depression and anxiety. *Archives of Women 's Mental Health, 6*, 15–22.

Pergamin-Hight, L., Bakermans-Kranenburg, M. J., van Ijzendoorn, M. H., & Bar-Haim, Y. (2012). Variations in the promoter region of the serotonin-transporter gene (5HTTLPR) and biased attention for emotional information: A meta-analysis. *Biological Psychiatry, 71*, 373–379.

Pischek-Simpson, L. K., Boschen, M. J., Neumann, D. L., & Waters, A. M. (2009). The development of an attentional bias for angry faces following Pavlovian fear conditioning. *Behavior Research and Therapy, 47*(4), 322–330. https://doi.org/10.1016/j.brat.2009.01.007

Pizzagalli, D. A. (2014). Depression, stress, and anhedonia: Toward a synthesis and integrated model. *Annual Review of Clinical Psychology, 10*, 393–423.

Post, R. M. (1992). Transduction of psychosocial stress into the neurobiology of recurrent affective disorder. *American Journal of Psychiatry, 149*, 999–1010.

Pulvermüller, F., Hauk, O., Nikulin, V., & Ilmoniemi, R. J. (2005). Functional interaction of language and action: A TMS study. *European Journal of Neuroscience, 21*(3), 793–797.

Rasch, B., Spalek, K., Buholzer, S., Luechinger, R., Boesiger, P., de Quervain, D. J.-F., & Papassotiropoulos, A. (2010). Aversive stimuli lead to differential amygdala activation and connectivity patterns depending on catechol-O-methyltransferase Val158Met genotype. *NeuroImage, 52*, 1712–1719.

Rasch, B., Spalek, K., Buholzer, S., Luechinger, R., Boesiger, P., Papassotiropoulos, A., & de Quervain, D. (2009). A genetic variation of the noradrenergic system is related to differential amygdala activation during encoding of emotional memories. *Proceedings of the National Academy of Sciences of the United States of America, 106*(45), 19191–19196.

Richard, J. M., & Berridge, K. C. (2011). Metabotropic glutamate receptor blockade in nucleus accumbens shell shifts affective valence towards fear and disgust. *European Journal of Neuroscience, 33*, 736–474.

Riskind, J. H., & Alloy, L. B. (2006). Cognitive vulnerability to emotional disorders: Theory, design, and methods. In L. B. Alloy & J. H. Riskind (Eds.), *Cognitive vulnerability to emotional disorders*. Earlbaum.

Robinson, M. J. F., & Berridge, K. C. (2013). Instant transformation of learned repulsion into motivational "wanting.". *Current Biology, 23*, 282–289.

Roiser, J. P., Elliott, R., & Sahakian, B. J. (2012). Cognitive mechanisms of treatment in depression. *Neuropsychopharmacology, 37*, 117–136.

Sadeh, N. S., Spielberg, J. M., Warren, S. L., Miller, G. A., & Heller, H. (2014). Aberrant neural connectivity during emotional processing associated with posttraumatic stress. *Clinical Psychological Science, 2*(6), 748–755. https://doi.org/10.1177/2167702614530113

Sarabdjitsingh, R. A., Kofink, D., Karst, H., de Kloet, E. R., & Joëls, M. (2012). Stress-induced enhancement of mouse Amygdalar synaptic plasticity depends on glucocorticoid and ß-adrenergic activity. *PLoS One, 7*(8), e42143. https://doi.org/10.1371/journal.pone.0042143

Schachter, S., & Singer, J. (1962). Cognitive, social, and physiological determinants of emotional state. *Psychological Review, 69*, 379–399.

Scher, C. D., Ingram, R. E., & Segal, Z. V. (2005). Cognitive reactivity and vulnerability: Empirical evaluation of construct activation and cognitive diathesis in unipolar depression. *Clinical Psychology Review, 25*, 487–510.

Segal, Z. V., Williams, J. M., Teasdale, J. D., & Gemar, M. (1996). A cognitive science perspective on kindling and episode sensitization in recurrent affective disorder. *Psychological Medicine, 26*, 371–380.

Sheikh, H. I., Hayden, E. P., Singh, S., Dougherty, L. R., Olino, T. M., Durbin, C. E., & Klein, D. N. (2008). An examination of the association between the 5-HTT promoter region polymorphism and depressogenic attributional styles in childhood. *Personality and Individual Differences, 45*, 425–428.

Siemer, M., Mauss, I., & Gross, J. J. (2007). Same situation—Different emotions: How appraisals shape our emotions. *Emotion, 7*, 592–600.

Soares, J. M., Marques, P., Magalhães, R., Santos, N. C., & Sousa, N. (2014). Brain structure across the lifespan: The influence of stress and mood. *Frontiers in Aging Neuroscience, 6*, 330. https://doi.org/10.3389/fnagi.2014.00330

Soares, J. M., Sampaio, A., Ferreira, L. M., Santos, N. C., Marques, P., Marques, F., … Sousa, N. (2013a). Stress impact on resting state brain networks. *PLoS One, 8*, e66500. https://doi.org/10.1371/journal.pone.0066500

Soares, J. M., Sampaio, A., Marques, P., Ferreira, L. M., Santos, N. C., Marques, F., … Sousa, N. (2013b). Plasticity of resting state brain networks in recovery from stress. *Frontiers in Human Neuroscience, 7*, 919. https://doi.org/10.3389/fnhum.2013.00919

Stroud, C. B., Davila, J., & Moyer, A. (2008). The relationship between stress and depression in first onsets versus recurrences: A meta-analytic review. *Journal of Abnormal Psychology, 117*, 206–213.

Suvrathan, A., Bennur, S., Ghosh, S., Tomar, A., Anilkumar, S., & Chattarji, S. (2014). Stress enhances fear by forming new synapses with greater capacity for long-term potentiation in the amygdala. *Philosophical Transactions of the Royal Society B: Biological Sciences, 369*, 151–159. https://doi.org/10.1098/rstb.2013.0151

Suzuki, H., Luby, J. L., Botteron, K. N., Dietrich, R., McAvoy, M. P., & Barch, D. M. (2014). Early life stress and trauma and enhanced limbic activation to emotionally Valenced faces in depressed and healthy children. *Journal of the American Academy of Child and Adolescent Psychiatry, 53*(7), 800–813.e10. https://doi.org/10.1016/j.jaac.2014.04.013

Swartz, J. R., Knodt, A. R., Radtke, S. R., & Hariri, A. R. (2015). A neural biomarker of psychological vulnerability to future life stress. *Neuron, 85*(3), 505. https://doi.org/10.1016/j.neuron.2014.12.055

Taylor, C., Simmons, A. N., Aupperle, R. L., Amir, N., Stein, M. B., & Paulus, M. P. (2013). Neural correlates of a computerized attention modification program in anxious subjects. *Social, Cognitive, and Affective Neuroscience, 9*(9), 1379–1387. https://doi.org/10.1093/scan/nst128

Todd, R. M., Mueller, D., Lee, D. H., Robertson, A., Eaton, T., Freeman, N., … Anderson, A. K. (2013). Genes for emotion enhanced remembering are linked to enhanced perceiving. *Psychological Science, 24*(11), 2244–2253.

Tomasino, B., Fink, G. R., Sparing, R., Dafotakis, M., & Weiss, P. H. (2008). Action verbs and the primary motor cortex: A comparative TMS study of silent reading, frequency judgments, and motor imagery. *Neuropsychologia, 46*, 1915–1926. https://doi.org/10.1016/j.neuropsychologia.2008.01.015

Tottenham, N., & Sheridan, M. A. (2009). A review of adversity. The amygdala and the hippocampus: A consideration of developmental timing. *Frontiers in Human Neuroscience, 3*, 68. https://doi.org/10.3389/neuro.09.068.2009

Trumpp, N. M., Kliese, D., Hoenig, K., Haarmaier, T., & Kiefer, M. (2013). Loosing the sound of concepts: Damage to auditory association cortex impairs the processing of sound-related concepts. *Cortex, 49*, 474–486.

Tupler, L. A., & De Bellis, M. D. (2006). Segmented hippocampal volume in children and adolescents with posttraumatic stress disorder. *Biological Psychiatry, 59*, 523–529.

Vergne, D. E., & Nemeroff, C. B. (2006). The interaction of serotonin transporter gene polymorphisms and early adverse life events on vulnerability for major major depression. *Current Psychiatry Reports, 8*, 452–457.

Vermeulen, N., Godefroid, J., & Mermillod, M. (2009). Emotional modulation of attention: Fear increases but disgust reduces the attentional blink. *PLoS One, 4*(11), e7924.

Watkins, E. R. (2008). Constructive and unconstructive repetitive thought. *Psychological Bulletin, 134*(2), 163–206. https://doi.org/10.1037/0033-2909.134.2.163

Webb, T. L., Miles, E., & Sheeran, P. (2012). Dealing with feeling: A meta-analysis of the effectiveness of strategies derived from the process model of emotion regulation. *Psychological Bulletin, 138*(4), 775–808.

Wells, T. T., Beevers, C. G., & McGeary, J. E. (2010). Serotonin transporter and BDNF genetic variants interact to predict cognitive reactivity in healthy adults. *Journal of Affective Disorders, 126*(1–2), 223–229. https://doi.org/10.1016/j.jad.2010.03.019

Whittle, S., Vijayakumar, N., Dennison, M., Schwartz, O., Simmons, J. G., Sheeber, L., & Allen, N. B. (2016). Observed measures of negative parenting predict brain development during adolescence. *PLoS One, 11*(1), e0147774. https://doi.org/10.1371/journal.pone.0147774

Zhang, J. Y., Liu, T. H., He, Y., Pan, H. Q., Zhang, W. H., Yin, X. P., … Pan, B. X. (2019). Chronic stress remodels synapses in an amygdala circuit-specific manner. *Biological Psychiatry, 85*(3), 189–201. https://doi.org/10.1016/j.biopsych.2018.06.019

Zoccola, P. M., & Dickerson, S. S. (2012). Assessing the relationship between rumination and cortisol: A review. *Journal of Psychosomatic Research, 73*, 1–9.

Chapter 5
Embodying Rigid Motivational Appraisals

5.1 Embodying Rigid Motivational Appraisals

Disturbed motivation is a central symptom of emotional disorders (EDs). It is involved in the psychopathology of drug-related disorders (i.e., addiction and intense cravings; Berridge and Robinson 2003; Dichter et al. 2012), depression (i.e., decreased motivation; Drevets et al. 2008), anxiety disorders (i.e., avoidance impulses and urges, Cha et al. 2014; Levita et al. 2012), and in many other disorders of behavior and cognition (personality disorders, schizophrenia, and so forth). Moreover, disturbed motivation has been proposed as a vulnerability mechanism in drug relapse episodes (Berridge and Robinson 2003), affective (Drevets et al. 2008), and anxiety disorders (Cha et al. 2014; Levita et al. 2012).

Rational emotive and behavior therapy (REBT), the oldest form of cognitive behavior therapy (CBT), proposes rigid motivational cognition as a primary vulnerability to EDs (Ellis 1994). Rigid appraisals of motivational relevance or demandingness are beliefs expressed in absolute terms such as "*I should get important things*" (David et al. 2002; David 2014; David et al. 2019; Ellis 1962; Dryden 2009, 2019). In addition, Ellis suggested that rigid appraisals result in another important vulnerability, exaggerated appraisals. Exaggerated appraisals (i.e., awfulizing, frustration intolerance, depreciative beliefs) are seen as secondary cognitive vulnerabilities that result from rigid appraisals. Together, these appraisals are named irrational beliefs (IBs). In short, escalating preferences or desires into "demands" or "cravings," "musts or must not," "shoulds" or "needs" (David 2014; Ellis et al. 2010) as a response to adversities lies at the basis of cognitive vulnerability to EDs.

Traditionally, in REBT, the transformation of desires into cravings or musts as responses to negative situations is considered a form of cognition (e.g., rigid motivational appraisals). Although in the initial proposals of A. Ellis (Ellis 1958), the founder of REBT, IBs are defined consistently with definitions of embodied mental states (cognition is identical with the experiences it references; see Tiba and Manea 2018 for a detailed discussion), the development of the theories of motivational

A. Tiba, *Embodied Hot Cognitive Vulnerability to Emotional Disorders*,
https://doi.org/10.1007/978-3-030-53989-4_5

cognition in REBT followed the dominant amodal view thinking (e.g., Fodor 1975). Thus, motivational appraisals have been considered by default being based on amodal representations, in which motivational cognition is transduced from experiences and translated into a new language-like propositional symbolic form (Ellis et al. 2010; Szentagotai et al. 2005). Cognitions based on amodal symbols are independent of the particularities of our brain and body. They are implemented by the brain, but their quality (rigid or not) follows from individual differences in learning, not from differences in our brain and body. They are disembodied types of cognition. As disembodied cognition, rigid motivational cognition is distinct from the processes of disturbed motivation.

On one hand, we have a worldwide recognized evidence-based treatment for emotional disorders based on targeting distorted motivational cognition (REBT is one of the most practiced forms of CBT; David et al. 2008; David 2014). On the other hand, we have substantial research about disturbed motivation in behavioral and emotional disorders. Between them, we have an understanding of motivational cognition as disembodied types of motivational cognition, based on amodal symbols, which is relatively independent of differences that exist in the characteristics of our motivational experiences and underlying neural implementations. This distinction keeps the research about processes of disturbed motivation and motivational appraisals and their treatment as two independent lines of inquiry.

In contrast, focusing on unique types of motivational cognition, embodied motivational cognition, as revealed by the embodied simulation view of motivational cognition (in which motivational cognition involve similar processes as those involved in motivation; Papies and Barsalou 2015), allows the translation of the knowledge from research on disturbed motivation (both as a subjective experience and basis of neural implementation) into the models of cognitive vulnerability to emotional disorders.

An embodied simulation perspective points to the partial re-enactment of motivational states as the representational basis for motivational appraisals. Accordingly, this theory suggests the existence of an important type of motivational cognition that is embodied by the partial re-enactment of motivational states: embodied motivational cognition (Papies and Barsalou 2015). Specifically, embodied motivational cognition is represented by the recruitment of partial activation of the neural states that were active during the motivational experiences corresponding to the context-dependent cognitive content (Barsalou 2008; Papies and Barsalou 2015). Paralleling the description of emotional cognition, disturbed embodied motivational cognition is represented by the partial re-enactment of disturbed motivational states (i.e., cravings or dreads). Specifically, it is represented by partial activation of neural states in hyper-reactive motivational distributed networks (motivational central embodiments) underlying disturbed motivation. When individuals react to adversities with a craving for what they missed or dreads to avoid threats, they become emotionally disturbed. When they think of adversities, they mentally re-enact states of disturbed motivation as reactions to adversities leading to affective and behavioral disorders. Nowadays, we have an increasing scientific consensus about how disturbed motivation as a response to rewards and adversities maintain emotional and behavioral disorders (Cabib et al. 2020; Douma and de Kloet 2020; Ironside et al. 2018). REBT is a main form of evidence-based treatment used in the treatment of emotional disorders that is based on changing rigid and exaggerated motivational appraisals. In this chapter, I describe rigid appraisals as embodied rigid motivational appraisals or distorted motivational cognition, and I translate research from altered motivational processes involved in emotional pathologies into the concept of demandingness as cognitive vulnerability to emotional disorders.

5.2 Abnormal Motivation and Embodied Rigid Motivational Appraisals

Both human (Cha et al. 2014; Siep et al. 2012; Kober et al. 2010a, b) and nonhuman animal (Berridge and Robinson 2003) research have rooted incentive (Berridge and Robinson 2003) and aversive (Cha et al. 2014; Cohen et al. 2012; Levita et al. 2012; Ventura et al. 2007, 2008) disturbed motivational states in the hyper-reactivity of mesolimbic dopaminergic distributed network. There are various conditions that may alter the mesolimbic system (drugs, stimuli characteristics, acute, and chronic stress, catecholamines, glucocorticoids, hormones, homeostatic states, and so forth) and result in sensitized or hyper-reactive mesolimbic dopaminergic responses. Later, when encountering specific stimuli (which acquired incentive properties due to classical conditioning) the sensitized mesolimbic system is activated in a hyper-reactive state and results in disturbed motivation. Furthermore, the development of a sensitized state depends on a large diversity of conditions (hormones, immune response, stress, regulatory control) that act at that very moment (Berridge and Robinson 2003). There are several interconnected brain regions whose states of activation determine a hyper-reactive response of the mesolimbic systems resulting in intense motivational states: (1) the activation of a hyper-reactive mesolimbic system, (2) the activation of the medial frontal cortex norepinephrine input to the mesolimbic system (Pascucci et al. 2007; Puglisi-Allegra and Ventura 2012), and (3) dysfunctional recruitment of regulatory hippocampal (Cha et al. 2014), prefrontal (Motzkin et al. 2014a, b), and the habenula circuits (Matsumoto and Hikosaka 2009). When these systems and their interaction are altered, the use of motivational cognition may recruit motivational disturbances in the conceptualization of external and internal sensations and build ongoing experience as disturbed motivation. Probably when they are over-activated because of recent stress, any type of motivational cognition will recruit them in conceptualization and will cause disturbed motivation (i.e., cravings or dreads). Nonetheless, distorted motivational cognition such as demandingness preferentially recruits a sensitized state of motivational systems over other types of motivational cognition.

In other words, the specific ways we think about our desires under adversities may differentially recruit states in large distributed areas of the brain including the mesolimbic dopamine (DA) system and the regulatory prefrontal brain regions. As a result, our motivation-related thinking has unique influences on motivation and emotion.

There are many studies that converge on the idea that changing thinking results in a reduction or in an increase of the activity in the mesolimbic and associated regulatory system changing the desire for natural (e.g., foods; Giuliani et al. 2013; Hollmann et al. 2011; Siep et al. 2012) or drug (i.e., cigarette cravings, Kober et al. 2010b) rewards.

In one of these studies, Siep et al. (2012) used functional magnetic resonance imaging (fMRI) as methodology. They showed that upregulating motivation by thinking of the properties of food recruits medial prefrontal cortex and mesolimbic DA activation coupled with the deactivation of regulatory prefrontal cortex regions. Instead, reappraisal (i.e., thinking of long-term negative costs) and suppression of motivational impulses engaged a different neural activation pattern in which regulatory regions common to those involved in emotion regulation are activated along with deactivation of the mesolimbic DA system (Giuliani et al. 2013; Kober et al. 2010a; Siep et al. 2012). Subsequent neuroimaging studies reinforced these ideas. They showed that an increase in subjective craving at rest is linked to an enhanced coupling between medial prefrontal network and other reward brain regions such as dorsal prefrontal, striatum, or hippocampus (Janes et al. 2014). Furthermore, increased craving has been associated with lower functional connectivity between nucleus accumbens and a network of frontal cortical regions involved in cognitive control in people with substance use disorders (Motzkin et al. 2014b).

Here I suggest that IBs such as demandingness determine disturbed emotions because they recruit as simulations over-activated neural states of sensitized motivational systems (involving deficient downregulation or an excessive upregulation mode of prefrontal brain regions). In other words, they function as embodied rigid appraisals. If the recruited neural states are in a sensitized mesolimbic system (activated probably due to the concomitant stress hormones or by conditioned memory) and decoupled from inhibitory control, then IBs may fully activate sensitized mesolimbic states that will result in the experience of strong impulses, cravings, emotions, and compulsive active coping. If simulations run on normal reactivity mesolimbic states, probably they may not be sufficient to activate intense dopaminergic states and result in increased but not exaggerated desires or cravings. Language has a central role in the recruitment and engagement of the simulations of experiences (Lindquist and Gendron 2013). Thus, the linguistic expressions of "musts, should, and needs" are primary (along with conditioned learning) in the control of simulations in the mesolimbic system. In the embodied simulation framework, linguistic types of beliefs are not the only mechanisms that may control and recruit exaggerated motivational embodiments. Other mechanisms may function as controls by recruiting and activating exaggerated embodied simulations in the conceptualization of the world. Conditioned perceptual stimuli, body expressions and gestures, gait patterns, intonation, memory tasks requirements (percept, associations, conditioning, and episodic memory tasks), or processing rules (i.e., meta-cognition) may also recruit the activation of exaggerated motivational embodiments from memory in the conceptualization of activating events. Moreover, the over-reactive incentive salience system may be triggered unconsciously and influence behavior without conscious awareness. This may be referred to as unconscious embodied demandingness.

I mentioned the role of several types of cognitive controls (language, memories, perceptions, and so forth) that select motivational embodiments in the conceptualization process. Yet biochemical mechanisms may also change the states in the brain regions recruited by simulations and determine exaggerated motivational embodiments. Such factors may be changes in homeostasis, reward deprivation, stress, uncertainty, immune responses, hormonal and neurohormonal changes, drugs, depending on their effects on mesolimbic sites and the regulatory brain regions (Berridge and Robinson 2003; Cabib et al. 2020). From this point of view, the motivational value of a situation is an online computed state depending on the corresponding activated knowledge, the state of the organism and homeostasis, the environment and the processing context (including language) at that time (Berridge and Robinson 2003; Papies et al. 2015).

Let us consider the following example of demandingness: "*I must not be rejected by significant others.*" The embodied simulation frameworks suggest that in order to express and understand this belief, we use unconscious partial activations of the neural states in disinhibited affective systems that were active during experiences such as avoidance of rejection.

Developmentally, some individuals have repeated experiences of disinhibited avoidance of negative events or obtaining positive ones. As a result, they develop motivational simulators of disinhibited needs and motivation. Other people may have repeated experiences of inhibition of the desire to avoid negative stimuli or to obtain rewards. These inhibitory experiences are captured in memory along with stimuli and retrieved during later processing of the stimulus (Mayr and Buckner 2007; Tipper 2001). Memories of inhibited desires are formed based on inhibitory experiences. Memories of disinhibited desires are formed when the recruitment of inhibition in motivational regulation is deficient. Thus, differences in the inhibited or disinhibited affective memories may occur between individuals. Nonetheless, the propensity for an early experience of intense disinhibited motivational states may result from an interaction between an already present biological susceptibility (e.g., deficient prefrontal cortex inhibition or mesolimbic excitability) and repeated experience of self- or other- induced motivational upregulation or nonregulation habits. Through repeated disinhibited experiences, prefrontal inhibitory networks develop poor plastic connections with mesolimbic regions (Castillo et al. 2011; Frias and Wierenga 2013). Given that acute stress profoundly alters inhibitory synaptic plasticity over mesolimbic neurons (Niehaus et al. 2010), it is possible that in people with untrained inhibitory networks, stress effects will result in "trait-like" deteriorations in inhibition.

Some individuals (e.g., showing dopamine D2 receptor gene A1 allele or COMT polymorphisms; Blum et al. 2012; Pani et al. 2000) are more susceptible to the effects of stress on the dopaminergic system and develop sensitization of motivational brain regions (context-dependent hyper-reactivity). Non-susceptible people are not so easily affected and do not develop such a sensitization under stress. In later encounters, motivational brain regions may re-enter hyper-reactive states by exposure to stress hormones, conditioned stimuli, and, as I suggest, by embodied simulations. Thus, these hyper-reactive states of the motivational brain are not only an output (desires/cravings and compulsive coping) but may also be recruited, used, and partially activated for representational proposes by embodied motivational appraisals. In this case, the understanding of the motivational relevance of rejection recruits sensitized states of motivational brain regions which result in exaggerated motivational and emotional experiences. For instance, understanding the motivational relevance of aversive situations (e.g., rejection) by demandingness or other upregulation cognition will result in disturbed disinhibited motivational and emotional states. On the contrary, understanding the motivational relevance of rejection by preferences recruits simulations of the past "pleasure" memories and additional regulatory regions (e.g., dorsolateral prefrontal cortex). These systems compensate for the deteriorated regulatory system and hyper-reactive mesolimbic activation. The result will be regulated motivational and emotional experiences.

In summary, recognizing the importance of avoiding dangers or obtaining rewards by activating disinhibited need simulators, partially re-instantiates a neural pattern of disinhibited motivation and emotion. In sensitized people, activation of disinhibited motivational simulators may result in the full and prolonged activation of a hyper-reactive mesolimbic neural response. The result is a perseveration of active coping (compulsive coping) and intense emotions. In non-sensitized individuals, partial activation induced by cognitive motivational simulations may not result in full activation and not produce an emotional response (Barsalou 2003, 2008, 2009).

Usually, the stress of rejection does not appear as a single event, but it overlaps with the context of other problems. Some parts of this context may be already present states of stress (e.g., from work or other problems) or other negative conditions (i.e., sleep deprivation).

Exposure to stress results in important neuroadaptations in both limbic and prefrontal regulatory systems. Thus, stress exposure results in hyper-reactive responses in mesolimbic brain regions and in deterioration or decoupling of regulatory areas (Peters et al. 2009) such as the medial prefrontal cortex (Niehaus et al. 2010) or deterioration of the habenula neurons (Matsumoto and Hikosaka 2009) involved in the regulation of motivational response when rewards are no longer available (i.e., resulting in a deficit of automatic regulation).

In addition to causing regulatory deficits (either by long-term or acute effects), acute stress states may directly activate the past sensitization of affective brain regions (Berridge and Robinson 2003). When the simulations are run by sensitized systems, they engage this sensitization in the conceptualization of desires. Thus, the current emotional negative states further alter the reactivity of limbic brain regions recruited for the conceptualization of importance (Pichon et al. 2014). Conceptualization of desires by the recruitment of simulations in the acute stress-induced hyper-reactive affective brain will augment the altered motivational and emotional response. Prolonged and context inappropriate disinhibited emotional responses characteristic of emotional pathologies may be promoted by core emotional simulations running over sensitized affective brain regions. The sensitized emotional brain may promote in turn the use of emotional simulations over other simulations in the conceptualization of the world (or knowledge) making emotional-based understanding more available and accessible. In turn, dysfunctional knowledge may continuously recruit sensitized systems and promote sensitization response. Thus, a sensitization cycle may be promoted by reciprocal patterns of emotional negativity.

On the contrary, recognizing the desire of not being rejected as a preference (expectations based on past "pleasure" experiences) rather than a "need" may bring in working memory other contents and recruits both "pleasure" based brain regions and regulatory prefrontal cortex in conceptualization, promoting a regulated state in responding to the situation and the downregulation of mesolimbic DA activation (Giuliani et al. 2013; Puglisi-Allegra and Ventura 2012; Siep et al. 2012). In sensitized individuals, promoting the recognition of desires by preferences and the recruitment of additional inhibitory processes needed to overcome the hyper-reactive mesolimbic responses due to deficits in automatic inhibition may help emotional and motivational regulation. Repeated preference-like motivational experiences may result in building regulated motivational simulators (memories; Barsalou 1999) that will be further recruited by automatic processes in the conceptualization of importance. Indeed, changing the language of "demanding and needing" with the language of "wanting and preferring" in the recognition of importance is a core intervention in appraisal-focused cognitive restructuring (i.e., REBT). Other simulation-control mechanisms such as conditioning, action or body expressions, conscious simulations, rules, perceptions, and meta-cognitions may activate "want"-like simulators in the conceptualization of desires.

5.3 Incentive Wanting, Hoping, and Dreading: Toward Salience Appraisals

When a very important reward is signaled, we need that reward. Sometimes we consciously feel that we need it (i.e., incentive wanting; Berridge and Robinson 2003). When we unexpectedly miss a reward or the reward is uncertain, we also start to "need" that reward and sometimes also consciously feel that we need it (i.e., incentive hope; Anselme and Güntürkün 2019). When we unexpectedly encounter a threat or aversive situation, we start to need to control and avoid that threat (i.e., incentive dread; Cabib and Puglisi-Allegra 2012; Douma and de Kloet 2020). Incentive salience or the mesolimbic-based motivation for rewards was initially thought as a process exclusively involved in the response to natural or drug reward cues. However, recent developments showed that the same process (dopamine release in ventral striatum) makes the organism to need the rewards when they are omitted (or uncertain) or in response to unexpected aversive stimuli (norepinephrine-induced dopamine release; Cabib and Puglisi-Allegra 2012; Ventura et al. 2007, 2008). There is extensive research on how dysregulation of the incentive salience system in response to proximal rewards results in pathologies such as addiction and depression (Berridge and Robinson 2003). Although not so extensive, research consistently supports the involvement of the dysregulation of the incentive hope and dread system in emotional disorders (Douma and de Kloet 2020).

In the following section, I describe the dysregulation of the mesolimbic incentive system as a response to threats and omitted rewards. I propose that *embodied demandingness* is a type of salience appraisal that recruits an oversensitive incentive salience system as part of its embodiment. By this path, embodied demandingness results in craving, compulsive active (approach or avoidance) coping, and emotional dysregulation (disturbed emotions) as a response to omitted rewards or threats. Thus, an embodied conceptualization of demandingness translates data from the affective science of motivation into the field of rigid and exaggerated appraisals. The dysregulation of the mesolimbic DA system supporting incentive salience and craving responses have been commonly linked to behavioral, food, and drug addiction (Berridge and Robinson 2003). As I mentioned above, convincing evidence from affective sciences suggests that dysregulation in the same system is involved in responses to adversities and rigid approach or avoidance coping linked to stress-related pathologies (Cabib and Puglisi-Allegra 2012; Douma and de Kloet 2020; Ironside et al. 2018; Pizzagalli 2014) and in response to the omission of rewards (incentive hope; Anselme and Güntürkün 2019).

5.3.1 Incentive Hope

Anselme (2010) observed that signaling the omission of a reward does not necessarily result in a decrease in mesolimbic DA but often sets the mesolimbic system on "fire," resulting in increased DA release. Most often, when a reward is uncertain or when behaviors have been intermittently reinforced, missing the reward results in an increase in motivation and efforts of animals to obtain the reward. Because incentive salience attribution refers to "wanting" for immediate reward, Anselme termed this increase in DA-based motivation *incentive hope*. When a reward is omitted, the animal wants it more and is mobilized to obtain it. When the mesolimbic DA response is sensitized, this wanting becomes excessive. The animal starts to crave for the omitted reward. Similarly, in vulnerable individuals (sensitized), when a reward is omitted (not receiving expected money) a motivational surge is set off to support obtaining the reward (Anselme and Güntürkün 2019). In this case, the release of a high amount of stress hormones places the mesolimbic system in a hyper-reactive state and the understanding of the salience of the missed reward is dominated by the ventral striatum DA system. The missed reward is not just wanted (based on being valued due to experiences) but it is *craved* or *needed* (i.e., incentive hope). It is an intense "urgent" desire. And coping becomes more than a learned response. It becomes a compulsion.

5.3.2 Incentive Dread

Excellent reviews (Cabib and Puglisi-Allegra 2012; Douma and de Kloet 2020; de Kloet et al. 2019; Ironside et al. 2018) that deal with mesolimbic activation in response to aversive stimuli (stress-coping) have been published. Although some of these findings have been replicated in human subjects, animal studies are extensively reported due to the use of invasive methodology. These reviews conclude that mesolimbic DA activation is essential in the support of active coping (animals persist to change the situation based on previously learned behaviors) when individuals (both humans and nonhuman animals) are confronted with stressors. Yet a flexible coping response (changing from active coping oriented to control and change of the stressor to a passive coping) is required for adaptation when the stressor cannot be controlled by previously learned behaviors (Douma and de Kloet 2020). Furthermore, after context-dependent hyper-dopaminergic states triggered by acute stressors (Grace 2016), an accentuated inactivation of DA system and a hypo-dopaminergic state may result in rigid passive coping and depression (Cabib and Puglisi-Allegra 2012; Cabib et al. 2020).

There are many conditions in susceptible organisms that result in a hyper-reactive mesolimbic DA response and rigid/compulsive active coping with the stressor. In turn, a prolonged response further results in emotional dysregulation and associated pathologies such as anxiety and stress-related disorders (Douma and de Kloet 2020). In contrast to omitted reward situations that trigger cravings, aversive stimuli trigger dreadful motivation (fearful incentive salience) to avoid and control the stressor. If missing an expected food sets you to crave more food (when you are hungry), you feel you need to escape from being socially rejected (dread).

Thus, we crave to control and escape from adversities as well. More importantly, the stress hormones (previous emotional states, the alarm system activation, the context-a sudden noise, Grace 2016) prime the incentive salience motivation to deal with a stressor. When a stressor is encountered, the general alarm response is triggered and stress hormones are released (e.g., norepinephrine, glucocorticoids; Douma and de Kloet 2020). The stress hormones sensitize the incentive salience system to motivate to change the stressor (active coping). Due to high mesolimbic DA release, the organism is mobilized and invigorated to control the stressor. When the organism is in a particular condition (due to external or internal states such as drug-cues, deprivation, sensitized neural system, low or altered prefrontal cortex/PFC control, inherited or acquired individual differences), the mesolimbic system DA becomes hyper-reactive and the organism experiences intense craving and compulsive behaviors.

Among the conditions that result in a shift from a PFC flexible coping response (George and Koob 2013) to a rigid striatal response to stressors are early chronic stress, environmental conditions, hormonal states or deprivation, emotions, expectations, and perceptions of availability of rewards. From this perspective, demandingness is a form of salience appraisal that is consciously experienced as a craving to control the adversities and is behaviorally expressed as rigid active coping implemented by hyper-dopaminergic mesolimbic states.

In short, based on the review of the existing research, a stressful situation (activating situation) triggers the incentive salience system to motivate active coping and the control of the stressor. In some conditions, this response results in the conscious experience of craving. The stressor can be an unexpectedly omitted reward or a threat. An overactive incentive salience response can appear as a craving for obtaining the reward (in the case of missing a reward) or as a dread for avoiding the threat (in the case of a threat; Berridge 2018).

5.4 Theoretical and Empirical Arguments for Embodied Rigid Motivational Appraisals

In the following section, I will review theoretical and empirical arguments for the embodiment of rigid motivational appraisals or demandingness in dysregulated motivational systems.

5.4.1 Theoretical Arguments

An embodied simulation view of demandingness suggests that it is not what you say to yourself that disturbs you emotionally but how you embody what you say. In other words, it is the meaning of demandingness (e.g., *I must be approved*) in terms of the re-enactment of craving/dread experiences that disturbs us emotionally. Verbal statements, no matter what form they take, impact emotions only when they recruit motivational and emotional embodiments into their meaning. They have a "hot" affective semantic core built on the partial reactivations of the affective states they refer to. In the case of demandingness, this *embodied core meaning* is built up on dysregulated motivational states or craving. It is not that I say "*I must be respected*" that disturbs me, but the understanding of the necessity of being respected based on my past cravings. It is *embodied demandingness,* that in the traditional literature it is referred to as *absolute demandingness*. When I understand my desires or necessities in terms of non-craving experiences, no emotional disturbance occurs.

Let us remember the experiment of Oosterwijk et al. (2010) described in Chap. 2. In their experiment, Oosterwijk et al. instructed participants to unscramble fear sentences in a scrambled sentence task by determining which word does not belong to the presented sentence (e.g., "*Bite poisonous is death*"). During the task, they monitored the electrodermal and corrugator activity as embodiments of the presented sentences (Oosterwijk et al. 2010). They found a higher electrodermal response and corrugator activity for the fear sentences which occurred in the absence of subjective fear experience. After concept activation, they presented participants with negative and neutral pictures in combination with startling sounds and measured electrodermal and startle response. The results showed that the level of emotional embodiment during the fear concepts task mediates the magnitude of emotional response when viewing negative pictures. In other words, fear sentences are embodied by partial emotional activations that are responsible for their effect on negative emotions. In the case of demandingness, we expect that the effect of demandingness on our responses will depend on its embodiment by dysregulated motivation. There are several arguments from observations of demandingness in clinical and nonclinical situations that support such a view.

The first theoretical argument for an embodied view of demandingness lies in the statement that it is not actually what we say to ourselves or the verbal expression of demandingness that disturbs us but it is the meaning of absolute demandingness that disturbs us. This claim is made both by A. Ellis and his most distinguished scholars (Dryden, DiGiuseppe, and David, among many others), being an accepted assertion among REBT practitioners.

Dryden and Branch (2008) present an excellent description of the difference between absolute (that disturb us emotionally) and non-absolute shoulds or musts (that do not disturb us emotionally). According to Dryden and Branch (2008), absolute "shoulds" refer to disturbance-creating demands (e.g., "I absolutely must win this contest").

Non-absolute shoulds include *recommendatory* (specifies a recommendation for self or other: "You should see the movie"), *predictive* (estimations about the future: "I should not get sick"), *ideal* (ideal viewpoint "People should be nice to each other"), *empirical* ("Because I did not study for the exam I should get a bad grade"), *preferential* ("My wife preferably should cook the dinner"), and *conditional* ("I *should* work to get paid") (Dryden and Branch 2008). It is not what you say to yourself that disturbs you, but what you mean when you say *things absolutely should be* as you want them to be. Thus, the standard REBT model agrees that is the meaning of the "must" which is important (not the verbal expression of the "must"). By this logic, the standard model is compatible with the embodied simulation model by asserting that the meaning of IBs is what disturbs us. Yet the meaning of demandingness can be represented both amodally (propositions in a language-like format, Fodor 1975) and modally (embodied) in the form of simulations of experiences labeled by verbal forms (Barsalou 1999, 2008).

For embodied demandingness, the meaning is situated (there can be different meanings depending on the context) and based on simulations of previous experiences. This implies that the meaning of verbal demandingness can be based on reactivation of different experiences and of different brain implementation systems and processes depending on the context. The meaning of demanding *being loved* is based on how the situation (the person present, being in a church or not; past experience, personal goals) structures and compositionally organizes from memory the experiences about love and the brain systems that are reactivated to simulate (represent) *I must be loved*. If I repeat *I must be loved* forty times in different tonalities like a song (e.g., the semantic satiation method), saying *I must be loved* will recruit for implementation auditory brain systems, and not affective systems. As a result, saying *I must be loved* will not result in disturbed emotions. The problem is that when I encounter cues related to the lost partner (looking at their pictures), these cues can trigger (based on conditioning) an incentive salience system-based embodiment. Different other internal and external contexts besides conditioned cues can set the incentive wanting system in overdrive. Some examples are prolonged exposure to stress hormones in constitutionally predisposed individuals, low of inhibitory control, craving memories, and so on. Understanding the desire for the loved person in this context will be based on simulations of craving (embodiment). Then, the person will truly believe that he absolutely must be loved. If the simulation fully activates the craving experience, the person will experience a full craving for being loved, think that he must be loved, will have an urge to be loved, compulsively seek for love, and will become obsessed with being loved.

The second argument lies at the very heart of REBT: the revised ABC model of REBT proposed by A. Ellis (1991, 2001). Ellis advanced a revised ABC model based on his early descriptions of beliefs in which beliefs are at the same time feelings and behaviors (Ellis 1991, 2001). In Ellis's revised ABC model, demandingness is at the same time believing-emoting-behaving. This is overlapping the concept of an embodied representation of demandingness as a multidimensional affective reaction. According to Ellis, demandingness is represented as a composite of feelings, behaviors, and beliefs. As demandingness can go into memory, so do experiences of feelings and behaviors be stored in memory and reactivated. Thus, the revised model of demandingness proposed by Ellis advances an embodied type of rigid appraisal or demandingness. Embodied emotional beliefs, similar to what A. Ellis suggested, are represented by simulations or reactivations of emotional and behavioral experiences captured in memory. Beliefs are at the same time thoughts, feelings, and urges to get what one must have. Moreover, Ellis asserted that demandingness, as a belief, is at the same time feelings and behaviors. This assumption is one of the core assumptions of the embodied simulation view of constructed emotions (Barrett 2017). In this view, emotions are psychological states which can be experienced as feelings when the focus of attention is to interpret interoceptive sensations based on emotion concepts (I feel anger); as cognition when the focus of attention is to what we believe (anger thoughts); as perception when the attention focuses on how to describe the object (e.g., It is an upsetting situation) or as behavior (e.g., "I tend to hit"). Similarly, demandingness is a subjectively constructed psychological state that can be experienced as a belief (e.g., "I must be appreciated"), a feeling (e.g., "I feel the need to be appreciated"), a behavior (e.g., the urge or the compulsion to get appreciation). The specific way of experiencing demandingness depends on the context, memories, and the focus of attention.

The third argument is based on suggestions that in REBT theory, demandingness is proposed to be a motivational experience: cravings. Thus, according to Ellis, individuals "choose to disturb themselves by escalating their preferences into demands and cravings…" (Ellis et al. 2010, p. 11). Referring to beliefs in terms of experiences suggests demandingness as an embodied type of appraisals. Beliefs about motivation are at the same time motivation.

The fourth argument lies in the conditions for assessing demandingness. Demandingness (e.g., I should be respected) can truly be seen when activated by a situation (e.g., being humiliated) and result in disturbed emotions (e.g., anger, Ellis 1994).

These conditions of demandingness are similar to conditions of disturbed motivation. Excessive salience is under the control of stimuli and stress hormones. Stress hormones (norepinephrine, corticotropin-releasing factor, or cortisol) can set off the incentive DA system in overdrive in susceptible individuals (increase in tonic DA signal). Subsequently, a situational cue triggers an exaggerated incentive salience phasic signal (Grace 2016). Thus, the incentive salience and the associated conscious (or unconscious) experience of craving appear in the presence of cues and stress.

5.4.2 *Empirical Arguments*

There are several empirical arguments for the embodiment of demandingness in altered motivational states: correlation of demandingness with genotypes that determine the control of motivational systems, the dissociation of positive and negative demandingness based on approach and avoidance motivational systems, the link between demandingness and sign-tracking-like reactions, difficulties in behavior-outcome reversal learning in high demanding individuals, and state dependency of demandingness.

5.4.2.1 Positive and Negative Rigid Thinking Can Be Dissociated Based on Approach and Avoidance Motivational Systems

If demandingness is embodied in partial states of disinhibited and sensitized motivational systems, then we can evidence an organization of demandingness based on principles of motivational systems. To this end, I investigated whether demandingness can be dissociated based on the approach and withdrawal (respectively) motivational systems. In a cross-sectional study, I asked 45 healthy participants to respond to measures of both positive (e.g., "*I must obtain approval*") and negative (e.g., "*I must not be rejected*") demandingness (Ellis and Dryden 1997) and approach-withdrawal motivation (e.g., BIS/BAS scale; Carver and White 1994). Results showed that positive demandingness and irrationality strongly correlated with *approach system* sensitivity (BAS scores), while negative demandingness and irrationality strongly correlated with *withdrawal system* sensitivity (BIS scores). This study has suggested that individuals tend to develop positive and negative demandingness depending on the *approach/withdrawal* motivational systems' sensitivity (Tiba 2005). Both positive and negative rigid beliefs have positively correlated with the drive-impulsivity scale suggesting that demandingness may engage dysregulated motivational systems for its representation (Tiba 2005).

5.4.2.2 Individuals with High Rigid Thinking Show Sign-Tracking Tendencies

If demandingness is embodied in dysregulated motivational systems, individuals with high levels of demandingness will manifest characteristics of individuals with sensitized motivational systems. Well-recognized indicators of the presence of sensitization of the mesolimbic system are sign-tracking behaviors. Sign-tracking reactions refer to the tendency of the animal to display consummatory behaviors toward cues of rewards (liking the lever) or relief (safety signals; Leclerc and Reberg 1980) instead of going to the location of reward delivery (go where sugar is delivered) or engage in safe behaviors. Sign-tracking behaviors or approach behaviors toward conditioned stimuli (e.g., attentional bias toward conditioned stimuli) versus unconditioned rewards (goal tracking) have been evidenced in humans as well in various forms of conditioned cue driven behaviors (e.g., attentional biased toward conditioned cues). Sign-trackers have the tendency to assign motivational value to cues of reward which become rewarding and attract approach and consummatory behaviors toward themselves. They show several characteristics such as tendency for addiction (Anderson et al. 2013), impulsivity (Pearson et al. 2015), trait reward seeking (Hickey et al. 2010), and compulsivity (Albertella et al. 2019), being predisposed to many psychopathologies (Morrow 2018).

In 2005, Tiba and Szentagotai showed that demandingness is linked to increased consummatory behaviors in a reward approach phase similar to sign-tracking reactions.

Tiba and Szentagotai (2005) asked participants to complete measures of trait and state IBs and approach-consummatory emotions in two situations: (a) remembering a situation in which the participant worked toward attaining an important personal goal (i.e., approach condition) and (b) remembering attaining an important goal (i.e., consummatory condition). Results showed that people with high demandingness levels manifest more consummatory positive feelings to the anticipation of positive outcomes and approach emotions when already have attained goals (consumption of rewards). Given that consummatory responses to reward cues are an index of sign tracking (Berridge and Robinson 2003) and mesolimbic sensitization is reflected in the presence of sign tracking (Anselme et al. 2013), these results suggest that demandingness may be grounded in sensitized mesolimbic systems and may be associated with sign-tracking tendencies in vulnerable individuals.

This interpretation is further supported by the finding that individuals with higher levels of BASdrive subscale of the BIS/BAS scale (Carver and White 1994) have high levels of positive and negative demandingness (Tiba 2005). Previous studies showed that individuals with high levels of BASdrive impulsivity scale show marked sign-tracking reactions (value enhanced visual priming; Hickey et al. 2010). The fact that higher scores at BASdrive impulsivity subscale are related with higher levels of demandingness and sign tracking suggests the possibility that a common factor may underlie both sign tracking and demandingness.

By embodying the representation of demandingness, individuals with high levels of rigid thinking may be characterized by the same factors that predispose people to a highly reactive mesolimbic system, the most common being stress and impaired prefrontal control over limbic brain regions (Berridge 2018). Although direct evidence is required, grounding of demandingness in the over-reactive dysregulated mesolimbic system suggests that factors that influence the mesolimbic system also influence demandingness (frontal deficiency or upregulation, stress, cross-overs from drugs, delivery modality, context, hormones, immune stimulation, genes polymorphisms; Berridge and Robinson 2003). Furthermore, it suggest that activated IBs are more a state-feeling concept (craving; Naqvi et al. 2014) related to states of the brain mesolimbic regions (this is not in opposition with "demanding" philosophies and explicit knowledge in people but distorted affective influence of these philosophies results only when demandingness runs over sensitized mesolimbic systems). Although the linguistic representations of salient stimuli may express various confound processes (e.g., liking or "pleasure" memories, conscious desires, reasoning) and cannot be reliable in the study of incentive salience, in vulnerable people, the use of linguistic expressions of demandingness may recruit a sensitized motivational system (similar to perceptions) in the conceptualization of ongoing sensations and promote disinhibited emotional and motivational responding.

5.4.2.3 Individuals with Met/Met COMT Genotypes Have Higher Levels of Rigid Appraisals

Another source of support for the idea that rigid thinking is embodied in hyper-reactive motivational systems comes from studies investigating the relations of irrational cognitions with genetic polymorphisms that promote over-reactive DA responses when individuals encounter negative events.

Podina et al. (2015) have investigated the relation between COMT 158Val Met genotypes and irrational beliefs. Participants completed trait measures of irrational beliefs, anxiety (STAI-Trait), and depression (Beck Depression Inventory) measures. Results have shown significant associations between genotype and irrationality (overall irrationality, rigid thinking, awfulizing and self-downing) for the high and mean levels of emotional distress but not for the low levels of emotional distress. Overall, the level of irrational cognition (overall irrationality, rigid thinking, awfulizing and self-downing) was higher in individuals with both Met alleles relative to the Val carriers. These results have been interpreted as evidence for IBs as cognitive phenotypes. Yet they also support an embodied view of IBs in neural hyper-reactivity of affective systems. It is well known that individuals with Met/Met alleles have hyper-reactive neural states in emotional regions in response to stressors (Serrano et al. 2019), higher levels of dopamine in ventral striatum and difficulties in cognitive flexibility than individuals with Met/Val or Val/Val individuals (Drabant et al. 2006). The (Val66Met) single nucleotide polymorphism (SNP) impairs BDNF (*Brain-Derived Neurotrophic Factor*) signaling and is associated with psychopathology (Douma and de Kloet 2020). BDNF is an important regulator of VTA-DA function and of the effects of stress on mesolimbic reactivity (Douma and de Kloet 2020), its effects being related to the extent of controllability, duration, and severity of the stressor.

5.4.2.4 The Dependency of IBs and COMT Relationship on High-Trait Stress

In the study of Podina et al. (2015), IBs were related to Met/Met genotypes only in individuals with high trait levels of distress (anxiety and depression). This stress-dependency of the genotypes X IBs relationship points to an embodied simulation account of rigid and exaggerated thinking. Accumulating evidence shows that COMT genotype individuals are susceptible to the effects of stress on various neural mechanisms including the hypothalamic-pituitary-adrenal axis (HPA; Zubieta et al. 2003) and mesolimbic DA activity (Jabbi et al. 2007). Specifically, stress results in hyper-reactivity of both HPA and DA neural systems to stress (along with many other neural systems). Thus, hyper-reactive neural embodiments of irrational beliefs are developed in genetically susceptible individuals (Met carriers) because of exposure to stress. Also, these individuals are susceptible to develop high emotional reactivity to stress. Some COMT individuals, probably not exposed to chronic stress, neither develop stress-related neuroadaptations such as HPA hyper-reactivity (indexed by STAI and BDI self-report measures) nor hyper-reactive incentive salience related to a sensitized mesolimbic DA response (self-reported as rigid demands). Thus, no relation between COMT genotype and IBs can be seen in people who did not develop a sensitized mesolimbic response that embodies IBs.

5.4.2.5 Individuals with High Levels of IBs Have Difficulties in Reward Reversal Learning

An important source of support for the idea that demandingness is embodied by a hyper-reactive mesolimbic system comes from the finding that individuals with high levels of IBs are characterized by increased behavioral inflexibility in tasks of reversal learning (which is a marker of increased mesolimbic excitability).

For example, Tiba (2003) investigated the association between verbal expressions of demandingness and difficulties of updating stimulus-reinforcement associations. Participants completed a verbal measure of demandingness, an emotional rating scale, and a monetary incentive delayed reverse task taxing the functioning of the prefrontal systems involved in the regulation of the mesolimbic dopamine systems in response to rewards (Knutson et al. 2001). The results showed that participants scoring high at verbal measures of demandingness have reduced performance in updating stimulus reinforcements associations compared to participants scoring low in demandingness.

Moreover, in high demanding individuals negative emotions were inversely related to stimulus-reinforcer updating performance (but not in the low demandingness group). This finding suggests a possible mediation of the relationship between verbal demandingness and emotional reactions by updating the difficulty of stimulus-reinforcement associations that is dependent on both mesolimbic system activation and inhibitory control mechanisms (Tiba 2003).

These results are consistent with the presence of difficulties of updating in the salience attribution process characteristic of an over-reactive mesolimbic system and a behavioral inflexibility phenotype. Furthermore, the results can be interpreted based on a reverse translation approach (Holmes et al. 2018). Once a behavioral trait is identified in humans, research of that trait in animals allows for detailed investigations of molecular mechanisms and pathophysiological mechanisms. Recent reviews of the effect of stress on mesolimbic VTA-DA (ventral tegmental area-dopamine) system suggest that (1) stress results in sensitization of mesolimbic system, (2) stress-induced VTA-DA neuronal plasticity promotes a behavioral inflexibility of coping with stress, and (3) behavior inflexibility affects the ability to change behaviors when the context changes, produces intense emotional reactions, and contributes to stress-related disorders (Douma and de Kloet 2020).

5.4.2.6 Emotional Situations and States as Amplifiers of Rigid Thinking

Albert Ellis proposed that true IBs can only be seen in situations of stress (Ellis 1994). According to this proposal, when people do not encounter a stressful situation, one cannot distinguish between high and low irrational individuals. Exposure to stressful events is necessary to reveal irrational beliefs in vulnerable individuals. In line with this proposal, studies show that irrational beliefs are usually higher with both state (Bridges and Harnish 2010) and trait emotional distress (e.g., Chang 1997; Deffenbacher et al. 1986). In the classical view of irrational beliefs, demandingness is stored in forms of propositions in a schematic form (Szentagotai et al. 2005). When they are activated from semantic memory, they can influence the response to both the stressor and the IBs tests.

In standard measures of IBs, individuals are presented with verbal sentences that describe (general or situation-specific) irrational beliefs (e.g., *"I must succeed"; "I must be loved"*) and are asked to rate the degree they agree or not with the sentence content (e.g., how much you agree with the sentence on a scale where 1 means totally disagree and 5 totally agree). Discrepancies between verbal reports of IBs under stress or non-stress situations are assumed to appear because under no-stress situations, IBs are not activated from memory. The embodied view of IBs suggests otherwise. When IBs are embodied, stress (hormones) puts the brain in a different state in genetically and epigenetically vulnerable individuals. Thus, the understanding of the importance of the stressful situation runs over a stress-induced dysfunctional affective embodiment. When an individual encounters a stressor, stress hormones (glucocorticoids/GC and norepinephrine) are released. In genetic (e.g., individuals with Met allele of COMT genotypes) and/or epigenetic (individuals with early stress neuroadaptations of PFC and mesocorticolimbic systems) vulnerable individuals, glucocorticoids or norepinephrine release sets the incentive wanting system in a hyper-responsive state and rigid active stress-coping results. Prolonged rigid reaction to a stressor further results in disturbed emotions (Cabib et al. 2020). Thus, in vulnerable individuals stress controls the neural embodiments (incentive salience system activation) that are used in the understanding of the stressful situation. The individual experiences this change *as an urge* to control the situation or a craving. When the individual is exposed to no stressful situation or is under no emotional states, the incentive salience system may not be activated and the ratings for IBs run over a *conscious desire* system rather than a *craving* system (Berridge 2018). Although embodied IBs are under the control of other top-down (memory, stimulus-driven, linguistic, etc.) and bottom-up (context, deprivation) control mechanisms of embodied simulations, hormonal control mechanisms are of importance. Below I describe a study that elegantly illustrates the action of stress hormones on mesolimbic DA level in vulnerable individuals.

Hernaus et al. (2013) used a positron emission tomography (PET) methodology to investigate the DA levels in response to stress in individuals carrying the COMT Met allele compared to individuals carrying the COMT Val/Val genotype. Participants underwent a stress task in which they performed mental arithmetic exercises (stressful feedback about the total number of errors, expected average number of errors, time spent on the current problem were given) (Hernaus et al. 2013). At every 12 minutes, they measured the levels of stress (i.e., ratings of "I feel relaxed", "I'm in control"). Results showed that in individuals with COMT Met/Met genotype, the stress task resulted in an increase in PFC and mesolimbic DA levels. They interpreted the results based on a U inverted function of PFC DA. Individuals with COMT Met/Met genotype have increased PFC DA levels due to reduced breakdown of DA (up to 40%). A stress-induced increase of DA in PFC will push the prefrontal DA over the optimal levels and will result in increased mesolimbic DA response to stress and higher stress responsiveness. Individuals with COMT Val/Val genotype have low baseline levels of PFC dopamine because of higher DA breakdown enzymatic activity. In these individuals, a stress-induced increase in DA in PFC will push the DA to optimal levels and will result in reduced mesolimbic DA response to stress and stress reactivity.

A higher increase in mesolimbic DA levels in response to stress reflects a higher rigid active coping (de Kloet et al. 2019; Douma and de Kloet 2020), in which the individuals persist in controlling the stress by changing it. In other words, they more readily and persistently *demand* to control the stressor.

Similar responses to those of genetically vulnerable individuals to acute stress (as above mentioned) can be seen in individuals who underwent early stress-related epigenetic changes (Arnsten 2009, 2015). In their case, long-term effects of stress decrease the PFC DA function and connectivity which (based on an inverted U function of PFC DA levels) results in hyper-reactive mesolimbic responses to stressors and rigid active coping (Deutch et al. 1990). In other words, stress exposure (by glucocorticoids release; de Kloet et al. 2019) primes a hyper-reactive mesolimbic system in response to stress. Understanding the importance of situations in vulnerable individuals is implemented by a hyper-reactive neural embodiment (not a "cognitive wanting"-based neural system). As a result, they experience these reactions as a necessity/urge to change the stressor.

5.5 Summary

Behavioral and genetic evidence suggests that demandingness, when it acts as vulnerability to emotional disorders, is a rigid appraisal embodied in over-reactive mesolimbic neural states. Embodied demandingness is a cognitive inflexibility phenotype implemented by over-reactive mesolimbic states associated with dysregulated emotions, rigid/compulsive active (approach or avoidance) coping, increased salience attribution, compulsivity, and sign tracking. This chapter advanced the ideas that: (1) rigid appraisals are embodied in hyper-reactive dopaminergic motivational states in genetically susceptible individuals, (2) rigid appraisals overlap with the concept of craving and rigid active coping, and (3) rigid appraisals, when embodied in disturbed motivation, are core trans-diagnostic processes involved in behavioral and emotional pathologies. The chapter described studies that support demandingness as embodied rigid motivational appraisals. Embodied rigid motivational appraisals can be implemented by different neural systems, the neural system selected to implement rigid appraisals being context-dependent. Rigid appraisals impact emotion and behavior when it is implemented by simulations of disturbed motivation. Disturbed motivation is recruited as simulations for rigid thinking based on several biased top-down (deficient recruitment of PFC or upregulation by PFC) and bottom-up (context, stress hormones, emotional states, epinephrine, glucocorticoid receptors, etc.) simulation-control mechanisms in vulnerable individuals.

References

Albertella, L., Le Pelley, M. E., Chamberlain, S. R., Westbrook, F., Fontenelle, L. F., Segrave, R., … Yücel, M. (2019). Reward-related attentional capture is associated with severity of addictive and obsessive-compulsive behaviors. *Psychology of Addictive Behaviors, 33*(5), 495–502. https://doi.org/10.1037/adb0000484

Anderson, B. A., Faulkner, M. L., Rilee, J. J., Yantis, S., & Marvel, C. L. (2013). Attentional bias for non drug reward is magnified in addiction. *Experimental and Clinical Psychopharmacology, 21*(6), 499–506. https://doi.org/10.1037/a0034575

Anselme, P. (2010). The uncertainty processing theory of motivation. *Behavioral Brain Research, 208*(2), 291–310.

Anselme, P., & Güntürkün, O. (2019). Incentive hope: A default psychological response to multiple forms of uncertainty. *Behavioral and Brain Sciences, 42*(e35), 40–59.

Anselme, P., Robinson, M. J. F., & Berridge, K. C. (2013). Reward uncertainty enhances incentive salience attribution as sign-tracking. *Behavioural Brain Research, 238*, 53–61.

Arnsten, A. F. (2009). Stress signalling pathways that impair prefrontal cortex structure and function. *Nature Review Neuroscience, 10*(6), 410–422.

Arnsten, A. F. T. (2015). Stress weakens prefrontal networks: Molecular insults to higher cognition. *Nature Neuroscience, 18*(10), 1376–1385. https://doi.org/10.1038/nn.4087

Barrett, L. F. (2017). *How emotions are made: The secret life of the brain*. Houghton Mifflin Harcourt.

Barsalou, L. W. (1999). Perceptual symbol systems. *Behavioral and Brain Sciences, 22*, 577–609.

Barsalou, L. W. (2003). Situated simulation in the human conceptual system. *Language and Cognitive Processes, 18*, 513–562.

Barsalou, L. W. (2008). Grounded cognition. *Annual Review of Psychology, 59*(1), 617–645.

Barsalou, L. W. (2009). Simulation, situated conceptualization, and prediction. *Philosophical Transactions of the Royal Society B: Biological Sciences, 364*(1521), 1281–1289. https://doi.org/10.1098/rstb.2008.0319

Berridge, K. C. (2018). Evolving concepts of emotion and motivation. *Frontiers in Psychology, 9*, 1647. https://doi.org/10.3389/fpsyg.2018.01647

Berridge, K. C., & Robinson, T. E. (2003). Parsing reward. *Trends in Neurosciences, 26*(9), 507–513.

Blum, K., Werner, T., Carnes, S., Carnes, P., Bowirrat, A., Giordano, J., … Gold, M. (2012). Sex, drugs, and rock 'n' roll: Hypothesizing common mesolimbic activation as a function of reward gene polymorphisms. *Journal of Psychoactive Drugs, 44*, 38–55.

Bridges, K. R., & Harnish, R. J. (2010). Role of irrational beliefs in depression and anxiety: A 3 review. *Health, 2*(08), 862. https://doi.org/10.4236/health.2010.28130

Cabib, S., Campus, P., Conversi, D., Orsini, C., & Puglisi-Allegra, S. (2020). Functional and dysfunctional neuroplasticity in learning to cope with stress. *Brain Sciences, 10*(2), 127. https://doi.org/10.3390/brainsci10020127

Cabib, S., & Puglisi-Allegra, S. (2012). The mesoaccumbens dopamine in coping with stress. *Neuroscience & Biobehavioral Reviews, 36*(1), 79–89.

Carver, C. S., & White, T. L. (1994). Behavioral inhibition, behavioral activation, and affective responses to impending reward and punishment: The BIS/BAS scales. *Journal of Personality and Social Psychology, 67*(3), 19–333.

Castillo, P. E., Chiu, C. Q., & Carroll, R. C. (2011). Long-term plasticity at inhibitory synapses. *Current Opinion in Neurobiology, 21*, 328–338.

Cha, J., Carlson, J. M., DeDora, D., Greenberg, T., Hajcak, G., & Mujica-Parodi, L. R. (2014). Generalizing fear: Hyperactive ventral tegmental area and altered connectivity in human generalized anxiety. *Journal of Neuroscience, 34*(17), 5855–5860.

Chang, E. C. (1997). Irrational beliefs and negative life stress: Testing a diathesis-stress model of depressive symptoms. *Personality and Individual Differences, 22*(1), 115–117.

Cohen, J. Y., Haesler, S., Vong, L., Lowell, B. B., & Uchida, N. (2012). Neuron-type specific signals for reward and punishment in the ventral tegmental area. *Nature, 482*, 85–88.

David, D. (2014). Rational emotive behavior therapy. In D. S. Dunn (Ed.), *Oxford bibliographies in psychology*. Oxford University Press.

David, D., Schnur, J., & Belloiu, A. (2002). Another search for the "hot" cognition: Appraisal irrational beliefs, attribution, and their relation to emotion. *Journal of Rational-Emotive and Cognitive-Behavior Therapy, 20*, 93–131.

David, D., Szentagotai, A., Lupu, V., & Cosman, D. (2008). Rational emotive behavior therapy, cognitive therapy, and medication in the treatment of major depressive disorder: A randomized clinical trial, posttreatment outcomes, and six-month follow-up. *Journal of Clinical Psychology, 64*, 728–746. https://doi.org/10.1002/jclp.20487

David, D. O., Sucală, M., Coteț, C., Șoflău, R., & Vălenaș, S. (2019). Empirical research in REBT theory and practice. In M. Bernard & W. Dryden (Eds.), *Advances in REBT*. Springer. https://doi.org/10.1007/978-3-319-93118-0_8

de Kloet, E. R., de Kloet, S. F., de Kloet, C. S., & de Kloet, A. D. (2019). Top-down and bottom-up control of stress-coping. *Journal of Neuroendocrinology, 31*(3), e12675. https://doi.org/10.1111/jne.12675

Deffenbacher, J. L., Zwemer, W. A., Whisman, M. A., Hill, R. A., & Sloan, R. D. (1986). 3 irrational beliefs and anxiety. *Cognitive Therapy and Research, 10*, 281–292.

Deutch, A. Y., Clark, W. A., & Roth, R. H. (1990). Prefrontal cortical dopamine depletion enhances the responsiveness of mesolimbic dopamine neurons to stress. *Brain Research, 521*, 311–315.

Dichter, G. S., Damiano, C. A., & Allen, J. A. (2012). Reward circuitry dysfunction in psychiatric and neurodevelopmental disorders and genetic syndromes: Animal models and clinical findings. *Journal of Neurodevelopmental Disorders, 4*, 19. https://doi.org/10.1186/1866-1955-4-19

Douma, E. H., & de Kloet, E. R. (2020). Stress-induced plasticity and functioning of ventral tegmental dopamine neurons. *Neuroscience and Biobehavioral Reviews, 108*, 48–77. https://doi.org/10.1016/j.neubiorev.2019.10.015

Drabant, E. M., Hariri, A. R., Meyer-Lindenberg, A., Munoz, K. E., Mattay, V. S., Kolachana, B. S., … Weinberger, D. R. (2006). Catechol O-methyltransferase val158met genotype and neural mechanisms related to affective arousal and regulation. *Archives of General Psychiatry, 63*, 1396–1406.

Drevets, W. C., Price, J. L., & Furey, M. L. (2008). Brain structural and functional abnormalities in mood disorders: Implications for neurocircuitry models of depression. *Brain Structure and Function, 213*, 93–118.

Dryden, W. (2009). *Rational emotive behaviour therapy: Distinctive features*. Routledge.

Dryden, W. (2019). Rational emotive behavior therapy: Assessment, conceptualisation and intervention. In M. Bernard & W. Dryden (Eds.), *Advances in REBT*. Springer. https://doi.org/10.1007/978-3-319-93118-0_8

Dryden, W., & Branch, R. (2008). *The fundamentals of rational emotive behaviour therapy: A training handbook* (2nd ed.). Wiley.

Ellis, A. (1958). Rational psychotherapy. *The Journal of General Psychology, 59*, 35–49.

Ellis, A. (1962). *Reason and emotion in psychotherapy*. Lyle Stuart.

Ellis, A. (1991). The revised ABC's of rational-emotive therapy (RET). *Journal of Rational-Emotive and Cognitive-Behavior Therapy, 9*, 139–172. https://doi.org/10.1007/BF01061227

Ellis, A. (1994). *Reason and emotion in psychotherapy (rev sub ed.)*. Citadel.

Ellis, A. (2001). *Feeling better, getting better, staying better: Profound self-help therapy for your emotions*. Impact Publishers.

Ellis, A., David, D., & Lynn, S. J. (2010). Rational and irrational beliefs: A historical and conceptual perspective. In D. David, S. J. Lynn, & A. Ellis (Eds.), *Rational and irrational beliefs: Research, theory, and clinical practice* (pp. 3–22). Oxford University Press.

Ellis, A., & Dryden, W. (1997). *The practice of rational emotive behavior therapy* (2nd ed.). Springer Publishing.

Fodor, J. A. (1975). *The language of thought*. Cambridge, MA: Harvard University Press.

Frias, C. P., & Wierenga, C. J. (2013). Activity-dependent adaptations in inhibitory axons. *Frontiers in Cell Neuroscience, 7*, 219. https://doi.org/10.3389/fncel.2013.00219

George, O., & Koob, G. (2013). Control of craving by the prefrontal cortex. *Proceedings of the National Academy of Sciences of the United States of America, 110*, 4165–4166. https://doi.org/10.1073/pnas.1301245110

Giuliani, N. R., Calcott, R. D., & Berkman, E. T. (2013). Piece of cake: Cognitive reappraisal of food craving. *Appetite, 64*, 56–61.

Grace, A. A. (2016). Dysregulation of the dopamine system in the pathophysiology of schizophrenia and depression. *Nature Review Neuroscience, 17*, 524–532.

Hernaus, D., Collip, D., Lataster, J., Ceccarini, J., Kenis, G., Booij, L., … Myin-Germeys, I. (2013). COMT Val158Met genotype selectively alters prefrontal [18F]fallypride displacement and subjective feelings of stress in response to a psychosocial stress challenge. *PLoS One, 8*(6), e65662. https://doi.org/10.1371/journal.pone.0065662

Hickey, C., Chelazzi, L., & Theeuwes, J. (2010). Reward guides vision when it's your thing: Trait reward-seeking in reward-mediated visual priming. *PLoS One, 5*(11), 1–5. https://doi.org/10.1371/journal.pone.0014087

Hollmann, M., Hellrung, L., Pleger, B., Schlogl, H., Kabisch, S., Stumvoll, M., … Horstmann, A. (2011). Neural correlates of the volitional regulation of the desire for food. *International Journal of Obesity, 36*, 648–655. https://doi.org/10.1038/ijo.2011.125

Holmes, E. A., Ghaderi, A., Harmer, C. J., Ramchandani, P. G., Cuijpers, P., Morrison, A. P., … Craske, M. G. (2018). The lancet psychiatry commission on psychological treatments research in tomorrow's science. *The Lancet Psychiatry, 5*(3), 237–286. https://doi.org/10.1016/S2215-0366(17)30513-8

Ironside, M., Kumar, P., Kang, M. S., & Pizzagalli, D. A. (2018). Brain mechanisms mediating effects of stress on reward sensitivity. *Current Opinion in Behavioral Sciences, 22*, 106–113. https://doi.org/10.1016/j.cobeha.2018.01.016

Jabbi, M., Kema, I. P., van der Pompe, G., te Meerman, G. J., Ormel, J., & den Boer, J. (2007). Catechol-o-methyltransferase polymorphism and susceptibility to major depressive disorder modulates psychological stress response. *Psychiatry Genetics, 17*, 183–193.

Janes, A. C., Farmer, S., Frederick, B. B., Nickerson, L. D., & Lukas, S. E. (2014). An increase in tobacco craving is associated with enhanced medial prefrontal cortex network coupling. *PLoS One, 9*(2), e88228. https://doi.org/10.1371/journal.pone.0088228

Knutson, B., Adams, C. M., Fong, G. W., & Hommer, D. (2001). Anticipation of increasing monetary reward selectively recruits nucleus accumbens. *The Journal of Neuroscience: The Official Journal of the Society for Neuroscience, 21*(16), RC159. https://doi.org/10.1523/JNEUROSCI.21-16-j0002.2001

Kober, H., Kross, E. F., Mischel, W., Hart, C. L., & Ochsner, K. N. (2010b). Regulation of craving by cognitive strategies in cigarette smokers. *Drug and Alcohol Dependence, 106*, 52–55.

Kober, H., Mende-Siedlecki, P., Krossd, E. F., Weberb, J., Mischelb, W., Hart, C. L., & Ochsner, K. N. (2010a). Prefrontal–striatal pathway underlies cognitive regulation of craving. *Proceedings of National Academy of Sciences USA, 107*, 14811–14816.

Leclerc, R., & Reberg, D. (1980). Sign-tracking in aversive conditioning. *Learning and Motivation, 11*, 302–317. https://doi.org/10.1016/0023-9690(80)90003-X

Levita, L., Hoskin, R., & Champi, S. (2012). Avoidance of harm and anxiety: A role for the nucleus accumbens. *NeuroImage, 62*(1), 189–198.

Lindquist, K. A., & Gendron, M. (2013). What's in a word? Language constructs emotion perception. *Emotion Review, 5*, 66–71.

Matsumoto, M., & Hikosaka, O. (2009). Representation of negative motivational value in the primate lateral habenula. *Nature Neuroscience, 1*, 77–84.

Mayr, S., & Buckner, A. (2007). Negative priming as a memory phenomenon. A review of 20 years of negative priming research. *Journal of Psychology, 215*(1), 35–51. https://doi.org/10.1027/0044-3409.215.1.35

Morrow, J. D. (2018). Relevance of sign-tracking to co-occurring psychiatric disorders. In A. Tomie & J. Morrow (Eds.), *Sign-tracking and drug addiction*. Ann Arbor. https://doi.org/10.3998/mpub.10215070

Motzkin, J. C., Baskin-Sommers, A., Newman, J. P., Kiehl, K., & Koenigs, M. (2014b). Neural correlates of substance abuse: Reduced functional connectivity between areas underlying reward and cognitive control. *Human Brain Mapping, 35*, 4282–4292.

Motzkin, J. C., Philippi, C. L., Wolf, R. C., Baskaya, M. K., & Koenigs, M. (2014a). Ventromedial prefrontal cortex is critical for the regulation of amygdala activity in humans. *Biological Psychiatry*. https://doi.org/10.1016/j.biopsych.2014.02.014

Naqvi, N. H., Gaznick, N., Tranel, D., & Bechara, A. (2014). The insula: A critical neural substrate for craving and drug seeking under conflict and risk. *Annals of the New York Academy of Sciences, 1316*, 53–70. https://doi.org/10.1111/nyas.12415

Niehaus, J. L., Murali, M., & Kauer, J. A. (2010). Drugs of abuse and stress impair LTP at inhibitory synapses in the ventral tegmental area. *European Journal of Neuroscience, 32*, 108–117.

Oosterwijk, S., Topper, M., Rotteveel, M., & Fischer, A. H. (2010). When the mind forms fear: Embodied fear knowledge potentiates bodily reactions to fearful stimuli. *Social Psychological and Personality Science, 1*, 65–72.

Pani, L., Porcella, A., & Gessa, G. L. (2000). The role of stress in the pathophysiology of the dopaminergic system. *Molecular Psychiatry, 5*, 14–21.

Papies, E. K., & Barsalou, L. W. (2015). Grounding desire and motivated behavior: A theoretical framework and review of empirical evidence. In W. Hofmann & L. F. Nordgren (Eds.), *The psychology of desire*. Guilford Press.

Papies, E. K., Pronk, T. M., Keesman, M., & Barsalou, L. W. (2015). The benefits of simply observing: Mindful attention modulates the link between motivation and behavior. *Journal of Personality and Social Psychology, 108*(1), 148–170. https://doi.org/10.1037/a0038032

Pascucci, T., Ventura, R., Latagliata, E. C., Cabib, S., & Puglisi-Allegra, S. (2007). The medial prefrontal cortex determines the accumbens dopamine response to stress through the opposing influences of norepinephrine and dopamine. *Cerebral Cortex, 17*, 2796–2804. https://doi.org/10.1093/cercor/bhm008

Pearson, D., Donkin, C., Tran, S. C., Most, S. B., & Le Pelley, M. E. (2015). Cognitive control and counterproductive oculomotor capture by reward-related stimuli. *Visual Cognition, 23*(1–2), 41–66. https://doi.org/10.1080/13506285.2014.994252

Peters, J., Kalivas, P. W., & Quirk, G. J. (2009). Extinction circuits for fear and addiction overlap in prefrontal cortex. *Learning and Memory, 16*, 279–288.

Pichon, S., Miendlarzewska, E., Eryilmaz, H., & Vuilleumier, P. (2014). Cumulative activation during positive or negative emotional events predicts inertia of future amygdala reactivity. *Social Cognitive & Affective Neuroscience, 10*(2), 180–190. https://doi.org/10.1093/scan/nsu044

Pizzagalli, D. A. (2014). Depression, stress, and anhedonia: Toward a synthesis and integrated model. *Annual Review of Clinical Psychology, 10*, 393–423. https://doi.org/10.1146/annurev-clinpsy-050212-185606

Podina, I., Popp, R., Pop, I., & David, D. (2015). Genetic correlates of maladaptive beliefs: COMT VAL158MET and irrational cognitions linked depending on distress. *Behavior Therapy, 46*(6), 797–808. https://doi.org/10.1016/j.beth.2015.06.004

Puglisi-Allegra, S., & Ventura, R. (2012). Prefrontal/accumbal catecholamine system processes high motivational salience. *Frontiers in Behavioral Neuroscience*. https://doi.org/10.3389/fnbeh.2012.00031

Serrano, J. M., Banks, J. B., Fagan, T. J., & Tartar, J. L. (2019). The influence of Val158Met COMT on physiological stress responsivity. *Stress, 22*, 276–279.

Siep, N., Roefs, A., Roebroeck, A., Havermans, R., Bonte, M., & Jansen, A. (2012). Fighting food temptations: The modulating effects of short-term cognitive reappraisal, suppression and up-regulation on mesocorticolimbic activity related to appetitive motivation. *NeuroImage, 60*, 213–220.

Szentagotai, A., Schnur, J., DiGiuseppe, R., Macavei, B., Kallay, E., & David, D. (2005). The organization and the nature of irrational beliefs: Schemas or appraisal? *Journal of Cognitive and Behavioral Psychotherapies, 2*, 139–158.

Tiba, A. I. (2003). Rational and irrational beliefs from a neuroscience framework. *Romanian Journal of Cognitive and Behavioral Psychotherapies, 3*, 61–78.

Tiba, A. I. (2005). Demanding brain: Between should and shouldn't. *Journal of Cognitive and Behavioral Psychotherapies, 5*, 43–53.

Tiba, A. I., & Manea, L. (2018). The embodied simulation account of cognition in rational emotive behavior therapy. *New Ideas in Psychology, 48 C*, 12–20. https://doi.org/10.1016/j.newideapsych.2017.08.003

Tiba, A. I., & Szentagotai, A. (2005). Positive emotions and irrational beliefs. Dysfunctional positive emotions in healthy individuals. *Journal of Cognitive and Behavioral Psychotherapies, 5*, 53–73.

Tipper, S. P. (2001). Does negative priming reflect inhibitory mechanisms? A review and integration of conflicting views. *Quarterly Journal of Experimental Psychology: Human Experimental Psychology, 54A*, 321–343.

Ventura, R., Latagliata, E. C., Morrone, C., La Mela, I., & Puglisi-Allegra, S. (2008). Prefrontal norepinephrine determines attribution of "high" motivational salience. *PLoS One, 3*(8), e3044. https://doi.org/10.1371/journal.pone.0003044

Ventura, R., Morrone, C., & Puglisi-Allegra, S. (2007). Prefrontal/accumbal catecholamine system determines motivational salience attribution to both reward- and aversion-related stimuli. *Proceedings of the National Academy of Sciences of the United States of America, 104*(12), 5181–5186. https://doi.org/10.1073/pnas.0610178104

Zubieta, J. K., Heitzeg, M. M., Smith, Y. R., Bueller, J. A., Xu, K., Xu, Y., … Goldman, D. (2003). COMT val158met genotype affect mu-opioid neurotransmitter responses to a pain stressor. *Science, 299*(5610), 1240–1243.

Chapter 6
An Embodied Simulation Model of Irrational Beliefs: Embodied Irrational Beliefs

6.1 Introduction

Cognitive behavior therapies (CBTs) are "gold standard" psychological treatments of emotional disorders. CBTs advance a cognitive model of disturbed emotions (i.e., the ABC model). In the ABC model, A represents adversity, B cognition (dysfunctional cognition), and C dysfunctional reactions (emotional and behavioral disturbances). As it is assumed that B determines C, in order to change C, the therapist helps the client to change B. There are many forms of CBT. CBTs differ regarding the type of cognition they propose as vulnerability to emotional disorders (David and Szentagotai 2006): cognitive therapy focuses on interpretative negative thoughts (Beck 1976), rational-emotive behavior therapy (REBT) on rigid and exaggerated appraisals (irrational beliefs; Ellis 1962), schema-focused therapy on schema (Young et al. 2003), and so on (David and Szentagotai 2006).

The original ABC model of CBT (e.g., Ellis 1962) advances rigid and exaggerated appraisals of adversities as core cognitive vulnerabilities. A. Ellis named rigid and exaggerated appraisals *Irrational Beliefs*. In this model, A stands for activating events (adversities such as threats, missed or lost rewards), B (Beliefs) for appraisals that may be rational (preferences, continuous appraisals for how desired the things were, how bad adversities are, high frustration tolerance, and unconditional self, other, and life acceptance) or irrational (rigid and exaggerated appraisals: demandingness, awfulizing, frustration intolerance, and depreciation beliefs) beliefs, and C stands for emotional, cognitive, and behavioral consequences (Ellis 1962, 1994). According to the ABC model proposed by A. Ellis, when a situation contradicts our desires and goals (i.e., adversities), we become emotionally disturbed (including development of exaggerated thinking and dysfunctional behaviors) because we transform our rational desires into rigid demands or cravings (Ellis et al. 2010). To change emotional disturbance, one has to first change IBs into their rational counterparts (Ellis 1962). In this chapter, I will focus on the core rigid appraisals: demandingness.

A. Tiba, *Embodied Hot Cognitive Vulnerability to Emotional Disorders*,
https://doi.org/10.1007/978-3-030-53989-4_6

6.2 The Revised ABC Model

Beginning with 1991, Ellis proposed a revised ABC model of emotional disturbance (Ellis 1991, 1996, 2001). In the revised ABC model (see Chap. 5), Ellis has conceptualized Beliefs (Bs) as believing-emoting-behaving composites of responding to Adversities. The revised ABC model asserts that when people *think* they need important things (for instance, affection from a significant person) they also *feel* they need affection (along with accompanying feelings such as agitation) and *have urges to get* affection (action tendencies). Their reactions (believing-emoting-behaving) to adversities (e.g., not getting affection or being rejected by significant others) result in disturbed emotions (e.g., anger, depressed feelings).

The view of IBs as *cravings* (opposed to cognitive desires based on appraisal of past or expected pleasure) and the revised model of ABC in which IBs are believing-emoting-behaving (Ellis 2001) suggest that Ellis viewed IBs as appraisals grounded in affective experiences of cravings (the difference is that Ellis did not describe associated physiological body reactions). Individuals disturb themselves emotionally because they crave to get important things or avoid threats as a response to adversities.

Initially, craving and incentive salience motivation were exclusively associated with addiction and reward. Only in the seventies the mesolimbic system was evidenced as a reaction to stress (Fadda et al. 1978). Therefore, an affect-model of IBs as cravings did not receive further attention as a model of our response to adversities. A. Ellis developed REBT in the age of cognitive revolution in psychology (when theories tried to underline the distinctiveness of cognition from emotion and perception), favoring a focus on disembodied views of IBs. As I will describe below, the revised ABC model of IBs is in line with current models of craving as affect (Giuliani and Berkman 2015) and with new affective neuroscience models based on embodied simulations such as constructed emotion (Barrett 2017) and grounded cognition theory (Barsalou 1999; Papies and Barsalou 2015). Moreover, it is in line with recent human and nonhuman animal models in affective science that suggest that craving and underlying incentive salience systems are involved in response to threats (Cabib and Puglisi-Allegra 2012) and omitted rewards (incentive hope; Anselme and Güntürkün 2019) being a core process for psychopathology (Cabib et al. 2020). Given this, I suggest that IBs are embodied rigid motivational appraisals or incentive appraisals that individuals experience as cravings when they have fully activated embodiments.

In this chapter, I describe embodied IBs based on embodied simulation and grounded cognition theory. Previous work (Papies and Barsalou 2015) outlined a grounded cognition model of normal desires. Here, I describe this model as applied to embodied IBs. As such, I conceptualize IBs as simulations of cravings/urges in response to negative events. I present the model, discuss the advantages of using this model, and analyze the model, paralleling it with existing models of craving. At the end, I integrate research and processes from craving models into a model of embodied IBs.

6.3 The Affect Model of Craving and IBs

As mentioned above, early conceptualizations of IBs, such as IBs are cravings (Ellis 1994; Ellis et al. 2010) and multicomponent coupled reactions (believing-emoting-behaving) in the revised ABC model (Ellis 1991, 2001) similar to emotional reactions, suggest an affect model of IBs. We crave for more than sex, drugs, and sugar or food. We also crave in the face of adversities. We crave to get back important things we lost (linked with social or symbolic rewards such as social acceptance, power, and respect; Erk et al. 2003), to avoid threats and for relief.

> "… Again, suppose that people strongly feel deprived of money, keep thinking "I must have more money!" and frantically buy and sell stocks to try to make more money. Again, they have thoughts, feelings, and actions about making money. If they then fail to make any amount of money (at point A) we can hypothesize that they will often have obsessive thoughts about money, have strong feelings of frustration intolerance (FI), and will keep compulsively seeking for more money (at point C). In both these instances, we can hypothesize that *people's complex thoughts-feelings-actions lead to a disturbed complex of thoughts-feelings-actions.*" (Ellis 1996, p. 106)

Craving, as many other concepts in psychological and related sciences, falls under a definitional hazard (Giuliani and Berkman 2015). Various fields of research conceptualize craving as brain responses, physiological responses, negative emotions, or subjective feelings.

A recent model of craving brings some clarity into this definitional hazard. Giuliani and Berkman proposed an affect model of craving in which craving is an anticipatory affect (Giuliani and Berkman 2015). According to Giuliani and Berkman (2015), the concept of craving follows the definitional features of affect. They are affective states that involve a loosely interactive and coordinated set of responses/components (Gross 2015): cognitive, experiential, physiological reactions, action tendencies, and behavior (Giuliani and Berkman 2015; Moors 2009). The first component is the cognitive component (i.e., appraisals). Nowadays, the appraisal theories consider that appraisal is a component of the emotional episode that determines the other components of the emotional episode (Moors 2009). The other components of the emotional reaction (e.g., arousal) influence the appraisals as well. Several situations can trigger craving: salient reward-cues, omission/uncertainty of the reward or a threat, physiological states. These situations elicit appraisals that determine the arousal, bodily sensations, the urge to get the reward, and the subjective experience of needing and other associated negative feelings. The affect theory of craving considers cravings as important mechanisms that determine psychopathology (Giuliani and Berkman 2015).

6.3.1 Implications of the Affect Model of Craving for IBs

The affect model of craving (Giuliani and Berkman 2015) has important implications for the conceptualization and treatment of IBs. In the revised ABC model, Ellis suggests that what disturbs us emotionally is a full craving response: motivational appraisals with associated feelings and action tendencies/behaviors. Both the revised ABC model and the affect model of craving suggest that craving is a multi-componential believing-emoting-behaving response (at B) that emotionally disturbs us at C (consequences). As part of this response, appraisals have a causal role: they determine the intensity and the quality of the other elements. In the affect model of craving (and IBs), IBs are anticipatory affective feelings in response to adversity. Given that, the change of IBs would be like the change of affective feelings by targeting the components of the affective response (Padesky and Mooney 1990) or the processes of the affective response (Gross 2015) (Fig. 6.1).

Put it in A. Ellis' words "… When people's strong desires are balked or thwarted their dogmatic beliefs that these desires absolutely must at practically all times be fulfilled create *a complex of thoughts, feelings, and action tendencies that is significantly more likely to lead to emotional disturbance than is a complex of similar desires that only includes their preferences to be fulfilled*" (Ellis 1996, p. 106).

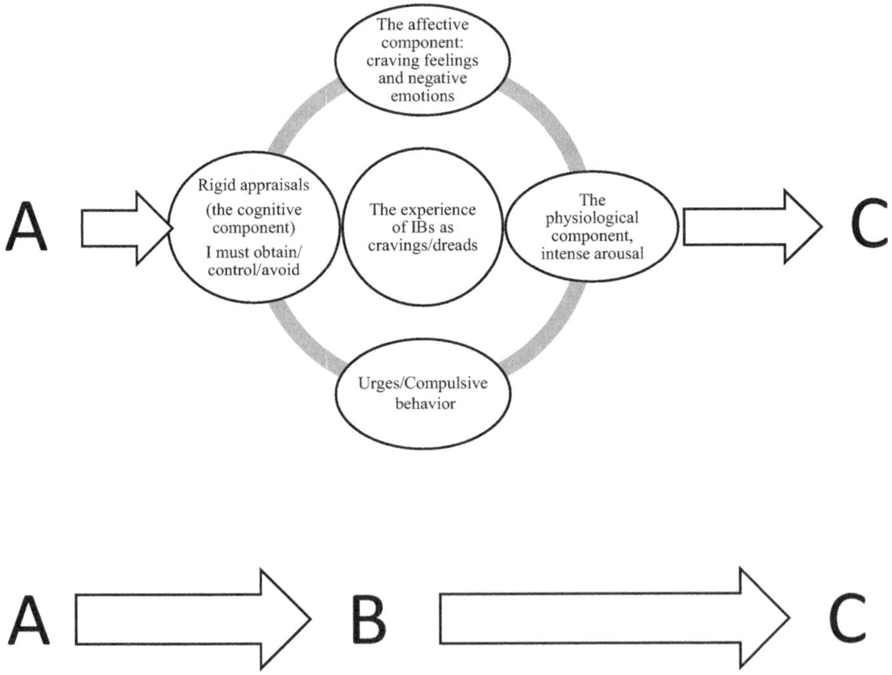

Fig. 6.1 The affect view of IBs in the revised ABC model

Let us consider the following situation. Frank gets separated from his beloved wife. She finds another man. Frank feels abandoned. Frank becomes emotionally disturbed, feeling angry when thinking about being abandoned. His feelings stacked for a month now, Frank feeling angry, stressed, anxious, and depressed. In therapy, Frank and his therapist agree that the problem they will work on is feeling angry for being left by his wife for another man. A cognitive-oriented CBT therapist will help Frank understand that he feels angry because of his exaggerated negative thoughts about being left by his partner. In an REBT intervention, the therapist will help him find and change specific types of thoughts such as rigid appraisals (irrational beliefs such "*I need her back*"). The main method to do this is to dispute the IBs he says to himself by *rational* (analyzing and reaching to the conclusion that "I need her" is not logical), *empirical* (is no empirical evidence that is true), and *pragmatic* (thinking this way is not helpful). Behavioral, emotive, and pragmatic (problem-solving) methods are used to help him overcome his anger.

Based on the affect model, craving is a conscious affective state (Giuliani and Berkman 2015), which has a dynamic dimension (develops and unfolds in time), involves valuation, and has a coordinated set of components (Gross 2015). It has a *cognitive component* (intrusive or deliberate perseverative thoughts and images about salient stimuli, rigid and exaggerated beliefs such as demands, attentional bias toward craved stimuli, consumption expectations), *a subjective feeling component* (the feeling of needing or craving and other negative feelings), *a behavioral component* (compulsive coping or urges), and a *physiological component* (arousal states and associated peripheral changes). Put it this way, the componential affect model of craving is consistent with the appraisal theories of emotion in which appraisal (cognitive part of composite irrational beliefs) is a causal component of an emotional episode, a component which directs the other components. Reactions in other components (motivational or behavior, arousal) influence appraisal as well (Moors et al. 2013). Rigid appraisal (demandingness) and cognitive elaboration determine a *craving response* that determines a *disturbed emotion*. In individuals with over-reactive affective and motivational brain systems, appraisals (thoughts about salient stimuli, rigid beliefs) easily trigger a full craving response. Moreover, under adversity and stress their desires easily transform into needs. Here, Frank not only believes he needs her back, he also feels he needs her back, and he verbally expresses his subjective experience as "*I need her back.*" He has a powerful urge or a compulsion to get her back.

In A. Ellis terms, it is the client's irrational *believing-emoting-behaving* response (IBs; Ellis 2001) which causes another disturbed *believing-emoting-behaving* response (unhealthy feelings; Ellis 1996). Helping Frank verbally change his demands and the labeling of his feelings of craving (e.g., "*I want to have her, but it is not a must or a need*") may help him reduce the craving response and adopt a flexible coping response appropriate to the situation. If Frank has a hyper-reactive motivational salience system (*trait craving*), he has a history of repeated experiences of craving for important things. Thus, Frank reflected on his feelings and developed a meta-cognitive belief system about cravings (e.g., "Needing is good or bad," "If you do not need important things you are superficial," "When something is awful you need to change it," "You must get what you want or you are a loser"). Frank has memories of craving along other elements of situations, acts, and contextual features that can become entrenched in a *craving schema* (Papies and Barsalou 2015). Using an affect model of IBs for helping Frank may add additional routes of change. First, a therapist can help Frank see he becomes emotionally disturbed because he craves for his partner as a response to "her leaving him" (e.g., "*Frank, first, you realized that you are angry because more than wanting her back, when you remember she left, you crave having her back. How does craving, instead of desiring make you feel? If you want to change feeling angry, we need to change your craving for her*"). Then, the therapist orients Frank toward changing the craving for his partner ("*Frank, what do you know about how we can change cravings*?"). Craving is an affective state built as anticipatory affective feelings. Thus, the primary focus is to change craving as an affective response by targeting cognitive (verbal beliefs and thoughts, imagery, memories, cognitive elaboration), behavioral (prevention of craving-driven behaviors, exposure), and physiological (arousal through relaxation methods) components. The therapist can use a component-targeted intervention for craving (targeting the cognitive, behavioral, and physiological dimensions of the craving response). He or she may educate Frank about changing the cognitive component of craving (a therapist may say: "Frank, one way to change "*needing her*" is to change what we are saying to ourselves. Sometimes we mistook desires with needs. If you say that you need her back, your brain reacts as it is an actual need such as the need for air or food. Let's analyze the reasons why you need her back"). Additionally, the therapists may target for the vivid images and the cognitive elaboration about getting what he lost, expectations, self-efficacy, memories of being with her and feelings of deprivation (May et al. 2004, 2012) or little linguistic differentiation for motivational states (the client does not have different verbal labels for different motivational states; Barrett et al. 2014). Craving is a *dynamic affective episode* dependent on cognitive and affective elaborations (e.g., rumination and vivid images in working memory). It grows in time.

The therapist may guide Frank to change cravings by preventing and changing craving-driven behaviors (emotion-driven behaviors; Barlow et al. 2011) or physiological arousal. Cognitive behavior therapy trained clinicians are familiar with these interventions as they apply these interventions to change emotional problems (e.g., the five-part cognitive model developed by Padesky and Mooney 1990).

The clinician may also change cravings based on the process-model of emotional regulation (Gross 2015; Giuliani and Berkman 2015). Thus, the clinician may help Frank by intervening at the level of *situation selection* (avoiding triggers that prime craving for his partner such as images), *situation modification* (changing the environment such as putting pictures of her in a folder or box, limiting access on social media and so on), *attentional deployment* (such as re-focusing attention on other things when he has intrusive images or distracting his attention), *cognitive reappraisal* (such as focusing on negative consequences of being with her after she left him, on positive consequences of moving forward, on changing verbal expression of demands and memories), or *response modulation* such as inhibiting his feelings of craving for his partner (restraining the expression of craving feelings) (Giuliani and Berkman 2015).

If we stick to an affect model of IBs (the revised ABC model of Ellis), then fully activated IBs are cravings (anticipatory affective states), demandingness being a causal cognitive component (appraisals) that determines the coordinated responses in other components of craving (Moors 2009). The change of cravings (*believing-emoting-behaving*) at B will cause changes in disturbed emotions (anxiety, anger, depression, guilt, etc.) at C. The main way to change cravings is by changing demandingness.

6.4 Embodied IBs: An Embodied Simulation Model of Hot Cognitive Vulnerability

In his first introduction of REBT theory (Ellis 1958), A. Ellis presented a view on cognition similar to the current embodied views (e.g., grounded cognition; Barsalou 1999). In his view, cognition includes emotional, behavioral, and perceptual ingredients.

> "thinking…, is, and to some extent has to be, sensory, motor, and emotional behavior … Emotion, like thinking and the sensorymotor processes, we may define as an exceptionally complex state of human reaction which is integrally related to all the other perception and response processes. It is not one thing, but a combination and holistic integration of several seemingly diverse, yet actually closely related phenomena (Ellis 1958, p. 35)".

In the section above I discussed the revised ABC model of IBs and showed that IBs are a form of dysregulated affective states (cravings or dreads) that promote emotional disturbances. This is in line with recent models of pathologies that point to aberrant functioning of motivational systems (craving/dread) at the core of addiction, affective disorders, anxiety, and compulsive (psychopathology promoting) stress-coping. However, how can we stick with IBs as cognition, not as affect? IBs as cravings may be cognition if IBs are embodied types of cognition. There are two important embodied simulation theories relevant for the cognitive vulnerability to emotional disorders: the constructed emotion theory (Barrett 2017) and the grounded cognition theory (Barsalou 1999; Papies and Barsalou 2015; Papies et al. 2020). According to embodied theories of affect and cognition (constructed emotion; Barrett 2017), depending on the focus of attention the individual can conceptualize craving simulations as a cognition (demands for the loved one), urge (action tendencies the compulsion and the urge to get the loved one), and a feeling (the feelings associated with the urge). Thus, IBs are embodied appraisals: embodied irrational beliefs.

In the previous chapters (see Chaps. 2, 3, and 5), I discussed the embodied simulation perspectives for both nonclinical and clinical hot cognition. Embodied simulation theories suggest that: (1) emotional cognitions are embodied by simulations of emotional experiences; (2) conscious emotional cognitions are psychological states constructed from basic ingredients in a situated conceptualization process; (3) embodied cognition involves as components embodied simulations, memories or simulators, and simulation-control mechanisms in a situated conceptualization process; (4) based on the activation states of underlying embodiments, embodied cognition may have different activation states; and (5) there are several simulation-control mechanisms that control the activation and composition of underlying embodiments (Tiba and Manea 2018). I presented the first two assertions in the previous chapters. In this part, I will compare the embodied model of IBs with existing models of craving and integrate in the embodied model of IBs relevant processes revealed by extant models of craving. I discuss the components of IBs, the activation states of the emotional embodiments, and the simulation control-mechanisms focusing on embodied rigid motivational appraisals.

6.5 Comparisons with Relevant Models of Craving

The main advantage of the embodied model of IBs is that of translating knowledge related to the concept of craving into the conceptualization and treatment of IBs. Original models of craving have put forward important processes involved in craving such as dynamic mental elaboration (May et al. 2004, 2012), neuroadaptations (Berridge 2018), cognitive processing (Tiffany 1999), stress hormones, meta-cognitions (Toneatto 1999), and associative learning (Drummond 2001). The embodied rigid salience appraisal model does not replace these models. It translates important mechanisms described by each model and explains fully activated rigid motivational appraisals in response to adversities. Thus, each model of craving suggests important simulation-control mechanisms that activate, organize, control, and structure the simulations of craving. I will discuss the processes advanced by these models with relevance for the embodied simulation affect model of IBs.

6.5.1 The Elaborated Intrusion (EI) Model of Craving

The EI model explains craving as an episode of cognitive elaboration of initial intrusive images. According to the model, intrusive images or thoughts (vivid images) of consumption of rewards enter working memory. These intrusions are pleasant, dominate the working memory and stimulate the person to elaborate (thinking about reward and planning to get it) and imagine consumption situations. If the person cannot satisfy the desire, unpleasant feelings appear, and these elaborations exaggerate the awareness of deprivation (May et al. 2004, 2012).

The EI model is similar to embodied IBs in accentuating mental simulations of consumption and deprivation in craving. The EI model suggests an episode view in which craving is dynamic, developing in time because of cognitive elaboration. This model has important implications for embodied IBs. First, it suggests that as craving, fully activated embodied IBs may develop in time as an episode because of elaboration on obtaining or controlling the adversity and deprivation, incongruence with goals and desires or loss. Second, it suggests that when vivid intrusive images persist and the person does not satisfy the desire, the feelings of deprivation are accentuated which intensify the feeling of craving and the embodied IBs.

6.5.1.1 Differences and Implications

The differences between the EI model and the embodied IBs model are like the differences between the EI model and the grounded cognition model of desires (i.e., Papies and Barsalou 2015). Thus, the embodied IBs model focuses on both conscious and unconscious multimodal simulations. The embodied IBs model stresses the role of the cognitive elaboration in recruiting and activating an overactive incentive salience system into desires. The EI model has important implications for the embodied IBs such as the episode view of fully activated IBs, the role of sustained cognitive elaboration, and the role of both the consumption (successful approach or avoidance) and deprivation images.

6.5.2 The Cognitive Model of Craving

The cognitive models of craving suggest that cognitive factors and processing are important for craving (Anton 1999; Drummond 2000; Tiffany 1999). For instance, expectancies about the positive or negative effects of consuming the reward, beliefs about coping with desire (self-efficacy), and perception of availability of rewards are important cognitive factors able to set off the craving response. Changing these factors causes changes in the experiences of craving. The embodied IBs model suggests that cognitive factors may have the role of triggers (e.g., perception of availability of consumption behavior) and as of a dimension of *desires and cravings* (e.g., I can obtain what I desire). *Thinking* may activate and control the ingredients of craving experiences in response to adversity (e.g., recruiting an overactive incentive salience system in active coping with adversity).

6.5.2.1 Differences and Implications

In the embodied model of IBs, cognitive factors are simulation-control mechanisms. Cognitive factors control whether the individuals desire (or not) to control the adversity and use active coping. Thus, cognitive appraisals of relevance, incongruence, availability of rewards, and self-efficacy are factors that can be targeted to modify the desire in the face of adversity. Cognitive factors can activate relevant craving meta-cognitive beliefs such as "When a situation is very incongruent with my goal, I have (must) to change it" and resulting meta-cognitive thoughts (e.g., "I must get the desired situation") that either describe or guide the simulations of cravings/dreads and not of wanting-like desire.

6.5.3 Conditioning Models

The conditioning models of craving assume that craving is a response to stimuli paired either with withdrawal reactions or with craving responses. In the conditioning withdrawal model (e.g., Ludwig et al. 1974), cues associated with consumption behavior are associated with withdrawal response (e.g., drop in the blood level of sugar). Later, these cues trigger a withdrawal response including craving to feel normal again (Drummond 2001). In the conditioned drug-like model (e.g., Stewart et al. 1984), cues become associated with drug-related response during consuming drugs including craving. Subsequently, the cues gain the ability to elicit conditioned responses, craving included (Drummond 2001).

6.5.3.1 Differences and Implications

The conditioning models suggest that consumption or withdrawal responses are paired with internal or external stimuli. Subsequently, these stimuli gain the ability to trigger a craving response. In the embodied IBs model, conditioned stimuli function as implicit simulation-control mechanisms. They trigger the activation of over-reactive incentive salience systems into embodied simulations by associative learning. Conditioned stimuli are important implicit controls. For instance, being in a park or riding a bicycle is paired with being with the person you love. A situated conceptualization including conditioned stimuli, unconditioned stimulus, and unconditioned responses is stored in memory. When the person encounters these stimuli again, they trigger, as an active inference in a pattern completion process (Papies and Barsalou 2015), a high state of activation of the incentive salience system in the understanding of the desire to be with the person he or she loves. A deprivation or availability-cue for reward alike may trigger an over-reactive incentive salience system in the multimodal simulation used to conceptualize the desire in the activating situation.

6.5.4 The Incentive Salience Model of Craving

The incentive salience model of craving considers the role of mesolimbic dopamine in motivational states and attribution of motivational value. High DA responses are composites of craving (involving cognitive mechanisms). Craving is a conscious state that refers to the subjective experience of the excessive incentive salience (Berridge and Robinson 2003). The over-reactivity of the incentive salience DA system and craving response are etiological mechanisms for addiction. The incentive salience model of craving is the first building brick of the embodied IBs model. According to the incentive salience model, there are two types of desires: (1) *conscious desires* based on the retrieval of past episodes of pleasure in specific situations and (2) *incentive wanting* based on DA mesolimbic system (Berridge 2018). Initial development of the model suggests incentive salience only in response to proximal incentive cues (or vivid images, Berridge and Robinson 2003). Recent developments show that incentive salience and sensitization occur in response to omitted rewards (Anselme et al. 2013) and threats (Berridge 2018).

6.5.4.1 Differences and Implications

The main implication of this model is evidencing the role of over-reactive incentive salience mesolimbic dopamine response in craving. Over-reactive mesolimbic dopamine is a basic ingredient of embodied simulations of craving. The response of the incentive salience system is stimulus-specific and depends on both learning (associative learning, vivid mental imagery) and the physiological states of the organism (deprivation, stress, etc.). The proponents of the incentive salience model suggest that conscious craving is a process based on cognitive interpretation of incentive salience attribution. They also argue that vivid consumption images (i.e., being with or having the lost reward or successful escaping images) may trigger an incentive wanting response. Yet they assert that incentive salience (unconscious craving) is an unconscious process. The embodied model of IBs suggests that embodied rigid appraisals are proximal factors for psychopathologies when the conscious states are being fully activated and experienced as cravings.

6.5.5 *The Affect Model of Craving*

The affect model of craving suggests that craving is an anticipatory affective state. Giuliani and Berkman (2015) suggest that craving fulfils the definition of affective states proposed by Gross (e.g., Gross 2015). They define craving as "a psychological state that involves valuation, unfolds over time, can be helpful or harmful, and involves loosely coupled changes in the domains of subjective experience, behavior, and peripheral physiology" (Giuliani and Berkman 2015, p. 49). According to this model, craving includes different affective dimensions (subjective, behavioral, cognitive, and physiological) and is regulated much like other negative emotions (Giuliani and Berkman 2015).

6.5.5.1 Differences and Implications

The affect model of craving is the second building brick of the embodied IBs model. Thus, the affect model of craving offers the advantage of considering craving from a dimensional affective perspective and to translate interventions from regulating negative emotions into the regulation of craving. In contrast to the affect model, the model of embodied IBs focuses on craving in response to adversity (threat and the omission of rewards). Thus, the fearful salience or dread (the need to avoid a threat) and incentive salience (intense desire to get a reward) alike are forms of affective feelings. Furthermore, the embodied IBs model suggests a *constructed emotion view of craving as affective feelings* (e.g., Barrett 2017).

6.5.6 The Grounded Cognition Model of Desire

The grounded cognition (GC) model of desire (Papies and Barsalou 2015) is the other foundational idea for the embodied IBs model. The GC model of desire suggests that desire appears when internal or external stimuli trigger a simulation of an experience of consumption of reward (Papies and Barsalou 2015). Simulating eating a cookie while watching TV could determine desire to eat a cookie again. Usually, simulations of desires are part of simulations of the entire situation (e.g., watching TV) and the simulations of desires result from a pattern completion inference process based on a modal reward memory. Craving is generated when a memory of reward consumption characterized by a deprivation state and intense desire is triggered (Papies et al. 2020).

6.5.6.1 Differences and Implications

The grounded cognition model is the other building brick of the embodied IBs model: craving results from embodied simulations in a situated conceptualization through a pattern completion process. The GC model of desire also offers a framework for explaining how thinking about desire recruits partial simulations of experiences of desires or cravings. Based on the GC model, thinking in terms of IBs involves partial reactivations of craving experiences. Differently from the GC model, the embodied IBs model aims to explain motivation to control adversities (either by approach or avoidance) and suggest that craving engages simulations of craving experiences that have as an ingredient the overdrive of the incentive salience system. Thus, in the embodied IBs model, desire and cravings have different ingredients. Desire engages simulations of consumption of rewards and past pleasures having as ingredients mildly reactive states of the incentive motivational system. Craving engages simulations of consumption of rewards having as ingredients the over-reactive states of the incentive motivational system. GC model explains how embodied simulations determine desires in a situated conceptualization process. Here, I focus on how embodied simulations of cravings/dreads are used for appraising adversity.

6.5.7 The Revised ABC Model of A. Ellis

Embodied IBs are consistent with the revised model of IBs presented by A. Ellis (Ellis 1991, 2001). A. Ellis often defined IBs in terms of cravings or needs. For instance, in one of the most important recent books on REBT *Rational and Irrational Beliefs*, edited by David et al. (2010), it is suggested that emotional disturbances arise when people escalate their preferences into cravings: "*REBT shows people that they consciously or unconsciously choose to disturb themselves by escalating their preferences into demands and cravings, and that they can train themselves not to do so and thereby create healthy feelings and emotions*" (Ellis et al. 2010, p. 11). Thus, integrating *craving* into the conceptualization of IBs and the ABC model follows naturally. Moreover, the revised ABC model suggests an affect model of craving in which craving is defined as a psychological state that involves linked cognitive, behavioral, and physiological dimensions (Gross 2015). In his revised ABC model, A. Ellis describes IBs as composite concepts of *believing-emoting-behaving* (Ellis 1991). Often, Ellis stated that emotional disturbances arise when people encounter Adversities that interfere with rigidly held goals as opposed with preferential goals.

For instance, in 2001, Ellis referred to goals as… "Goals include pronounced cognitive, emotive, behavioral, and physiological elements. Thus, the urge to eat is cognitive (e.g., "Food is good and nourishing, so I'd better get it"); is emotive (includes the pleasure of eating "good" and the displeasure of eating "bad" food); is behavioral (includes purchasing, cooking, and chewing "proper" food); and is physical (includes sensations of touch, taste, smell, and sight) (Ellis 1991, p. 162). Furthermore, Ellis asked, "Why are musts and shoulds that people accept, create and disturb themselves with often so difficult for them to surrender? Answer: they tend to have a special, interrelated kind of cognitive, emotive, and behavioral nature" (Ellis 1991, p. 162).

6.5.7.1 Differences and Implications

Although the revised ABC model and embodied IBs overlap, REBT focuses on the cognitive component of IBs, interventions targeting other components (e.g., arousal) being non-elegant interventions. Embodied IBs explains how verbal rigid appraisals (IBs) result in a full craving response in the process of active coping with adversity by recruiting embodied simulations of altered motivational experiences. A major difference is that embodied IBs suggest that fully activated rigid appraisals (i.e., must) are very intense "urgent" desires. Under adversities, people transform their desires into cravings. Thus, it is a continuum between the incentive salience motivational processes involved in normal desires and intensive "abnormal" desires. In normal desires, the incentive salience system is activated (but is not hyper-reactive). It makes the things we like (conscious desire based on past liking) also wanted. In cravings, the incentive salience motivation is sensitized or hyper-reactive.

Demandingness is a cognitive label that reflects the "urgency" of very intense desires and behaviors, an urgency that may develop in time. In the traditional ABC model of REBT, intense desires and demands are qualitatively different.

6.5.8 The Meta-cognitive Model of Craving

According to the meta-cognitive model, craving is a "meta-cognitive statement indicative of a strong desire to modify ongoing cognitive experience" (Toneatto 1999, p. 529). When individuals crave for something (alcohol, rewards etc.), in fact they crave to escape an aversive psychological state (the object of craving). Individuals experience a psychological state (image, emotion, thought, etc.). This psychological state is construed as aversive. The individual wishes to modify the state. The situation/object that is craved is able to change this discomfort rapidly. "The greater the discomfort, the greater the desire to escape discomfort, hence the stronger the urge or craving." (Toneatto 1999, p. 530). Craving is a result of the discomfort and the perceived relief from discomfort due to craved objects. To change craving, it requires to: (a) identify the object of craving ("What would happen if you have her back?"; Answer: "My anxiety will go away-anxiety is the object of craving"), (b) identify the meta-cognitive consequences of the object and change the aversiveness ("If you have anxiety and you don't get her back, what would happen with you anxiety?"), (c) identify the meta-cognitive effects of the object and develop alternative coping with an undesired psychological state ("If you get her back how is your anxiety relieved?"; "What are alternatives for relieving anxiety?") (Toneatto 1999).

6.5.8.1 Differences and Implications

Although the meta-cognitive model and the embodied models accentuate the role of the meta-cognitive factors, they are different in several respects. In the embodied simulation model, craving requires a sensitized mesolimbic system. The meta-cognitive model describes how verbal meta-cognitive labels reflect an intense desire. The embodied simulation model suggests that verbal labels (descriptive meta-cognitive thoughts) can recruit a craving state in sensitized individuals. The meta-cognitive model describes withdrawal and stress-induced craving and suggests that cognitive restructuring should target meta-cognitive beliefs about the consequences of getting the craved things, the aversiveness of discomfort, and the tolerance of distress.

6.6 The Components of the Embodied IBs

Each theoretical model describes specific components or processes based on a specific explanatory goal (plan an intervention; explain differences between healthy and unhealthy phenomena, etc.). For instance, the grounded cognition model of desire explains how we build an emotional state of desire based on situated simulations of consumption and rewards (Papies and Barsalou 2015). CBT treatments (i.e., REBT) focus on changing conscious verbally expressed appraisals (cognitive restructuring of IBs). Given this reason, I focus on how verbally expressed IBs are based on embodied simulations of craving (and implications for change) and how these situated conceptualizations (in the form of embodied simulations) result in the experience of craving in stress-coping. Papies and Barsalou have previously described the grounded cognition model of nonclinical desire (Papies and Barsalou 2015). Because my goal is to refine mechanisms involved in vulnerability to emotional disorders, I focus on cravings. The grounded cognition theory of desire and the theory of constructed emotion and emotion regulation (Barrett 2017; Barrett et al. 2014) explain how we consciously build the experience of craving as a conscious affective state based on situated conceptualizations in the form of embodied simulations (Barrett 2017). From this point of view, we build the experience of cravings as we build other affective feelings. The difference is that cravings have as ingredients an over-reactive incentive salience system. Compared to a standard component-based model of affective states (as described above), from an embodied simulation framework, the intervention at each component of an affective state is an intervention targeting a different simulation-control mechanism (cognitive, behavioral/expressive behaviors, and peripheral) by which we change the situated simulations. Thus, the interventions aimed at changing craving states target the change of situated conceptualization of motivational states (in form of embodied simulations) based on a different mechanism such as executive control (Barrett et al. 2014; Papies and Barsalou 2015) or implicit processes (physiological states, associative learning, environment, peripheral changes, behaviors). Verbally reappraising motivational states as desires (and not needs) will change the situated conceptualization based on executive control of simulation of desires and not needs. Changing the physiology (e.g., by medication), the environmental cues or the behavior will change the situated conceptualization of the ongoing motivational states resulting in changes of the subjective feelings of craving or desire.

6.7 Situated Conceptualizations, Simulators, and Embodied Simulations

We are not passive recipients of what happens to us. We react to what happens to us. And as A. Ellis claims, maladaptive *believing-emoting-behaving* reactions are the foundation of emotional disturbances (Ellis 2001). Recent theories of psychological phenomena suggest that people do more than just reacting. They prospectively react. They are ongoing trying to explain the things that their internal and external sensations stand for (Barrett 2017). In finding an answer to this question people simulate experiences based on multimodal (e.g., perceptual, motor, affective) simulations (Barsalou 2008). Grounding cognition theory of desire has suggested the general brain processes of situated conceptualization, multimodal simulations, and pattern completion inference in constructing the experience of desire (Papies and Barsalou 2015; Papies et al. 2020). Desire results from simulations of consumption and reward based on situated conceptualizations and embodied simulations in a pattern completion inference process (Papies and Barsalou 2015; Papies et al. 2020).

According to the grounded cognition theory of desire (Papies and Barsalou 2015; Papies et al. 2020), we capture our experiences in our memory in the systems involved in our experiences. When we answer the phone, we have the experience of visual perception of the phone, auditory perception, our movement or reaching the phone, the desire to answer if we wait for an important phone, the associated positive feelings. These experiences are stored, or better said, captured, in modal brain areas (not represented as language-based representations in a semantic memory) along with introspective states and interpretations as situated conceptualizations. They are organized by our language in an entrenched situated memory depending on the various factors such as allocation of attention, repetition, and so on (i.e., situated conceptualization). When the phone rings, a person predicts what that sound stands for to select the best action (answer) based on a *pattern completion inference*. A multimodal simulation is used to build the understanding of the current sounds based on experiences. Thus, each feature of a situation can activate an entire situated conceptualization stored in memory, retrieving the other elements in a situated way. Various factors work as constraints of the simulations, such as the context and the ongoing states of the organism. We also understand the importance of a situation such as desire, urge, need, or craving. During our experiences about important situations, we capture, besides other parts of the experience, our motivational states. When we become separated by a parent we love, we may experience the desire to see him. Sometimes, not seeing them for a lengthy period may cause intense desire.

Other factors such as not sleeping or stress can set off the motivational brain system hyper-reactive, making us react to adversities with intense dysregulated desires that we label as craving. A simulator (an experience-based memory) of craving or need-like experiences is developed capturing our motivational experience. Later on, when we understand the importance of other situations, activating simulations of previous craving experiences may cause craving-like desires of the ongoing situation. Language about motivational states (words such as craving, need, desire, and urge) is of importance. It acts as a glue building a motivational category of craving. Statistical similarities of various experiences of craving are captured and later represent the conceptual core that guide the understanding of our motivational states in a situation (Barsalou 2008). Motivation may have different related types of associated conscious experiences. As with other types of affective feelings (Barrett 2017) when the focus is on understanding of what the body states stand for during appraising the importance of a situation, *a craving as a feeling* will emerge.

When the focus of attention is on perceiving and describing an encounter (the importance of the person who left), craving will be experienced as a feature of the situation (*"It is an extremely important person"*). When the focus of attention is on the behavior, the behavior will be experienced as an urge (the urge to see the person). When the focus of the attention is on *appraisal* as a cognitive act, we can experience craving as a belief such as *I must have him/her back/see him/her.* Sometimes individuals appraise an automatic thought (not being appreciated) as "*I must have appreciation.*" When simulations of craving states are used to build the meaning of *I must be appreciated*, depending on how strong they are, individuals will also feel they need appreciation. In some conditions (the hyper-reactivity of the incentive salience system), these simulations are so powerful that they become conscious. Then, at the same time, individuals will *believe* they need appreciation, *feel* they need appreciation, and *have the urge* to get appreciation. The conscious experience of craving emerges during the process of situated conceptualization based on embodied simulations. Different ingredients can give the "flavor" of the subjective experience of craving. When the motivational simulations have as an ingredient an over-activation of the incentive salience system (due to various state and trait factors) being accompanied by a state of arousal, the flavor will be that of craving. When the incentive salience system is mildly activated, the "flavor" will be of desire.

6.8 The Activation of Embodied Simulations

Embodied simulation perspective explains how we can develop a full emotional response starting with an appraisal. For instance, we may think of us as being anxious in an emotionally disembodied way. We find a rhyme for anxious (i.e., conscious) and sing it (it is embodied by phonetic but not emotional systems). Or we can say we are anxious for communication goals. Yet we can think we are anxious in an emotionally embodied way. We think we are anxious based on simulations or reactivations of experiences of being anxious tuned to the context. Although these activations are partial, in some conditions (residual arousal, reactivity of the autonomic nervous system, deficient regulatory control, upregulation mode) they can be powerful. Then, we can say that we do not just think we are anxious but we can feel it too. When the emotional simulations are fully activated, they capture the focus of our attention and we have a fully experienced affective feeling depending on the situated conceptualization involved (Barsalou 2008; Niedenthal 2007). We can observe the same processes with IBs. For instance, Frank can use a (emotionally) disembodied rigid appraisal. He says to his therapist he needs his wife back (we can understand this as a non-absolute must or IBs for communication purposes). Yet when Frank is also emotionally disturbed, most of the time his IBs will be embodied by partially (yet not fully) activated experience-related brain and body systems. Here, Frank will also feel he needs her back and he will tend to act on getting her back (absolute must or IBs). When emotional simulations are fully activated, the appraisals become an emotional experience (craving for her). Thus, when Frank thinks he lost his wife, he starts craving for her and his craving disturbs him emotionally (he has a fully activated absolute must or IBs). He appraises adversity based on embodied simulations of craving experiences. When simulations are powerful enough or run over sensitized motivational and affective brain systems (for instance, because of prolonged exposure to stress hormones such as norepinephrine and glucocorticoids), a full motivational and affective experience develops. Frank feels he needs her and has the urge and compulsion to get her back, not only he demands getting her back.

Building on the idea that craving experiences are constructed by the process of situated conceptualization based on embodied simulations, the therapist can plan to use changes targeting mechanisms that control simulations in the situated conceptualization process (simulation-control mechanisms). Thus, we may understand therapy interventions at each level (cognitive, behavioral, affective, and physiological) as simulation-targeted interventions based on deliberate executive or automatic control processes. For instance, when targeting the cognitive dimension of craving, we can base cognitive reappraisal on both deliberate, executive control (e.g., "vigorous" disputation methods) and automatic processes (cognitive training). In the same time, the embodied simulations involved in situated conceptualizations of cravings are under the control of different implicit control mechanisms. While expectations influence situated conceptualization based on the executive control system, stress hormones (implicit control process) influence the situated conceptualization automatically. With embodied IBs, verbal IBs have a meaning based on *the embodied simulations of cravings and disturbed emotions*. When Frank says to himself that *he needs her back*, he partially reactivates the affective states of craving (embodied simulations) and of being with her to understand the importance of missing her (situated conceptualizations). In certain conditions (and Frank is in one of them) such as the overactivation of the incentive salience (consciously experienced as craving) system (because of stress hormones, sensitization, inherited differences, loss of inhibitory control or upregulation by excessive perception of availability of rewards), verbal beliefs are powerful enough and fully activate *a craving response* to get her back. Craving for his loved one further promotes maladaptive coping (rigid, perseverative, and compulsive active coping) persistently trying to get her back by any method he can try (i.e., "trial by error"; Cabib and Puglisi-Allegra 2012) and emotional dysregulation. In time, the sensitization of mesolimbic DA systems may lead to changing the balance of simulation-control mechanisms toward the amplification of affective and biological controls of craving simulations and less involvement of cognitive controls. As I described in the beginning of the chapter, fully activated craving simulations are conscious affective states (Giuliani and Berkman 2015) which have a dynamic dimension (develops and unfold in time having temporal dimensions), involve valuation, and have a coordinated set of components (Gross 2015). They have a *cognitive component* (intrusive or deliberate perseverative thoughts and images about salient stimuli, rigid and exaggerated beliefs such as demands, attentional bias toward craved stimuli, consumption expectations), *a subjective feeling component (*the feeling of needing or craving and other negative feelings), *a behavioral component* (compulsive coping or urges), and a *physiological component* (arousal states and associated peripheral changes) (Fig. 6.2).

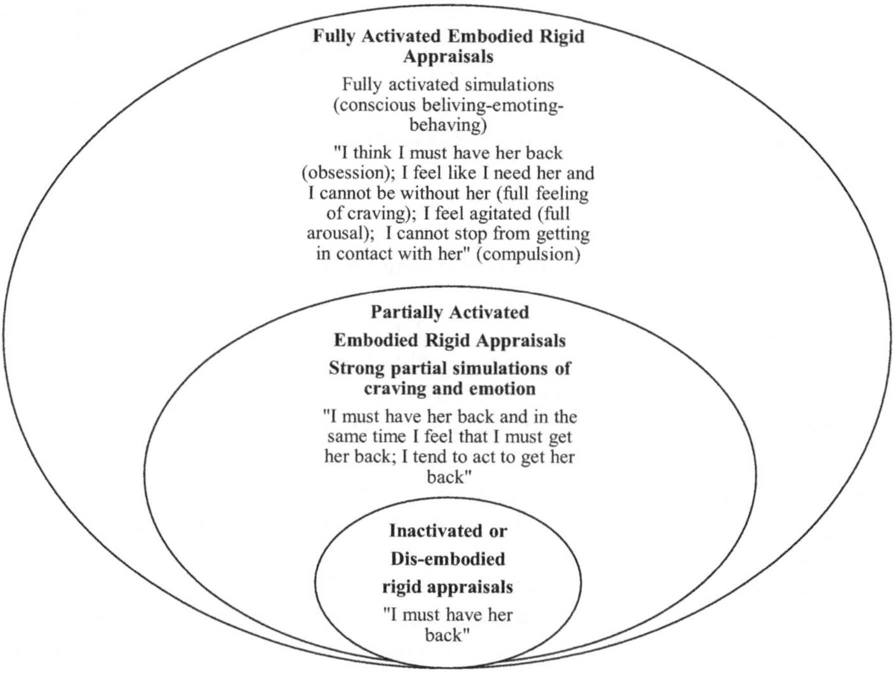

Fig. 6.2 The embodied rigid appraisals/embodied IBs

6.9 Processes that Control Embodied Simulations

6.9.1 Deliberate Processes in the Control of Craving Simulations

Deliberate or top-down simulation-control processes are those mechanisms based on the executive attentional system (Barrett et al. 2014). The attentional executive control system allows individuals to activate the conceptualizations that fit their behavioral goals (Barrett et al. 2014; Papies and Barsalou 2015; Papies et al. 2020). There are two types of deliberate processes that control craving simulations: upregulation and downregulation controls. Conscious upregulation controls are those conscious processes that result in activation of craving/dreads simulations and recruitment of an overactive incentive salience system in the understanding of the motivational relevance of situations. Conscious downregulation controls are those conscious processes that prompt the activation of the simulation of different motivational states without recruiting an overactive incentive system in understanding. Dysfunctional craving simulations result from either excessive upregulation (e.g., based on excessive perceptions of control over adversities) or deficient downregulation in individuals with sensitized incentive salience systems. In highly stressful situations, hormonal changes determine an override of executive controls by limbic affective controls. Thus, the affective and biological simulation-control mechanisms dominate the function of the deliberate control mechanisms over the mesolimbic system. In vulnerable individuals, re-establishing the balance is very difficult. The role of the therapist is to restore the balance of deliberate simulation-control mechanisms over affective and biological (implicit) simulation-control mechanisms.

6.9.1.1 Deliberate Upregulation of Craving Simulations

Cognitive models of craving suggest different types of cognition that act as simulation-control mechanisms (Tiffany 1999). Conscious cognitive processes that control consumption simulation are based on executive attentional systems. Outcome expectations (perceptions of positive effects of consuming the rewards) and perceptions of availability of consumption of salient stimuli may use the top-down control system to prompt an amplified incentive salience neural systems response (George and Koob 2013) as an active ingredient of understanding incentive salience.

For instance, in a landmark study that focused on craving for cigarettes, Hayashi et al. (2013) told participants from one group that after the fMRI session they can smoke cigarettes. To the other group they told participants that they cannot smoke cigarettes. The authors observed that the perceived availability of cigarettes increased craving and the activation of the incentive salience motivational systems because of activation of the dorsolateral prefrontal cortex (DLPFC). The inactivation of DLPFC by repetitive transcranial brain stimulation reduced cravings and the activation of the incentive salience system.

Although some models are focused on how we experience cravings (Tiffany 1999), here are of importance those processes that select ingredients for mental states that promote the use of amplified responses of the incentive salience system in the control of behavior. Cognitive elaboration based on vivid conscious simulations of having (i.e., consumption simulations) the missed important thing (vivid imagery of reward such as images of contact with a loved one, consuming chocolate, gambling) may also impact the use of the incentive salience system in motivation and result in cravings and urges. Acute perception of deprivation of salient stimuli may further amplify the response of the incentive salience system (May et al. 2004, 2012). Evaluative beliefs and labels of motivational states are other important cognitive processes that may prompt the over-activation of the incentive salience system (saying such as "*I need her love*" "*I must have him/her*"). Labeling situations as needs or urges (descriptive meta-cognitive thoughts) may drive the activation of past reward memories (memories of the experience of needing love based on incentive salience system) and re-instantiation of an amplified incentive salience-based motivation in the understanding of the significance of that adverse event. Examples may be schema for needs and urges such as *you cannot live without love, if you don't need the other person or crave when you lose her means you do not love her*. Most individuals with sensitized incentive salience systems will experience desires more often as cravings (instead of regular desires). Thus, they will be predisposed to use craving/needs labels and develop a need-based interpretation system for the importance of situations. They also may have more craving or needs-based memories about the importance of significant events. Conscious verbal beliefs about needing important things and conscious memories will act as deliberate controlled processes that may amplify the incentive salience of obtaining what is important in activating situations.

For instance, a person craving for appreciation as an adolescent will develop beliefs that "*we need others to be happy; being deprived (lonely) is awful*" and memories about needing instead of just wanting others or of being lonely and feeling deprived. In future social situations, when someone important is missing, they will understand missing others as a deprivation and a need for the other. These beliefs will act as conscious control mechanisms that will amplify the incentive salience system response in understanding the value of missing others. Most often this amplification will overlap individual trait vulnerability (already sensitized incentive salience system in vulnerable individuals because of inherited differences, sensitization, and neuroadaptations because of early life stress) and/or individual state vulnerability such as an over-activation of the incentive salience system because of prolonged exposure to the stress situation (because of inappropriate coping and prolonged norepinephrine release). Conscious perception of the physiological responses of craving will determine, besides the awareness of the thought "*I must get or avoid,*" the awareness of the feeling that the person needs to get the missed reward or to avoid a threat. Here, the person will have a fully activated need (irrational belief) instead of just wanting (based on perceived pleasure of being with that person). Different factors will set the perception of the availability of getting back important people in their life when they are missing such as: near-misses ("If I wouldn't miss that date we would still be together"; Sescousse et al. 2016), the perceptions of easy-to-change conditions to get that person back ("*If I will go out with the other person I will make him/her jealous and get him/her back*"), exaggerated personal control and self-efficacy ("*If I try enough, I will succeed*"; Tiffany 1999), exaggerated illusion of control (Ly et al. 2019), or coping development-oriented cognitions under adversity (similar to gambling skills-oriented cognition, the individuals may perceive that coping or knowledge may be acquired to increase the likelihood of controlling the adversity and getting back the lost rewards; Billieux et al. 2011).

Rational motives for being with that person ("*He/her promised we will be together*"; "*It is awful*") will also set cognitive upregulation and an amplified response of the mesolimbic system in the understanding of his/her desire in an activating (losing a person in this example) situation.

In their Elaborated Intrusion Theory, May et al. (2004) emphasize sustained conscious elaboration in the development of craving. At first, individuals may experience an intrusive vivid image of lost reward/consumption of that reward. Then, they become preoccupied and ruminate about obtaining the things they missed and they maintain a top-down upregulation of the incentive salience system (by both images of obtaining/consuming the things they lost and deprivation).

For individuals with sensitized incentive salience systems this sustained elaboration sets the stimulus-related response of the incentive salience dopaminergic system into overdrive. Prolonged elaboration and rumination about getting desired stimuli and deprivation/incongruence may maintain the stress system activated, the stress hormones (or other implicit upregulation controls) further amplifying the response of the incentive salience system (for instance, stress hormones increase the tonic DA release—background less frequent firing rates at 1–5 Hertz—and those neurons will enter phasic bursts—stimulus-related high firing rates from 5 to 100 Hertz—to subsequent cues or mental images; Grace 2016). Thus, in people with already over-reactive salience systems (because of state and/or trait factors) upregulating instead of downregulating the DA system will set off the DA system in overdrive and craving and compulsive active coping will emerge. An overdrive of the mesolimbic system will result in the alteration of the efficiency of cognitive control. In time, the balance of the simulation-control mechanisms of craving simulations will change to a dominance of affective and biological mechanisms over the cognitive-control mechanisms.

In short, because of prolonged stress, stress hormones sensitize the incentive salience system in vulnerable individuals (inherited differences, sensitization because of early stress) that become hyper-reactive when individuals encounter negative stressful events. Using conscious language-based controls that amplify the DA system will result in over-reactive responses in negative situations and cravings that promote perseverative coping and dysregulation. In time, the balance in the control of craving simulations will be inclined toward the dominance of the affective and biological mechanisms and less efficient cognitive control mechanisms. There are many types of conscious controls (prolonged mental elaboration of conscious consumption simulations, multisensory imagery of obtaining/consuming the salient stimulus, perceived availability of the stimuli, perseverative beliefs, exaggerated self-efficacy and perceived control, self-motivating beliefs, conditions/reasons for urgency) that may upregulate the craving response to adversities. Sustained conscious elaboration has a larger impact because of sustaining the activation of the incentive salience systems over prolonged time intervals. From this view, although sometimes automatic and unconscious, the time-framed mental construction by elaborative processes is important for the building of embodied irrational beliefs. Thus, IBs are amplified by a time-dependent accumulation based on conscious elaboration of consumption representations, deprivation, incongruence, and stress hormones.

6.9.1.2 Deliberate Downregulation of Craving Simulations

Cognitive factors that result in the downregulation of craving simulations are: cognitive distraction instead of elaboration over salient stimuli, negative instead of positive expectancies for reward, perceptions of no-availability of reward, lack of perceived control over obtaining reward, etc.

Cognitive load

One type of conscious control supported by research over many types of rewards (food rewards, cigarettes, cocaine, etc.) is cognitive load or distraction. Van Dillen and van Steenbergen (2018) examined the effect of cognitive load on appetitive, high-calorie food stimuli. In an fMRI study, they asked participants to categorize high-calorie and low-calorie food pictures as edible or inedible. At the same time, participants performed a digit-span task that varied between low and high cognitive load (i.e., memorizing six digits vs. one digit). They found that exposure to high-calorie compared to low-calorie food pictures led to increased activation in the nucleus accumbens (NAcc) only when participants memorized one digit (low cognitive load) and not six digits (high cognitive load). In addition, connectivity analyses showed that asking participants to memorize six digits altered the coupling between NAcc and right DLPFC during presentation of the high-calorie versus low-calorie food pictures.

Expectations

Expecting negative long-term consequences decreases cravings (Kober et al. 2010a, b). In a laboratory model of craving, Kober et al. (2010a) presented cigarette smokers with pictures of cigarettes and foods and then to either think of immediate feelings of smoking/eating ("feeling good") or to long-term negative consequences of regular consumption smoking/eating ("I will get a disease"). Participants reported reduced food cravings (controls) and cigarette cravings (cigarette smokers) when focusing on the long-term consequences associated with eating or smoking. In a subsequent study, Kober et al. (2010b) used the same task, but they analyzed the brain of the participants by an fMRI methodology. Compared with the facilitation of craving, regulating craving by negative consequences in response to smoking-related pictures increased the activation in lateral prefrontal areas (DMPFC, DLPFC, and VLPFC) and decreased the activation in ventral striatum/VS, amygdala, subgenual anterior cingulate cortex/ACC, and ventral tegmental area/VTA. The decrease in the ventral striatum activity mediated the effect of DLPFC increases on craving reduction.

Reappraisal

Reappraisal involves thinking differently about the reward stimuli. There are multiple strategies used for reappraisals. In a study investigating tailored reappraisal strategies of food items and their effect on cravings, Giuliani et al. (2013) found that several reappraisal strategies have the same efficacy in reducing cravings. Giuliani et al. (2013) presented participants pictures of foods and asked them either to consider the food is real and imagine consuming foods or to use one of four reappraisal strategies. 50% participants imagined that something bad had happened to the pictured food (e.g., sneezed on), 30.45% focused on the negative consequences of eating that food (e.g., weight gain), 9.75% imagined that they are very full, 7.32% reminded themselves that they can save that food for later, and 2.44% choose other strategies (Giuliani et al. 2013). All strategies were effective in reducing craving and recruited brain areas involved in emotional regulation.

In a study comparing different strategies of reappraisal, Yokum and Stice (2013) presented participants caloric-food pictures and asked them to think of long-term costs of eating the food, the long-term benefits of not eating the food or to suppress the craving. Results showed that *focusing on long-term benefits of not eating the food* increased inhibitory region activity and reduced craving more (Yokum and Stice 2013).

Demos McDermott et al. (2019) presented participants high caloric food pictures and compared the effect of four cognitive strategies on reduction of cravings: (1) simulation of consumption of foods ("*As you see the foods come up on the screen, imagine what they taste like, smell like, and what actually consuming them would be like*", Demos McDermott et al. 2019, p. 2), (2) distract by thinking ("*As you see the foods come up on the screen, change your thoughts by distracting yourself with thoughts of something else such as imaging doing something you enjoy, or thinking about what you have to do today*", Demos McDermott et al. 2019, p. 2), (3) mindful attention ("*Try to observe your thoughts and recognize these thoughts as creations of your mind, a part of a mental process that is happening that you do not need to do anything about. For example, if you find yourself having thoughts about the foods or feeling like you want to eat, try to notice these thoughts. You may practice by mentally noting "I'm having the thought that…or even picture each thought going through your mind like a ticker tape or seeing those thoughts up on a screen like at a movie theater, where you don't try to change them or direct them in any way*", Demos McDermott et al. 2019, p. 2), and (4) thinking of long-term negative consequences (*"As you see the foods come up on the screen, imagine the long-term negative consequences of repeatedly eating these foods. For example, you might think about how eating these foods could affect your appearance, your quality of life and mobility, and/or lead to health problems such as diabetes or cardiovascular disease"*, Demos McDermott et al. 2019, p. 3). Results showed that *thinking of long-term negative consequences* is the best strategy that efficiently recruits DLPFC and reduces cravings (Demos McDermott et al. 2019). This is followed by the "distract by thinking" strategy, the least effective in reducing cravings (though significantly) being mindful instruction (Demos McDermott et al. 2019). Reappraisal strategies are effective in cravings overlapping the reappraisal of emotions (Giuliani and Berkman 2015).

Mindfulness

Mindfulness refers to paying attention to moment-to-moment experience while having a nonjudgmental, accepting attitude toward that experience (Bishop et al. 2004). It is a strategy that separates craving from the associated behavior (Giuliani and

Berkman 2015). In a landmark fMRI study, Westbrook and her colleagues trained 47 treatment seeking cigarette smokers to view images passively or with mindful attention. Then, they presented participants smoking or neutral images and instructed them either to view them passively or with mindful attention. Results showed that mindful attention reduces the craving intensity and the reactivity of brain regions involved in craving decoupling the craving neural-circuitry when viewing smoking cues (Westbrook et al. 2013).

6.9.2 Implicit Processes in the Control of Craving Simulations

Simulations of getting important things are situated (Papies and Barsalou 2015). This means they are under the control of an ongoing changing state of the external or internal environment (Papies and Barsalou 2015). I will refer to these contextual factors as implicit controls of simulations. Implicit control over simulation may function both to promote/activate an upregulated craving-based simulation and to inhibit or downregulate craving-based simulations. As the brain and body change, simulations change. When different concepts are activated, simulations change again. As the environmental or behavioral requirements change, different simulations of motivational states may be selected. Implicit downregulation controls are processes that recruit an *inhibited incentive salience system or other systems* in the conceptualization of motivational states. Implicit upregulation controls over craving simulations are those implicit processes that activate craving simulations or recruit an overactive incentive salience system in the conceptualization of motivational states. For instance, when the organism is in a state of deprivation, the simulations used for the conceptualization of the motivation for a cigarette recruits motivational systems based on deprivation brain states and a craving response instead of wanting to smoke a cigarette is constructed (Papies and Barsalou 2015). Thus, physiological states of body and brain systems are implicit controls of simulations. There are many upregulation control mechanisms of craving simulations. The most common are abstinence and withdrawal, lack of sleep, stress hormones, contextual features (e.g., near-misses), and associative learning (operant and classical conditioning).

6.9.2.1 Abstinence and Withdrawal

Withdrawal-induced craving is a particular type of craving based on classical conditioning associations. Deprivation and withdrawal modulate the neural reactivity to rewards such as cigarettes or nondrug rewards (food). In an fMRI study, McClernon et al. (2005) asked participants to rate cravings in response to cigarette cues after smoking as usual or overnight abstinence. In the same participants, the authors observed that abstinence increased cravings and brain (medial DLPFC, ACC and inferior frontal) reactivity to cigarette cues. Subsequent studies showed that participants with greater smoking-cue reactivity in the ACC during acute abstinence were more likely to relapse (Allenby et al. 2019, 2020).

6.9.2.2 Sleep Problems

Difficulty falling asleep and staying asleep result in increases of both drug and nondrug cravings (Greer et al. 2013). In an fMRI study, Greer et al. (2013) measured cravings for foods and brain responses of healthy participants after a normal sleep and after a sleepless night. Results showed an increase in the cravings for high caloric foods and a decrease in frontal areas related to regulatory of food cravings (Greer et al. 2013). Thus, sleep deprivation may decrease inhibitory control required for suppressing craving simulations.

6.9.2.3 Cues Associated with Consumption

Presenting cues such as images of nondrug (e.g., images of eating) or drug (e.g., images of people smoking) rewards is the dominant paradigm of researching mechanisms of craving. Stimuli associated with consuming drug or nondrug rewards gain the power to trigger incentive salience systems and become powerful attractors. Thus, the environmental cues associated with consumption become factors that control the simulations of consumption and trigger the incentive salience system. Cue-induced craving is a recognized type of craving contrasted with withdrawal-induced craving. There are two features of the contextual cues that facilitate an over-reactivity of mesolimbic DA system and amplify the craving response: *near-misses* and *uncertainty*.

Sescousse et al. (2016) tested for the first time the idea the near-misses involve an increase in the DA response. The authors asked pathological gamblers and healthy controls to play a slot machine task. While the participants were inside an fMRI machine, the researchers measured their brain responses to wins, near-misses, and full-misses. Each participant gambled first under placebo and then under a dopamine D2 receptor antagonist (sulpiride 400 mg). All participants showed increased striatal responses (and higher motivation to continue gambling) to near-misses when compared with full-misses. Pathological gamblers showed amplified striatal responses to near-misses.

Conditioning refers to the fact that pairing a neutral stimulus (bell sound) with unconditioned stimulus (US; food) gives the neutral stimulus (now the bell sound is a conditioned stimulus/CS) the power to elicit a response (conditioned response/CR; salivation) similar to the response to unconditioned stimulus (the unconditioned response/UR such as salivation) (Pavlov 1897). Research showed that intermittently pairing the CS with the US strengthens the conditioned response which is more persistent and resistant to extinction (partial reinforcement effect, Anselme 2015). This is consistent with the observations of Amsel in the 1950s in which animals show an invigorated behavior when a previous reward is no longer presented. The effect was named the "frustration effect" (Anselme 2015). Based on a thorough analysis, Anselme suggested that uncertainty of reward results in an increase in the activation of the incentive salience system (mesolimbic dopaminergic system). Thus, the receipt of an unexpected reward amplified the value of that reward (Anselme 2015). The animal develops an *incentive hope*. Uncertainty increases the incentive motivation to reward cues. Uncertainty about the effort to get a natural reward (e.g., saccharin) results in the sensitization and the neuroadaptations of the incentive wanting system to natural rewards similar to that observed to drugs (Singer et al. 2012).

Yet powerful responses to the uncertainty of situations (intolerance responses) are trans-diagnostic vulnerability factors to stress-related disorders such as generalized anxiety (Rosser 2019). Recent neuroimaging studies show that motivational and craving-related brain areas such as insula are over-reactive to uncertainty in individuals with high levels of intolerance to uncertainty (Kim et al. 2017; Tanovic et al. 2018). Thus, it is possible that over-reactive incentive salience in response to uncertain rewards or threats and associated craving (amplified incentive salience) to get rewards or avoid threats (control) may underlie intolerance of uncertainty (Fig. 6.3).

6.10 Embodied Rigid Appraisals

Based on reviewed theories, I argue that irrational beliefs are embodied rigid appraisals. When embodied rigid appraisals are fully activated, they are experienced as cravings in response to adversities. Given this conceptualization of irrational beliefs, the theories of clinical cognition that inform evidence-based psychological treatments (the cognitive model of A. Ellis) and affective neuroscience theories converge on the same process as core vulnerability to emotional disorders and addiction: embodied rigid motivational appraisals. Because psychological treatments targeting the change of embodied rigid appraisals are already validated treatments (through randomized clinical trials; David et al. 2017), optimizing the model of irrational beliefs has an increased success (and low risk) potential to improve existing psychological treatments. There are several ideas based on the concept of embodied rigid appraisals that can inform cognitive-oriented psychological treatment of emotional disorders:

(1) Embodied rigid appraisals are forms of appraisals embodied by hyper-reactive states of the incentive salience affective brain systems.
(2) Embodied rigid appraisals function in both unconscious and conscious ways.
(3) Embodied rigid appraisals involve embodied simulations, simulators, and simulation-control mechanisms in a situated conceptualization process of salience appraisal.
(4) Embodied rigid appraisals can be in several states of activation: inactive (disembodied), partially activated, or fully activated.

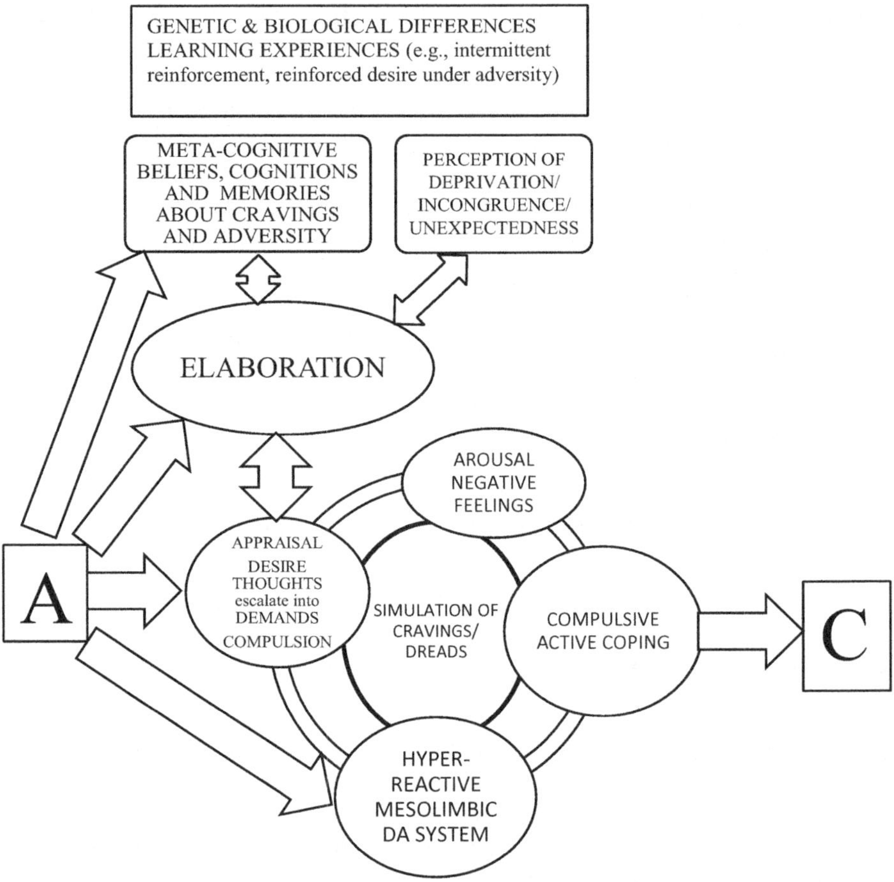

Fig. 6.3 The cognitive–affective model of episodic embodied rigid appraisals. When individuals meet an adversity (A; distress feelings, unexpected omitted rewards or aversive stimuli), they start to crave (transform their desire into craving) to actively control *A* because of different cognitive, affective, and biological factors that recruit for simulation a hyper-reactive mesolimbic dopamine (DA) system. The adversity triggers (directly or indirectly) a response in the mesolimbic system, a cognitive elaboration process or/and meta-cognitive and cognitive beliefs (rigid or flexible thoughts about the importance of A; unexpectedness). There are several mechanisms that interact and result in the escalation of desires into demands under adversity: (a) linguistic expression of urges (e.g., demands that describe and/or organize the motivational simulations), (b) meta-cognitive beliefs that facilitate an upregulation mode of control over a sensitized mesolimbic DA system in response to adversity, (c) appraisals of the situations (e.g., salience, unexpectedness, incongruence), (d) prolonged elaboration (by verbal rumination or vivid imagery) that engages simulations of cravings/dreads and deprivation, (e) aversive emotions and reactions, discomfort, hormonal and stress states, (f) associative memory-based activation of a sensitized mesolimbic DA system, and (g) body and brain states that promote dysregulation and a hyper-reactive DA response in the mesolimbic system. In vulnerable individuals, the executive system-based controls of simulations are overridden by the affective and biological-based bottom-up controls. When a craving/dread response develops, compulsive and perseverative active coping results in disturbed and dysregulated negative emotions (C). The task of the therapist is to restore the top-down control over the craving simulations in response to A

(5) Fully activated embodied rigid appraisals are forms of dysregulated craving/dread in response to adversities accompanied by intense affect and compulsive active coping.
(6) The proximal determinants of emotional disorders are fully activated embodied rigid appraisals. In psychopathology, affective and biological control mechanisms outruns the executive system-based controls over craving simulations resulting in dysregulated craving/dread simulations.
(7) Activation of embodied rigid appraisals is often a dynamic episode-like process resulting from cognitive elaboration (repetitive thinking and imagery about successful approach/avoidance and deprivation/incongruence), metacognitive beliefs (reasons to crave/demand, positive consequences of perseveration and active coping and negative consequences of passive coping; perception of getting the desired situation as a mean to escape aversive states), cognitive beliefs (appraisal of a novel uncontrollable/unescapable stressor/loss; unexpected uncertainty; relevance and incongruence; exaggerated illusion of control; exaggerated perceptions of deprivation, dysfunctional self-efficacy of response to adversity; perception of hope based on adversity characteristics such as near-misses, exaggerated importance of the adversity; exaggerated perception of consequences of getting the missed reward or escaping the threat; exaggerated averseness of negative states), affective determinants (e.g., prolonged exposure to stress, arousal), and biological processes (biological conditions that induce the hyper-reactivity of mesolimbic systems to adversity).
(8) Both deliberate and implicit simulation-control mechanisms determine and control the activation of embodied rigid appraisals. In vulnerable individuals and psychopathology, the balance of simulation-control mechanisms is toward affective and biological implicit controls.
(9) Changes of embodied rigid appraisals result from changes in deliberate (e.g., reappraisal, deliberate and automatic cognition) and implicit (e.g., stress hormones, sleep, conditioning) simulation-control mechanisms.
(10) Fully activated rigid embodied appraisals may be changed based on component or process-driven interventions that target craving responses to adversities.
(11) Embodied rigid appraisals are implemented by dysregulated adversity-related (hyper) reactivity of the mesolimbic dopamine system.
(12) An important developmental pathway of the embodied rigid appraisals consists in individual biological differences and stress-related neuroadaptations in susceptible individuals regarding regulatory control and mesolimbic dopamine brain system.

6.11 Summary

The revised ABC model proposed by A. Ellis advances an affect model of IBs in which IBs are thinking, feelings, and behavioral composites. This model of IBs is consistent with affect models of cravings which consider cravings as anticipatory affect and with IBs as fully activated embodied types of emotional cognition. Embodied IBs may be in different states of activation: inactivated (disembodied cognition regarding motivational experiences), partially activated (feeling, action tendencies are also activated but not fully experienced), and fully activated IBs (experienced as affective feelings). Embodied IBs are based on embodied simulations of disturbed motivational states or cravings. There are many deliberate and implicit simulation-control processes involved in embodied IBs. Comparisons with relevant models of craving reveal important mechanisms that control the simulations involved in embodied rigid appraisals. Embodied IBs unfold as dynamic episodes in which cognitive, hormonal, and affective factors interact to determine fully activated embodied IBs. Although embodied IBs are in line with the revised ABC model on IBs, in a framework of embodied IBs, normal desire and demandingness are on a continuum. On this continuum, normal desires involve a mild activation of the mesolimbic dopamine system in response to stimuli and craving involves a very intense activation of a dysregulated mesolimbic dopamine system. Amplification of the affective and biological controls over craving simulations reduces the efficiency of executive control resulting in dysregulated craving states. The demanding feature related to desire reflects the "urgency" associated with an overdrive of mesolimbic dopaminergic systems.

References

Allenby, C., Falcone, M., Ashare, R. L., Cao, W., Bernardo, L., Wileyto, E. P., … Lerman, C. (2019). Brain marker links stress and nicotine abstinence. *Nicotine Tobacco Research, 22*, pii: ntz077. https://doi.org/10.1093/ntr/ntz077

Allenby, C., Falcone, M., Wileyto, E. P., Cao, W., Bernardo, L., Ashare, R. L., … Lerman, C. (2020). Neural cue reactivity during acute abstinence predicts short-term smoking relapse. *Addiction Biology, 25*(2), e12733. https://doi.org/10.1111/adb.127

Anselme, P. (2015). Incentive salience attribution under reward uncertainty: A Pavlovian model. *Behavioural Processes, 111*, 6–18.

Anselme, P., & Güntürkün, O. (2019). Incentive hope: A default psychological response to multiple forms of uncertainty. *Behavioral and Brain Sciences, 42*, e35. 40–59.

Anselme, P., Robinson, M. J. F., & Berridge, K. C. (2013). Reward uncertainty enhances incentive salience attribution as sign-tracking. *Behavioural Brain Research, 238*, 53–61. https://doi.org/10.1016/j.bbr.2012.10.006

Anton, R. F. (1999). What is craving? Models and implications for treatment. *Alcohol Research & Health: The Journal of the National Institute on Alcohol Abuse and Alcoholism, 23*(3), 165–173.

Barlow, D. H., Farchione, T. J., Fairholme, C. P., Ellard, K. K., Boisseau, C. L., Allen, L. B., & Ehrenreich-May, J. (2011). *The unified protocol for transdiagnostic treatment of emotional disorders: Therapist guide*. Oxford University Press.

Barrett, L. F. (2017). *How emotions are made: The secret life of the brain*. Houghton Mifflin Harcourt.

Barrett, L. F., Wilson-Mendenhall, C. D., & Barsalou, L. W. (2014). A psychological construction account of emotion regulation and dysregulation: The role of situated conceptualizations. In J. J. Gross (Ed.), *The handbook of emotion regulation* (2nd ed., pp. 447–465). Guilford.

Barsalou, L. W. (1999). Perceptual symbol systems. *Behavioral and Brain Sciences, 22*, 577–609.

Barsalou, L. W. (2008). Grounded cognition. *Annual Review of Psychology, 59*(1), 617–645.

Beck, A. T. (1976). *Cognitive therapy and the emotional disorders*. International Universities Press.

Berridge, K. C. (2018). Evolving concepts of emotion and motivation. *Frontiers in Psychology, 9*, 1647. https://doi.org/10.3389/fpsyg.2018.01647

Berridge, K. C., & Robinson, T. E. (2003). Parsing reward. *Trends in Neurosciences, 26*(9), 507–513.

Billieux, J., Van der Linden, M., Khazaal, Y., Zullino, D., & Clark, L. (2011). Trait gambling cognitions predict near-miss experiences and persistence in laboratory slot machine gambling. *British Journal of Psychology, 103*(3), 412–427. https://doi.org/10.1111/j.20448295.2011.02083.x

Bishop, S. R., Lau, M., Shapiro, S., Carlson, L., Anderson, N. D., Carmody, J., ... Devins, G. (2004). Mindfulness: A proposed operational definition. *Clinical Psychology: Science and Practice, 11*, 230–241.

Cabib, S., Campus, P., Conversi, D., Orsini, C., & Puglisi-Allegra, S. (2020). Functional and dysfunctional neuroplasticity in learning to cope with stress. *Brain Sciences, 10*(2), 127. https://doi.org/10.3390/brainsci10020127

Cabib, S., & Puglisi-Allegra, S. (2012). The mesoaccumbens dopamine in coping with stress. *Neuroscience & Biobehavioral Reviews, 36*(1), 79–89.

David, D., Coteț, C., Matu, S., Mogoașe, C., & Ștefan, S. (2017). 50 years of rational-emotive and cognitive-Behavioral therapy: A systematic review and meta-analysis. *Journal of Clinical Psychology*, 1–15. https://doi.org/10.1002/jclp.22514

David, D., Lynn, S. J., & Ellis, A. (2010). *Rational and irrational beliefs: Research, theory, and clinical practice*. Oxford University Press.

David, D., & Szentagotai, A. (2006). Cognition in cognitive behavior psychotherapies. *Clinical Psychology Review, 26*, 284–298.

Demos McDermott, K. E., Lillis, J., McCaffery, J. M., & Wing, R. R. (2019). Effects of cognitive strategies on neural food cue reactivity in adults with overweight/obesity. *Obesity (Silver Spring, Md.), 27*(10), 1577–1583. https://doi.org/10.1002/oby.22572

Drummond, D. (2000). What does cue-reactivity have to offer clinical research? *Addiction, 92*, 129–144.

Drummond, D. C. (2001). Theories of drug craving, ancient and modern. *Addiction, 96*(1), 33–46. https://doi.org/10.1046/j.1360-0443.2001.961333.x

Ellis, A. (1958). Rational psychotherapy. *The Journal of General Psychology, 59*, 35–49.

Ellis, A. (1962). *Reason and emotion in psychotherapy*. Lyle Stuart.

Ellis, A. (1991). The revised ABC's of rational-emotive therapy (RET). *Journal of Rational-Emotive and Cognitive-Behavior Therapy, 9*, 139–172. https://doi.org/10.1007/BF01061227

Ellis, A. (1994). *Reason and emotion in psychotherapy (rev sub ed.)*. Citadel.

Ellis, A. (1996). Responses to criticisms of rational emotive behavior therapy (REBT) by Ray Digiuseppe, Frank Bond, Windy Dryden, Steve Weinrach, and Richard Wessler. *Journal of Rational-Emotive and Cognitive-Behavior Therapy, 14*, 97–121. https://doi.org/10.1007/BF02238185

Ellis, A. (2001). *Feeling better, getting better, staying better: Profound self-help therapy for your emotions*. Impact Publishers.

Ellis, A., David, D., & Lynn, S. J. (2010). Rational and irrational beliefs: A historical and conceptual perspective. In D. David, S. J. Lynn, & A. Ellis (Eds.), *Rational and irrational beliefs: Research, theory, and clinical practice* (pp. 3–22). Oxford University Press.

Erk, S., Spitzer, M., Wunderlich, A., Galley, L., & Walter, H. (2003). Cultural objects modulate reward circuitry. *Neuroreport, 13*, 2499–2503. https://doi.org/10.1097/01.wnr.0000048542.12213.60

Fadda, F., Argiolas, A., Melis, M. R., Tissari, A. H., Onali, P. L., & Gessa, G. L. (1978). Stress-induced increase in 3,4-dihydroxyphenylacetic acid (DOPAC) levels in the cerebral cortex and n.accumbens: Reversal by diazepam. *Life Sciences, 23*, 2219–2224. https://doi.org/10.1016/b978-0-08-023768-8.51934-4

George, O., & Koob, G. (2013). Control of craving by the prefrontal cortex. *Proceedings of the National Academy of Sciences of the United States of America, 110*, 4165–4166. https://doi.org/10.1073/pnas.1301245110

Giuliani, N. R., & Berkman, E. T. (2015). Craving is an affective state and its regulation can be understood in terms of the extended process model of emotion regulation. *Psychological Inquiry, 26*(1), 48–53. https://doi.org/10.1080/1047840X.2015.955072

Giuliani, N. R., Calcott, R. D., & Berkman, E. T. (2013). Piece of cake: Cognitive reappraisal of food craving. *Appetite, 64*, 56–61.

Grace, A. A. (2016). Dysregulation of the dopamine system in the pathophysiology of schizophrenia and depression. *Nature Review Neuroscience, 17*, 524–532.

Greer, S. M., Goldstein, A. N., & Walker, M. P. (2013). The impact of sleep deprivation on food desire in the human brain. *Nature Communications, 4*, 2259. https://doi.org/10.1038/ncomms3259

Gross, J. J. (2015). Emotion regulation: Current status and future prospects. *Psychological Inquiry, 26*(1), 1–26. https://doi.org/10.1080/1047840X

Hayashi, T., Ko, J. H., Strafella, A. P., & Dagher, A. (2013). Dorsolateral prefrontal and orbitofrontal cortex interactions during self-control of cigarette craving. *Proceedings of the National Academy of Sciences of the United States of America, 110*, 4422–4427.

Kim, M. J., Shin, J., Taylor, J. M., Mattek, A. M., Chavez, S. J., & Whalen, P. J. (2017). Intolerance of uncertainty predicts increased striatal volume. *Emotion, 17*(6), 895–899.

Kober, H., Kross, E. F., Mischel, W., Hart, C. L., & Ochsner, K. N. (2010b). Regulation of craving by cognitive strategies in cigarette smokers. *Drug and Alcohol Dependence, 106*, 52–55.

Kober, H., Mende-Siedlecki, P., Krossd, E. F., Weberb, J., Mischelb, W., Hart, C. L., & Ochsner, K. N. (2010a). Prefrontal–striatal pathway underlies cognitive regulation of craving. *Proceedings of National Academy of Sciences U. S. A., 107*, 14811–14816.

Ludwig, A. M., Wikler, A., & Stark, L. H. (1974). The first drink: Psychobiological aspects of craving. *Archives of General Psychiatry, 30*, 539–547.

Ly, V., Wang, K. S., Bhanji, J., & Delgado, M. R. (2019). A reward-based framework of perceived control. *Frontiers in Neuroscience, 13*, 65. https://doi.org/10.3389/fnins.2019.00065

May, J., Andrade, J., Kavanagh, D. J., & Hetherington, M. (2012). Elaborated intrusion theory- a cognitive-emotional theory of food craving. *Current Obesity Reports, 1*(2), 114–121.

May, J., Andrade, J., Panabokke, N., & Kavanagh, D. (2004). Images of desire: Cognitive models of craving. *Memory, 12*, 447–461. https://doi.org/10.1080/09658210444000061

McClernon, F. J., Hiott, F. B., Huettel, S. A., & Rose, J. E. (2005). Abstinence-induced changes in self-report craving correlate with event-related FMRI responses to smoking cues. *Neuropsychopharmacology, 30*(10), 1940–1947. https://doi.org/10.1038/sj.npp.1300780

Moors, A. (2009). Theories of emotion causation: A review. *Cognition and Emotion, 23*, 625–662.

Moors, A., Ellsworth, P. C., Scherer, K. R., & Frijda, N. H. (2013). Appraisal theories of emotion: State of the art and future development. *Emotion Review, 5*(2), 119–124. https://doi.org/10.1177/1754073912468165

Niedenthal, P. M. (2007). Embodying emotion. *Science, 316*, 1002–1005.

Padesky, C. A., & Mooney, K. A. (1990). Presenting the cognitive model to clients. *International Cognitive Therapy Newsletter, 6*, 13–14.

Papies, E., Barsalou, L., & Rusz, D. (2020). Understanding desire for food and drink: A grounded cognition approach. *Current Directions of Psychological Science, 29*(2), 193–198. https://doi.org/10.1177/0963721420904958

Papies, E. K., & Barsalou, L. W. (2015). Grounding desire and motivated behavior: A theoretical framework and review of empirical evidence. In W. Hofmann & L. F. Nordgren (Eds.), *The psychology of desire*. Guilford Press.

Pavlov, P. I. (1897/2010). Conditioned reflexes: An investigation of the physiological activity of the cerebral cortex. *Annals of Neurosciences, 17*(3), 136–141. https://doi.org/10.5214/ans.0972-7531.1017309

Rosser, B. A. (2019). Intolerance of uncertainty as a Transdiagnostic mechanism of psychological difficulties: A systematic review of evidence pertaining to causality and temporal precedence. *Cognitive Therapy and Research, 43*, 438–463. https://doi.org/10.1007/s10608-018-9964-z

Sescousse, G., Janssen, L. K., Hashemi, M. M., Timmer, M. H., Geurts, D. E., Ter Huurne, N. P., ... Cools, R. (2016). Amplified striatal responses to near-miss outcomes in pathological gamblers. *Neuropsychopharmacology, 41*(10), 2614–2623. https://doi.org/10.1038/npp.2016.43

Singer, B. F., Scott-Railton, J., & Vezina, P. (2012). Unpredictable saccharin reinforcement enhances locomotor responding to amphetamine. *Behavioural Brain Research, 226*(1), 340–344. https://doi.org/10.1016/j.bbr.2011.09.003

Stewart, J., Dewit, H., & Eikelboom, R. (1984). Role of unconditioned and conditioned drug effects in the self-administration of opiates and stimulants. *Psychological Review, 91*, 251–268.

Tanovic, E., Gee, D. G., & Joormann, J. (2018). Intolerance of uncertainty: Neural and psychophysiological correlates of the perception of uncertainty as threatening. *Clinical Psychology Review, 60*, 87–99. https://doi.org/10.1016/j.cpr.2018.01.001

Tiba, A. I., & Manea, L. (2018). The embodied simulation account of cognition in rational emotive behavior therapy. *New Ideas in Psychology, 48*, 12–20.

Tiffany, S. T. (1999). Cognitive concepts of craving. *Alcohol Research & Health: The Journal of the National Institute on Alcohol Abuse and Alcoholism, 23*(3), 215–224.

Toneatto, T. (1999). A metacognitive analysis of craving: Implication for treatment. *Journal of Clinical Psychology, 55*, 527–537.

van Dillen, L. F., & van Steenbergen, H. (2018). Tuning down the hedonic brain: Cognitive load reduces neural responses to high-calorie food pictures in the nucleus accumbens. *Cognitive, affective & behavioral neuroscience, 18*(3), 447–459. https://doi.org/10.3758/s13415-018-0579-3

Westbrook, C., Creswell, J. D., Tabibnia, G., Julson, E., Kober, H., & Tindle, H. A. (2013). Mindful attention reduces neural and self-reported cue-induced craving in smokers. *Social Cognitive and Affective Neuroscience, 8*(1), 73–84. https://doi.org/10.1093/scan/nsr076

Yokum, S., & Stice, E. (2013). Cognitive regulation of food craving: Effects of three cognitive reappraisal strategies on neural response to palatable foods. *International Journal of Obesity, 37*(12), 1565–1570. https://doi.org/10.1038/ijo.2013.39

Young, J. E., Klosko, J. S., & Weishaar, M. E. (2003). *Schema therapy: A practitioner's guide*. Guilford Press.

Chapter 7
The Treatment of Embodied Rigid Appraisals: Restructuring Embodied Irrational Beliefs

7.1 Introduction

Early cognitive theories (the rational emotive behavior therapy/REBT revised model; Ellis 1991, 2001), empirical research from affective science (Douma and de Kloet 2020; Cabib et al. 2020; Cabib and Puglisi-Allegra 2012), and recent theoretical developments of psychological treatment (Ellis et al. 2010; Tiba and Manea 2018) suggest embodied rigid (motivational) appraisals as stress-related etiologic mechanisms that determine emotional disorders.

In nonhuman animal models of psychopathology and stress-coping, embodied rigid appraisals have been evidenced and conceptualized as incentive salience (Robinson and Berridge 1993), incentive hope (Anselme and Güntürkün 2019), incentive dread (Berridge 2018), or rigid coping (Cabib and Puglisi-Allegra 2012; Douma and de Kloet 2020). In human models of psychopathology, embodied rigid appraisals have been conceptualized as irrational beliefs (Ellis 2001; Ellis et al. 2010). For a lengthy period, these two lines of evidence were independent. Yet an embodied construction of rigid appraisals bridges data from affective science into cognitive models of psychopathology and psychological treatment.

Embodied appraisals are appraisals based on the recruitment of affective experience systems in representations (see Chap. 2). Embodied cognition (i.e., cognition based on embodied states) is a well-recognized type of cognition in human affective science literature (Barrett 2017; Barsalou 2008), classical models of appraisals (Moors et al. 2013; Leventhal and Scherer 1987), animal models in affective science (e.g., the concepts of incentive salience and hope from animal models are carried out in the motivational brain system, not in semantic brain systems, thus being by default types of embodied appraisals; Berridge and Robinson 2016), and consistent to early models of rigid appraisals in psychotherapy (e.g., Ellis 1958). Yet embodied cognition has been neglected in the mainstream cognitive models of evidence-based psychological treatments.

A. Tiba, *Embodied Hot Cognitive Vulnerability to Emotional Disorders*,
https://doi.org/10.1007/978-3-030-53989-4_7

Embodied rigid appraisals refer to the rigid evaluation of personal significance or desirability based on hyper-reactive states of incentive salience motivational system in response to adversities (threats or loss of rewards). They are rigid "salience" appraisals. For instance, when individuals encounter stress situations such as losing a partner, loss of money, or any other important things, because of individual differences, neurobiological adaptations to stress and situational factors, they appraise the desirability of situation based on (motivational) affective systems in states similar to those involved in response to drugs. They *crave* to control the stressful situation, relief from aversion, and get the lost reward resulting in compulsive active coping and emotional disturbance. Thus, the individuals appraise the aversive stimuli as things they must or should change. As a result, they also evaluate the adversity as intolerable and awful and are stuck in compulsive active coping to control the situation. Embodied rigid appraisals are primary appraisals embodied in dysregulated craving experiences (i.e., shoulds and musts in response to adversities). Embodied exaggerated appraisals (i.e., frustration intolerance and awfulizing) are secondary embodied appraisals. They result from primary appraisals.

Rigid embodied appraisals function in both unconscious and conscious ways. Moreover, they may be in different states of activation: (a) inactivated or disembodied regarding the recruitment of affective systems, (b) partially activated, and (c) fully activated. When their motivational embodiment is fully activated, they are experienced as *affective feelings of craving* including cognitive components (demands and vivid images of the activating situation, obsessing thoughts), behavioral tendencies (compulsive and perseverative active coping), physiological reactions (arousal states), and subjective components (feelings of extremely intense desire). These dysregulated affective feelings and compulsive coping result in emotional disturbances. Prolonged and frequent disturbed emotions affect the daily life functioning of individuals resulting in emotional disorders.

As described in the previous chapters of this book, embodied appraisals are a common type of appraisals (Chap. 2), they can be rigid and exaggerated (Chaps. 3 and 5), reflect both individual differences in affective (motivation) and regulatory brain systems and neuroadaptations related to excessive levels of stress hormones in susceptible individuals (Chap. 4), are involved in psychopathology, and are important targets for evidence-based psychological treatments (Chap. 6). In this chapter, I discuss the treatment of embodied rigid appraisals (embodied irrational beliefs/IBs).

Cognitive behavior therapy (CBT) is the "gold standard" of evidence-based psychological treatment. The original form of CBT is rational emotive behavior therapy (REBT). REBT and cognitive therapy (Beck 1976) are two main types (among many others) of what we call cognitive behavior therapy (David et al. 2017). REBT training model is an important provider of certification in cognitive behavior therapy, also being named rational-emotive cognitive behavior therapy (David et al. 2017).

In this chapter, I describe the process of assessment, conceptualization, and treatment of embodied rigid motivational appraisals. I describe new interventions targeting fully activated embodied IBs such as exposure and memory restructuring methods and discuss medication in the treatment of the embodied rigid appraisals or irrational beliefs.

7.2 The Assessment of Embodied Rigid Appraisals

The mainstream assessment of IBs includes well-known and validated tests such as the Attitudes and Beliefs Scale (The Attitude and Belief Scale 2/General Attitude and Belief Scale (ABS 2/GABS)—Burgess 1986; DiGiuseppe et al. 1988) and the Shortened General Attitude and Belief Scale (SGABS—Lindner et al. 1999), among many others (for a detailed description see David et al. 2019a; Macavei and McMahon 2010). These assessment measures are sound measures. Yet they were not safe from criticism. According to REBT theory, true IBs (absolute rigid beliefs) can be seen only in *activating situations* (i.e., measured when the individuals face the adversities) and when they result in *disturbed emotions* (Ellis 1994; Ellis et al. 2010). In this book, the main tenet is that the effect of IBs on disturbed emotions is because of their maladaptive embodiment. Thus, when we measure IBs we have to measure the underlying embodiments. Measuring embodied IBs is similar to measuring *absolute irrational beliefs*: in activating situations and when they result in emotional disturbance. Although previous literature has made absolute versus non-absolute distinction for demandingness only (Dryden 2019), I propose the same distinction for secondary exaggerated appraisals as well (awfulizing, frustration intolerance). For instance, an individual may say that losing a job is awful but does not mean it. He says it is awful for communication purposes only. When the individual says that *it is awful*, feels like it is awful, and feels to avoid the situation, then the "*awful*" exaggerated appraisal is said to be *absolute* or as I propose here, *an embodied exaggerated appraisal*. Because both traditional approaches (David et al. 2019b; Ellis 1994) and affective neuroscience (catastrophizing and distress intolerance recruit the craving systems overlapping the craving for relief from aversive states) argue that demandingness beliefs are core IBs (the other exaggerated beliefs being derivatives; David et al. 2019b; Ellis 1994, but see DiGiuseppe et al. 2014 for alternative models), I will focus on measurements of demandingness or rigid appraisals. As I described in Chap. 6, embodied IBs may be inactivated, partially activated, or fully activated. A partially activated embodiment of IBs may be measured mainly by implicit tasks (e.g., affective priming tasks). Often, a partially activated IB may be identified by verbal expressions of cognition as feelings (e.g., "*I also feel that I must have her back*"). Instead, a fully activated embodiment is assessed by measures of the embodied experience (intense urgent "abnormal desire" or craving and emotional response) comprising cognitive, affective, physiological, or behavioral components. For instance, the therapists may use open, theory-guided, or choice theory-guided questions for assessing embodied IBs at:

- Cognitive level (Dryden and DiGiuseppe 1990; Dryden 2019) (e.g., "*What thoughts did you have when you realized that she left you?*"; "*When she left, did you think you must not lose her?*"; "*When she left, did you have the specific thought that you must not lose her, or you just wanted her back?*"; "*Did you have vivid images of what you want?*"),
- Affective level (e.g., "*Did you have any feelings associated with your thoughts?*"; "*How strongly did you also feel that you needed her back?*"; "*Did you also feel*

that you needed her or was it just a thought you that you needed her back?"; "*When you thought you must not lose her, did you also feel that you have to get her back?*" "*How intense was that feeling?*"; "*How intense were the feelings of urgency of your desire?*"; "*Did you feel anxiety or agitation?*"; "*Did you feel your desire as a need or craving or just a regular desire for important things?*"),

- Behavioral level (e.g., "*Did you act in some way?*"; "*Did you have a strong feeling to act on getting her back?*"; "*Did you feel an urge to get her back?*"; "*When you thought of getting her back, did it feel like an urge, or more as a regular thing you do?*"; "*Did you feel an urge to have her back?*"),
- Physiological level (e.g., "*What sensations did you have in your body when you thought you needed her back?*"; "*How much tension/arousal did you feel in that moment?*").

Furthermore, the therapist may assess the distinction between partially or fully activated craving embodiments of IBs. The therapist may ask: "*When you thought you must have her back and felt that you needed to get her back, was this feeling like an impression or a fully feeling of needing her?*"

Moreover, the therapist may differentiate between various intensities of the affective component of embodied IBs (*the intensity of craving* for the lost rewards; "*How strongly did you feel that you needed her back on a 0 to 10 scale?*"), the *urgency of the desire/craving*; "*How urgent did you feel your desire/need to get her back to be?*; and the *intensity of urges and compulsions* (e.g., "*How intense was the urge to get her back?*"; "*Did you feel you cannot stop yourself in trying to get her back?*").

Nonetheless, the therapist may assess the dysregulation level of the embodiment. (e.g., "*Did you feel that your need for her was within your control?*"; "*Did you feel that you cannot stop needing her?*").

Another method to measure IBs is by psychometric scales. Scales based on conscious ratings such as short craving scales are important tools that can measure embodied IBs. I will illustrate the use of these measures with embodied rigid appraisals (demandingness). For instance, measures of the embodiment of demandingness may provide clues about quantitative aspects of craving under stress and adversities. The therapist may ask clients to complete situation-related craving questionnaires. For instance, The Brief Substance Craving Scale is such a measure (Somoza et al. 1995). This scale may be adapted as a situational measure of embodiment of IBs. With Frank, he may be instructed to endorse and rate: (a) the intensity of his craving to get back his wife (e.g., the intensity of my craving, that is, how much I needed to [*complete with the omitted reward*] in the past 24 h was from none at all to extreme), (b) the frequency (e.g., the frequency of my craving, that is, how often I needed [*complete with the omitted reward*] in the past 24 h was from never to almost constantly), and (c) the duration of craving (e.g., the length of time I spent craving for [*complete with the omitted reward*] during the past 24 h was from none at all to very long) (Somoza et al. 1995). Additional items may be added depending on the interest in the dynamic features of craving response.

Theory-driven measures of embodied IBs may be used. For example, one such measure that can be adapted to assessing embodied IBs is the Craving Experience Questionnaire (CEQ; May et al. 2014). The Elaborated Intrusion Theory proposes that craving for various situations begins with a spontaneous intrusive thought (triggered by cues from the environment, mind, and body), followed by the controlled processes of elaboration. Cognitive elaboration includes the construction of embodied imagery that is pleasurable at first but in time becomes distressing (May et al. 2014). Thus, CEQ measures the processes delineated by the theory (i.e., intensity, imagery, intrusiveness) in two forms: strength and frequency (May et al. 2014). For instance, when assessing the strength of the craving as an embodiment of his IBs, we can ask Frank about the intensity of his craving feelings (e.g., how much did he/want/need [*to have her back*]; how strong was the urge to have [*her back*]?), imagery (e.g., how vividly did he picture/imagine [*being with her*]), the sensations he would experience (e.g., what it would feel like [*to be with her*]), or intrusiveness (e.g., how hard was he trying not to think about [*her*]) (adapted after May et al. 2014, p. 733). Other scales can measure core IBs (for a detailed description of craving measures, see Sayette et al. 2000).

Although I described the traditional assessment methods, other methods may be used as well. For instance, virtual reality assessment, electronic mood diaries, and neuroimaging methods can be added in the process of assessing embodied IBs (Macavei and McMahon 2010). The embodied simulation model of IBs suggests that there are many determinants that result in activated embodied rigid appraisals. Therefore, the assessment should include cognitive, affective, and biological determinants of episodic development of demandingness. As I mentioned in Chap. 6, when faced with adversity (A), individuals transform their desires in cravings because of affective (emotions, compulsive coping), cognitive (mental elaboration, meta-cognitive beliefs and reasons, appraisals, demands, perception of deprivation), and biological (incentive salience system activation because of biological mechanisms) determinants. The appraisals of importance of A are dynamically changing in time as their affective, biological, and cognitive determinants change in the situated conceptualization process.

Although these determinants are interacting in the development of a demandingness episode, therapists would gain much insight if they assess each of these factors. For instance, if the client *persistently ruminate* about the lost things and not having them (deprivation/incongruence elaboration), imagine having and the "consumption" of the lost rewards (images of being with his lost partner), think of A in terms that exaggerate the importance and the consequences of active controlling the adversity, thinking that getting her back will result in escaping from negative feelings, frustration and thoughts, exaggerated perceptions of self-efficacy and control, thinking in terms of near misses and increased sense of control under adversity (e.g., "when are no chances to get what I want it is a sign that I have to persist; it is a challenge") may escalate his desires into cravings and demands. Targeting repetitive thinking and using repetitive thinking-control methods should reduce cravings over time. Toneatto (1999) suggests that meta-cognitive reasons associated with craving-related meta-cognitive descriptions should be assessed and modified. To this end, the therapists would identify the psychological object of craving (e.g., the aversive emotion, thoughts; "*You crave to get her back because getting her back would...* [relief from what psychological state-anxiety]"), ask about the meta-cognitive consequences of craving and find reasons of why the object of craving is aversive and change those reasons (e.g., "*If you don't get her back and you feel anxious about it, how bad that anxiety would be*?"), ask about the meta-cognitive effects of the external object of craving (getting her back) over psychological state and find alternative coping (e.g., "*If you don't get her back and have anxiety what can we do to decrease your anxiety*?"). At the meta-cognitive level, derivative beliefs (awful, frustration intolerance, self-depreciation) are meta-cognitive consequences of craving and function as reasons for craving. If these reasons are removed, then it is expected that clients will no longer demand and will not be emotionally affected. The therapist should further inquire about these beliefs (e.g., "*What is awful about this experience? What exactly is intolerable? Tell me more about how this situation is making you miserable?*").

Other conditions that result in increased aversiveness of psychological states perceived to be relieved by the external object (or action) should be assessed. Moreover, it is suggested that these meta-cognitive reasons should be targeted in the cognitive restructuring of demands. Thus, the proposal is in line with targeting the secondary emotional problems with priority in REBT (DiGiuseppe et al. 2014). Dealing with secondary emotional problems, sometimes (stress and relief-related craving) it would be enough to reduce the primary emotional problems (in the case of discomfort-related embodied rigid appraisals).

The affective determinants may escalate desire thoughts into demanding thoughts as well. Moreover, a biased dominance of affective and biological implicit control over craving simulations is proposed as indicative of vulnerability to emotional disturbances. Thus, the therapists can assess the emotions and feelings that unfold and determine an episode of demandingness. The clients may *demand about A* and have an episode of demanding and craving after they had anxiety, stress, or depressed feelings for extended periods. These feelings may escalate their appraisals of how much they desire important things into demands and urgent desires in negative situations. Affective determinants may be assessed based on questions targeting their feelings or by emotion-focused scales. At last, therapists may assess biological reactivity in terms of craving responses by asking clients about their craving history to various rewards such as foods, relations, sign-tracking, and drugs.

7.3 The Conceptualization of Embodied Rigid Appraisals

The conceptualization explains how the clients develop and maintain their problems (Persons 2008). Based on this explanation, the therapist develops and delivers the treatment (Persons 2008).

The traditional approach to the conceptualization of IBs considers IBs as something we say to ourselves because of what we have learned from others (i.e., social influences) and/or our biological inclinations (Ellis 1962, 1994). Although A. Ellis has stressed that we are biologically inclined to "demand," this explanation was less favored in the conceptualization of the origin of IBs when compared to the learning-based formation of IBs (for a detailed discussion, see Tiba and Manea 2018). Embodied IBs bring two major implications for how we explain IBs: (1) explain IBs in terms of its parts, opening the way of integrating many interventions in the change of IBs and (2) suggest the dynamic and episodic construction of IBs in our consciousness as psychological states. In a problem-focused REBT intervention, the conceptualization process follows several steps. First, the therapists start by educating the clients about how IBs determine disturbed emotions (education about the general model), then they link the IBs to disturbed emotions and rational beliefs/ RBs to non-disturbed emotions, and in the end, the therapists strengthen the explanation by linking the changes in IBs (the newly acquired RBs) to the regulated emotion (healthy negative emotion; sad but not depressed) and reduced disturbed emotion (Dryden 2019).

In the following section, I will illustrate the education part of the conceptualization process based on the embodied model of IBs. The education about the embodied IBs (the role of IBs in disturbed emotions and the link between IBs and disturbed emotions) may be delivered as in the traditional model of education in REBT (referring just to IBs but as strong needs). Yet the education about embodied IBs adds explanations of how the changes of embodied IBs may target different components of IBs (embodied simulations, simulation-control mechanisms, simulators, and biological brain states during simulations). Here I suggest that education about the parts of embodied IBs may be elegantly delivered before beginning to teach the clients how to change their IBs.

7.3.1 Educating the Clients About the ABC Model of Emotional Disturbances

Traditionally, an emotional problem is defined in terms of dysfunctional ("unhealthy") emotions triggered by an activating situation (the adversity or A). The client is told about the difference between the practical problem (A) and the emotional problem (the C or the "unhealthy" or disturbed/dysregulated emotion). Then, the client is guided through the cognitive mediation mechanisms in terms of IBs (Dryden and DiGiuseppe 1990). It is not the A (the adversity) that causes C (the unhealthy emotion), but the B (IBs) (Ellis 1994). Because the "lay" terms used by A. Ellis to explain clients the ABC model often involved needs to refer to IBs and wants to refer to RBs (Ellis 2001), a conceptualization based on embodied rigid appraisals is familiar to REBT therapists.

Embodied IBs are rigid appraisals of the importance of personal goals under A based on simulations that recruit the "need"-like states of motivational brain system (dysregulated sensitized states of incentive salience motivational system) in understanding, while rational beliefs are seen as "wants" based on a cognitive regulation system. Our (verbal) expressions disturb us emotionally when they recruit for the representation of their meaning experiences of desires based on needs and the hyperactive incentive brain system. The task is to switch between the two systems while appraising goals under adversity.

There are several methods that can be used for education in the traditional IBs model: didactic and Socratic methods, illustrations and metaphors (DiGiuseppe et al. 2014; Dryden 2019). In the following part, I illustrate an example of using the didactic method:

> "Frank, what do you know about how recognizing things important for you as something you need, not just something you want, affects your emotions? I think knowing how *the fact that we recognize important things as needs affects us emotionally* is important when we want to change these emotions. When we encounter an unexpected aversive situation, our brain releases stress hormones. These stress hormones affect how we process the importance of that situation and force us to understand how much we desire important things based on states of our brain usually involved in our needs rather than wants or goals. Thus, when we understand in this way the desire for things we cannot get, we end up in having very intense emotions (as we have when needs, such as the need for air, are not satisfied) that do not easily break off."

> "For instance, a common situation when we use the "*need mode*" rather than a "*desire mode*" of our motivational brain is not having air to breathe. We need air to breathe. We do not just want air. If we stop into actively getting air when we do not have air, we die. It is very disturbing, but at least, if we do not stop into getting air, we have more chances not to die. Just imagine the struggle. Now imagine that you consider not being respected or loved in the same way. The problem is that not being respected is a common problem that has proper solutions in our daily lives. We do not die from not being respected. Using our motivational brain in a "*need mode*" may be often very emotionally disturbing and may cause long-term problems such as stress-related disorders. Sometimes when we have had very stressful periods of stress in past years, our motivational brain system becomes more sensitive, being easily set off in a "need mode," and because of this, it is often used to understand how important things are for us."

7.3.2 Identifying Embodied Rigid Appraisals and Linking Them to Disturbed Emotions and Rational Beliefs to Regulated Emotions

This sequence is like the sequence used in the traditional REBT intervention. I will illustrate this process in the interaction between the therapist and the client.

THERAPIST: Let's see if you recognize your problem using a "*need mode*" of your motivational system to assess the importance of this situation for you. Sometimes we can identify that we use needs from our language or from our felt sensations as an *urgent need,* rather than just something that we want.

THERAPIST: The initial problem was that your colleagues do not respect you. How do you feel when you use your needs to understand the situation?

CLIENT: Angry.

THERAPIST: And if we are to replace being angry with being annoyed, what do you think we have to change?

CLIENT: If I understand being respected as a need and when I use my needs system it gets me angry, probably it will help me if I change my understanding of respect.

THERAPIST: Yes, we have to recognize that being respected is a desire or a "want" but not a need, and it is possible that you are not respected. If this is not good for you, it is best to focus on possible ways you could be dealing with your colleagues who do not respect you.

7.3.3 Orienting the Client for the Change of Embodied Rigid Appraisals

The next step is education about the cognitive restructuring process. Traditionally, the cognitive restructuring of IBs is done by cognitive disputation techniques. The resulting cognitive changes are further reinforced by imagery, affective, and behavioral interventions. For instance, at this step the therapist may describe the process of changing IBs by saying that: "*One way to change IBs is analyzing whether they are supported by evidence/are helpful/are logical*" (Dryden and DiGiuseppe 1990). There are two reasons for which the process of changing embodied IBs is more complex.

First, as discussed in Chap. 6, as psychological constructed states, partially activated embodied IBs may be conceptualized as qualitatively different mental states: cognition (beliefs, memories), behaviors (habits, self-determined behavior), motivational states (needs), and feelings. As such, therapists have the possibility to change IBs based on idiosyncratic simulation-control mechanisms used by clients to construct IBs (when IBs are conceptualized as feelings, the therapists can change IBs as they change feelings; when the clients conceptualize IBs as a behavior—verbal behavior such as "I tell myself they should respect me," the therapists can change IBs as they change behaviors). Additionally, the therapists may use a different conceptualization (e.g., "sometimes it is helpful to see these beliefs as needs and change them as you usually change needs") of the same IBs to reinforce the change by different simulation-control mechanisms.

Second, rigid thinking in response to stress is conceptualized as a composite psychological state. Because of this, the change process targets the simulation-control mechanisms, simulators, and brain/experience states involved in the embodied simulations. When IBs are targeted as composite psychological states based on embodied simulations of needs in understanding, the therapists may explain the process of cognitive change as follows:

> "Frank, we saw that when you remember she left you and consider that *her love* is important as something you need, you feel depressed feelings and despair rather than just sadness. Instead, when you understand that *her love* is important as something you want but it is not a need, you feel rather sad, not depressed. So what we have to do is to find ways to recognize *her love* as an important thing you want but not necessarily something you need.

What do you know about changing the use of needs in understanding the importance of this situation? Probably it would be helpful first to find what influences the use of our needs in understanding the importance of the situation and then to find a way to change this."

After explaining the process of changing IBs, the therapists may initiate the change of *each component* of the activated embodied IBs: simulation-control mechanisms (linguistic, memory-based, and peripheral mechanisms), body states, and emotional simulators. Furthermore, the therapists may target *the processes* (cognitive and affective elaboration processes) that make clients escalate from desires to cravings into their appraisals of adversities.

7.4 The Treatment of Embodied Rigid Appraisals

7.4.1 Healthy Brain and Body, Rational Mind

States of our body and brain can strongly influence the central embodiment of IBs. When IBs are embodied in states of neural systems involved in disturbed and dysregulated motivation and emotion, conditions that affect our bodies by promoting regulatory failures and affective hyper-reactivity are of importance. These are body-state implicit simulation-control mechanisms. For instance, sleep deprivation (Goldstein and Walker 2014), systemic and neuronal inflammation (Felger 2018; Mehta et al. 2018), lack of physical exercise (Kujach et al. 2018; Tsukamoto et al. 2016), hormonal dysregulation (Wu et al. 2016), obesity (Lowe et al. 2019), and high fat-sugar diet (Jacka et al. 2010; Lowe et al. 2019) are several examples of conditions that may result in maladaptive embodiment of appraisals or embodied IBs.

In this case, changing embodied IBs should start with changing body conditions that result in maladaptive embodiments (motivational and emotional dysregulation). In the early phases of the therapy, we may explain to clients about the importance of engaging in activities that promote efficient regulatory functions. For instance, the therapist can help Frank to start a physical activity program such as jogging, get an early hour for sleep, and solve his sleep problems. A diet supporting regulatory functions might be of help (Hernandez et al. 2018). The therapist may help Frank build a balanced diet and avoid high sugar-fat foods. The therapist may also help Frank to start activity scheduling including hedonic activities (Frank can appoint a relaxing massage session), social activities (Frank can spend time with his friends), and meaningful activities (Frank can start to do things to help others). Although it would not be the case of Frank, in the case of female clients they can discuss an awareness of premenstrual hormonal fluctuations and their possible impact on changing the embodiment of appraisals and the potential of their transformation into IBs.

Illustration for explaining the influence of hunger on IBs:

THERAPIST: Frank, have you understood that if you want to feel sad but not depressed you have to tell yourself that having her back is a *want* but not a *need*. Let's go over another mechanism that activates your motivational systems in a "need state" when you think about this situation.

THERAPIST: Frank, when you are hungry, what did you generally observe about your desires?

CLIENT: I am not ok when I am hungry. I am irritable and I struggle if things don't go my way.

THERAPIST: As they should or need to be. It's like you need not only food because you are hungry, but you need anything else that's important.

CLIENT: Yes.

THERAPIST: Usually, being hungry sets off your motivation system in a "need state" and when you face something important, you will use (due to being hungry) this "need state" of motivation to recognize the significance of other situations such as being respected and then you feel anger. So, what do you think we have to do to cool down your *"need state"*?

CLIENT: I usually calm down when I eat!

THERAPIST: and feel satiated....

CLIENT: I understand. When I eat I am not that frustrated....

THERAPIST: And yes, when you are satiated, the need system is cooled down and not recruited in your thinking. So what would help you to not feel so distressed about not being respected?

CLIENT: Eating when I feel bad?

THERAPIST: We wouldn't want you to get fat. What about drinking water? It gives you a satiation feeling and cools down your need states of your motivational system.

CLIENT: And perhaps thinking about how to best deal with the fact he didn't respect me, is best done after I eat and not when I am hungry.

THERAPIST: Yes, you got the idea. You can either use the time when you feel satiated to think and solve your problem or get satiated when you start to use your motivational system in a need state in your understanding.

7.4.2 Changing Language-Control Mechanisms of Embodied Rigid Appraisals

One common way to change embodied IBs and distorted embodied simulations is by changing the language-control mechanisms of the *simulation of the needs* in understanding the personal significance of situations. This procedure is like classic disputations methods from REBT. There are several major differences from the traditional approach. In the case of changing embodied IBs: (1) changing verbal IBs (i.e., demandingness) is expected to result directly in a change of a craving response (not emotional C), as verbal labels of craving responses describe, organize, and structure the motivational experience, (2) demandingness is a label or a meta-cognitive description of the intensity of motivation (desire) used to recognize the importance of a cognitive encounter that result from cognitive and affective elaboration processes, and (3) cognitive disputation is a form of meta-cognitive intervention that result in building meta-cognitive beliefs (e.g., "*Because it is not logical/not congruent with reality/not helpful, I better not demand*) and changing meta-cognitive descriptive thoughts (demands into preferences) is a way to regulate, organize, and control the simulations of motivational experiences.

Cognitive processes that escalate desires into demands (meta-cognitive reasons and elaborative processes for why individuals demand) often unfold in time (are episodic) and include repeated thoughts and vivid images of desired situations, poor linguistic differentiation between desires and needs, repeated verbal elaboration of the memory of consumption of the missed rewards, meta-cognitive reasons, activated meta-cognitive beliefs about desires under adversity, learned conditions for demanding such as high expectation to get important things by perseveration based on incongruence, reciprocity, fairness violations, escape from negatives, and so on. Although not all processes involved in the cognitive elaboration are verbal-based processes (e.g., visual and motor conscious simulations of past encounters), the use of verbal processes may take over cognitive elaboration to direct the conceptualization of the motivational responses as a desire and not a need. Changing verbal demands determines the change of craving-related simulations and the transformation of craving responses in regulated "desires."

W. Dryden, one of the most prolific authors in the REBT literature, has recently presented excellent descriptions of the verbal disputation methods (Dryden 2019). Traditionally, the process of changing IBs starts by suggesting logical, empirical, and pragmatic methods of disputation of IBs. In the case of Frank, it would be asking Frank if he knows how to change IBs and to guide him to conclude that one way to change IBs is to analyze if they are logical; if there is evidence supporting them; or if believing them helps Frank achieve his goals. Although these are some clinically proven ways to change IBs, the change of embodied IBs should additionally include the change of cognitive (including meta-cognitive) elaboration processes and meta-cognitive beliefs that result in IBs. Thus, the cognitive determinants of embodied IBs are those cognitive (including meta-cognitive) processes that trigger or maintain an over-activated incentive salience system in our conceptualization and escalate desires into demands in response to adversities. They can be appraisals, repetitive thinking, and meta-cognitive factors. The first type of cognitive determinants is appraisals that accentuate the cognitive discrepancy (appraisals of incongruence, deprivation, unexpectedness, aversiveness, coping potential/self-efficacy). The second type of cognitive determinants is repetitive thinking or elaboration processes about the cognitive discrepancy (in terms of deprivation, incongruence and unexpectedness and related consequences), positive-"consumption" (satisfying the desires blocked by adversity) and positive consequences of controlling the adversity or relief. The third type of cognitive determinants is meta-cognitive beliefs that promote rigid active (approach or avoidance) coping in response to adversity. For instance, they can be: meta-cognitive beliefs or reasons to crave/demand for the desired situation in the face of adversity based on negative reinforcement ("I must change A, otherwise it is awful"; "I must change A, otherwise I cannot stand it"), self/other/life-depreciation ("I must change A, or I am a failure"); positive reinforcement (arguments for demands based on positive memories-"It was too good," exaggerated self-efficacy or self-valuation about obtaining the lost reward/avoiding/controlling threats or persistence); idiosyncratic reasons (based on personal reasons to demand- reciprocity and fairness appraisals); adversity-based growth or reward overvaluation (e.g., when it is impossible, it means that I am almost close to succeed; the success is valuable if I persist in no win situations and I finally succeed; the value of controlling the adversity is greatest when the situation is impossible, every failure is a step closure to controlling the adversity); deficient meta-cognitive discrimination (e.g., lack of differentiation between wants and needs, between acceptance and giving-up) (e.g., Toneatto 1999).

In short, cognitive appraisals, elaboration, and meta-cognitive processes maintain an exaggerated and rigid active perseverance in response to adversity. Taking this approach would require asking Frank why he believes *he needs her* and then analyzing and disputing each reason provided by Frank. For instance, Frank may say he needs her because they were meant to be together, because they had their best time together, that she loves him, his anxiety is awful if he doesn't get her back, and so on. Each of these arguments or reasons may be disputed based on logical, empirical, and pragmatic methods.

The following example illustrates the change of language-control mechanisms to control the use of the simulation of the needs.

THERAPIST: "First, how much do you understand about the impact of what you tell yourself in a specific situation and how it can determine if you respond with a need or a desire in that situation?

THERAPIST: Let's see an example about how the things you say to yourself get you into *needing* or just *wanting* something. Let's consider that you go to buy food and you are hungry. Being hungry means that you are in a *need state* and you need food, not just want food. You observe this and you feel agitated. What do you say to yourself to get out of the need state?

CLIENT: That I don't need it. I don't die if I don't eat.

THERAPIST: Yes, so you push yourself in a wanting state based on your goal in that situation, which is not to eat because you don't want to get fat! And if you say that to yourself, how do you feel about not eating?

CLIENT: Probably not so agitated.

THERAPIST: … And you will likely think of other things, start other activities and calm down. Let's go back to the situation in which you say *you need her love.* What can you say to yourself to switch from a need state regarding her love to a less distressing want state for her love?

CLIENT: That I want her love, but I don't need it?

THERAPIST: Yes, it is true. And what reasons do you have to tell yourself *her loving you* is something you want but not something you need?

As I have mentioned in the beginning of the chapter, the cognitive elaboration processes also facilitate the escalation of desires into cravings. To change embodied IBs, the client should be helped to change the cognitive elaboration processes. After Frank understands that his IBs determine his anger and depression, and is asked about how to change IBs, Frank can be oriented to different sources of the development of the embodied IBs. To do so, the therapist uses theory-driven questions to identify different sources of IBs such as:

"When you remember her, do you think of your best times together?"

"Does your desire for her change after thinking of your best times together?"

"When you remember her, do you start vividly imagining being with her?"

"How do you feel about yourself if you do not want her anymore?"

Then, the therapist can help the client link these processes to an increase in state (activated) IBs. Examples of theory-driven questions in the case of Frank would be:

"When you thought of those splendid times together, what happened with how much you needed her?"; "When you imagined how you held her, how much did you want her? You've just wanted her or you needed her?"; "When you remembered how bad it was without her, how much did you want her? You've just wanted her or you needed her?"

After the clients understand that thinking of past moments of consumption of rewards (or mentally rehearsing, thinking it is a near-miss, too incongruent with his desires, etc.) and deprivation when those rewards are not present (in response to adversity) make them crave for instead of wanting the things they lost, then they can be guided to engage into several strategies to disrupt these IBs maintaining processes. Examples of theory-driven questions in the case of Frank would be:

"What (negative) things can you remember about you two, so you don't end up in needing her when you think of her?"

"What are the reasons you can remember about her, so you don't end up in needing her when you think of her?"

After learning how to change the IBs maintaining mechanisms, the clients may be helped to use these strategies.

Changing the language-control mechanisms to control the use of *simulation of needs* in the understanding of personal significance of situations overlaps with the verbal disputation techniques used in REBT. Thus, when changing embodied IBs, any form of disputation (logical, pragmatic, empiric) builds language-control mechanisms that direct the understanding of the significance of the situation based on desire-states and not need-states of the motivational system.

Traditional verbal interventions of changing demandingness are focused on changing demandingness as distorted evaluations of importance of an event for personal goals. When IBs are embodied, individuals demand from several other cognitive reasons (that recruit or set an over-reactive state of the incentive salience system in the representation of the importance of the situation). As I mentioned above, these reasons are: (1) repeated imagery of past or future memories with the lost reward stimuli or relief from stress, (2) deprivation simulations and cues, (3) environmental cues, (4) consumption and approach behavior, (5) meta-cognitive reasons, (6) cognitive appraisals (perception of the availability goals, self-efficacy over changing A or relief, near-misses, uncertainty, expectancy violation/unexpectedness, relevance, incongruence), and (7) intermittent reward schedules (uncertainty).

Embodied IBs are also under the control of *implicit simulation control-mechanisms* (besides the language-control mechanisms) that drive the use of an over-reactive state of the incentive salience (mesolimbic dopamine system) system in the understanding of the personal significance of a situation. Examples of implicit simulation-control mechanisms are stimulus and memory-based mechanisms, neurochemical (stress-related glucocorticoids release, ghrelin release, orexin, neuropeptide Y) mechanisms, and expressive action-based mechanism (e.g., the tonality of the voice). When the therapists identify such a mechanism, it can become a target of the intervention. The therapists can promote adaptive simulation-control mechanisms to strengthen the situated conceptualization process based on a desire-state instead of a need-state of the incentive salience motivational system.

7.4.3 Mindfulness and Embodied Rigid Appraisals

Mindfulness refers to observing our reactions (and feelings) without judging them or without judging ourselves (Bishop et al. 2004). Most common conceptualizations of mindfulness include present moment awareness, decentering (self-regulation of attention), and acceptance (Tapper 2017, 2018). Present moment awareness refers to allocating attention to present moment experience (self-regulation of attention to breathe, content of thoughts, bodily sensations, and feelings) (Tapper 2018). Decentering refers to viewing one's experiences as transient events separate to oneself (Tapper 2018). Acceptance refers to adopting a nonjudgmental attitude toward one's experience (thoughts, feelings, and bodily sensations) (Tapper 2018). Mindfulness entered the mainstream of evidence-based psychological therapies both as a method added to existing CBT protocols (see Barlow et al. 2011; Hayes and Hofmann 2018) and a form of treatment (mindfulness based CBT, Williams et al. 2007) being an evidence-based intervention (Tapper 2018). Yet mindfulness treatment has been recently criticized (Stefan and David 2020; David 2014). Given that mindfulness interventions are evidence-based procedures, they can be valuable procedures used to target partially or fully activated embodied IBs. Activated embodied IBs are multicomponent episode-like dynamic reactions comprising thoughts, feelings, bodily sensations, and compulsive coping tendencies. Thus, using mindfulness interventions focused on negative feelings and cravings may prove a useful procedure for changing the impact of embodied IBs on disturbed emotions. L. Barsalou suggested that decentering methods (seeing perceptions and thoughts as mere transient events) from the mindfulness procedure reduce the believability of conscious embodied reward simulations and their transformation into intense desire and cravings (Barsalou 2017). In two studies based on applying mindfulness on simulations of consumption of rewards, Papies et al. (2015) trained participants to observe thoughts in reaction to incentive stimuli as mental events (in Study 1 they presented pictures of attractive persons and in Study 2 pictures of foods). They asked participants to react to stimuli as to passive mental events. As such, they told them that when they encounter stimuli (persons or food pictures) they might experience various reactions (interacting with the persons, liking or disliking, etc.). Then, participants were asked "*to observe all these reactions and to consider them as momentary constructions of their minds, which arise and pass as transient mental events*" (Papies et al. 2015, p. 153). In study one, after using mindful attention to pictures of attractive individuals, the participants rated the individuals as less attractive and thought that it is less possible that the individual presented in each picture would be a potential partner for them (compared to a control group). In study two, after mindful observing their reactions to unhealthy food pictures, participants experienced less intense cravings and rated food pictures as less attractive. Moreover, mindful attention reduced the effect of deprivation (hunger) on developing cravings and food choices (Papies et al. 2015).

Based on these findings, mindful interventions result in the change of activated embodied IBs. In the case of embodied IBs, mindful procedure may be applied either as a distinct therapy procedure (as in studies of Papies et al. 2015) in a conceptualization-guided treatment (Persons 2008) or as a component of emotional awareness module (as in the unified protocol for emotional disorders; Barlow et al. 2011) in a treatment "package."

As a distinct procedure, mindfulness can be delivered to modify embodied IBs via both imagery and computerized training. For instance, during rational emotive imagery (a technique used for consolidating the change of IBs; Maultsby 1971), clients may be asked to let their feelings of craving to unfold and to observe them as they are transient mental events. Moreover, clients can be guided to observe how their feelings start and rise, transforming into very intense desire and feelings of must and how they decrease and transform into regular desires.

Another way to deliver mindful attention procedures in the treatment of embodied IBs is by computerized training. To this end, the clients take pictures representing different adversities that trigger embodied IBs based on ratings of IBs. Then, the clients undergo mindfulness training (they apply mindful attention to various problem-neutral sensations such as perception of foods, etc.). In the end, a mindfulness session is designed in which the clients use mindful attention to repeated presentations of pictures for a specific period (e.g., 10–20 min). Adrian Wells (2009) has provided valuable resources regarding detached mindfulness techniques that can be applied to change embodied IBs. For instance, in his book *Meta-cognitive Therapy for Anxiety and Depression*, Adrian Wells presents ten mindful detachment techniques (Wells 2009) that may be used to address embodied IBs. I will illustrate how several of these techniques can be used in the case of embodied IBs.

One of these techniques, the "*Meta-cognitive guidance*" comprises asking clients questions to promote a detached self-reflection to problematic stimuli (Wells 2009). Questions adapted to embodied IBs include: "*Can you look through your [demanding that…] at the outside world?*"; "*Can you see your thought [specify the demand] and what is going on around you in the situation at the same time?*"; "*Are you living by your [demands…] or by what your eyes reveal?*" (Wells 2009, p. 80).

There are many metaphors that may promote a detached response to embodied IBs: "cloud" metaphor, the "recalcitrant child" metaphor, the "tiger" metaphor, and the "passenger train" metaphor (Wells 2009). For instance, in the "cloud" metaphor clients are given the following instructions (Wells 2009):

> "One way to understand detached mindfulness and what it requires is to consider experiencing your thoughts as you would experience clouds passing you by in the sky. The clouds are part of the Earth's self-regulating weather system, and it would be impossible and unnecessary to try to control them. Try to treat your thoughts and feelings [*that you need; that it should....*] like you would treat passing clouds and allow them to occupy their own space and time in the knowledge that they will eventually pass you by." (Wells 2009, p. 83).

Clients are guided to observe non-volitional aspects of imagery as means of detaching from embodied IBs. It is important to mention that these techniques aim to induce a detached experience with embodied IBs, not to transform them. When a transformation of embodied IBs is targeted, the clients may be asked to imagine the embodied IBs being written on clouds (train or any other metaphor) and watch how they disappear.

Similarly, embodied IBs may be targeted by mindfulness-based procedures included in various treatment protocols. The unified trans-diagnostic protocol for emotional disorders includes a mindfulness intervention on three components: (1) monitoring feelings, (2) mindful meditation, and (3) mindful observing the induced feelings (Barlow et al. 2011).

In the beginning of this procedure adapted to the process of changing embodied rigid appraisals, clients can be guided to use a craving induction procedure and to notice and record their reactions. For instance, clients may use mood induction procedures to become aware of and practice noticing their thoughts, feelings, and sensations of craving. Thus, clients are asked to confront situations that trigger their embodied IBs and to note their reactions to their cravings. Then, clients write their reactions in a craving monitoring form to record the thoughts, sensations, or feelings they experienced. Also, clients may exercise anchoring in the present at least once per day (noticing at least one thing going around and record any thoughts, feelings and sensations) and to practice at least twice per day nonjudgmental present-focused awareness (Barlow et al. 2011).

As with other feelings, clients can be thought to observe the *feelings of need, what they missed, they lost or have to avoid* by focusing on the experience of their feelings without judging these feelings and without judging themselves. In the beginning of the procedure, clients notice the changes in their feelings, including the feelings of needing the lost person (in the case of Frank). Then, they practice body scanning methods and notice the intensity of the cravings for the lost things, relief or comfort (e.g., for Frank the intensity of his need to be with his wife). At the end, clients are asked to imagine the activating situations (e.g., being left by their partners), letting their reactions unfold while they observe them nonjudgmentally as transient mental events from their beginning to their end.

7.4.4 Exposure Interventions: Changing Embodied Rigid Appraisals by Cue-Exposure

Exposure is a treatment of choice for anxiety. During a typical exposure procedure, the client faces stimuli (in vivo or imaginary) that trigger an emotional response (anxiety or craving) and has to stay in the situation until emotion recedes. To be efficient, exposure needs to be graded, prolonged, repeated, and without distraction. In the case of craving, exposure is considered being more efficient if the person adds to exposure the skills to manage cravings (Drummond 2000).

There are several steps in applying exposure and response prevention strategies: (1) education about the role of avoidance of the encounter, (2) building a craving situation hierarchy, (3) rehearsing the craving management strategies, (4) choosing a situation to practice, and (5) starting the exposure session and in-session application of the strategies (Dharmadhikari and Sinha 2015).

Education about craving involves explaining to the client the cycle of craving and consumption (in the case of stress, consumption refers to the interaction with the activating situation such as the problem is solved, getting the missing reward, relief or successfully avoiding the aversive stimulus). When craving is followed by consumption, craving is reinforced. Every time the person gives in, the craving is reinforced. To break this circle, the person is exposed to a mental of environmental cue (the adversity) and has to stay with the craving response until it recedes while restraining from engaging in consumption behaviors (Dharmadhikari and Sinha 2015).

For instance, Frank believes that he should have his wife back. Every time when he thinks like this, he calms down by thinking he will be again with her, remembering the pleasurable time together (action tendencies). The therapist explained to Frank that every time when he imagines, or remembers being with his wife, he feels he should have her back. When he does things as "*he is having her back,*" he calms down for short-term but in long-term he reinforces the craving response. To break this cycle, Frank has to let his feelings "*he should have her back*" go down without comforting himself with the idea that he will have her back.

To build a hierarchy, it helps to go through a list of activating situations. Then, each situation is rated according to the intensity of associated craving (Dharmadhikari and Sinha 2015). For instance, Frank identifies situations when he meets her (100%), when he visits the park where they used to run together (75%), watching movies (50%), seeing her picture (25%). He rated each situation according to the level of craving.

The therapist then guides the client to choose a situation and to confront it either in real life or using imagery. For instance, Frank chose first to go over the situation in which they watched movies. He imagined the situations and let himself feel that he needs her and they should be back together, but they are not. Then, Frank paid attention and remained with his feelings of needing her ("*Let the feelings unfold and follow their course*").

Another component of the intervention is response prevention applied to the urge to "consume." Every time Frank craved being with his wife, he comforted himself by thinking they will be together again. Frank learned that he can stop thinking of them if he simply remembers not to think they will be together again.

Usually, exposure follows learning the skills of coping with craving. Thus, Frank may use responding to his thoughts, detached observing his feelings together with response prevention to manage his feelings of craving (Dharmadhikari and Sinha 2015; Stalcup et al. 2006).

7.4.5 *Memory-Based Interventions: Targeting Simulators*

A simulator is a memory schema (Barsalou 1999). Previous research has suggested that rigid thinking is a schema stored in memory (Szentagotai et al. 2005). An embodied simulation view suggests that this schema is not stored in a semantic memory system but rather in the modality systems involved in the experience of IBs (including introspection). Thus, the "incentive salience" system is locked in a type of experience-based memory of the personal significance of a specific situation. Usually, once the mesolimbic dopamine system becomes sensitized to a stimulus, another encounter to that stimulus retrieves the mesolimbic DA system in a sensitized state. From this point of view, interventions that focus on changing memory-based processes (memory encoding, consolidation, reconsolidation and retrieval) are promising interventions that may change the embodied rigid appraisals.

CBT interventions targeting memory re-scripting have been proven as beneficial for emotional disorders. Examples of these treatments are schema-based therapy (Young et al. 2003), emotional-schema therapy (Leahy 2015), emotional processing therapy (Foa and Kozak 1986), and schema-focused interventions in cognitive therapy (Beck 1976). Young et al. suggest that a deeper level of cognitive interventions is the memory restructuring of schema (Young et al. 2003). In schema-restructuring interventions, after clients learn how to deal with a problem, they are guided to relieve the memory associated with that problem but now when dealing with the situation based on their new cognitive perspectives and skills.

Currently, treatments based on restructuring craving-based memories proved to be efficient for changing cravings related to cocaine addiction (Marsden et al. 2017, 2018, 2019). In these treatments, once the identification of craving-related experiences is done, the memory restructuring of those episodes follows. The focus is the most salient consumption memories in which craving elaboration processes can be identified (e.g., adapted to Frank would be "if I am with her, I will finally be happy and my misery will end," "being with her is what makes me happy") (Marsden et al. 2018). Marsden et al. (2018) have suggested several components of the memory reconsolidation and development of coping strategies phase to deal with memories of cravings (for cocaine).

The first component is socializing the client with the model. During this component, the therapist may discuss the rationale for reliving and updating the memories (Marsden et al. 2018). The second component of the intervention is *reliving the craving-memory.* During reliving, memories are vividly imagined and the client rates the level of craving and emotional response (0-10 strength scale). Moreover, the client is guided to pay attention to emotional "hotspots" (sensory images or meaning) similar to imagery re-scripting interventions in PTSD (Marsden et al. 2018).

The third component is cognitive restructuring and imagery re-scripting. Marsden et al. (2018) included four subcomponents of craving-memory re-scripting: (1) in vivo exposure (drug-related objects and photographs are presented and clients respond with alternative nonconsumption appraisals), (2) cognitive disputation outside of memory reliving (discrimination of neutral from conditioned cues; mental countering facilitative beliefs), (3) cognitive disputation within reliving (holding an image in working memory and responding with adaptive appraisals or new information), and (4) imagery re-scripting (e.g., the mental transformation of the episode from a moment when desire is high to the end of the episode, using positive images) (Marsden et al. 2018). The fourth component is stopping dysfunctional behaviors and promoting coping strategies (Marsden et al. 2018). The client is guided to engage in recovery-promoting activities (spending time with family members, diary of positive experiences), behavioral experiments (new social activities, testing reactions), and applying coping strategies (responding to craving by noticing sensations images and feelings, shifting attention) (Marsden et al. 2018).

Similarly to restructuring the memories of craving related to drugs, the therapist can restructure memories related to the embodied IBs. For instance, in the case of Frank, memories of being with his wife that are activated during his cravings for her may be targets for memory re-scripting. Reliving these memories while focusing on sensations and feelings may be followed by re-scripting the memory based on new appraisals of the fact that she left, she doesn't love him anymore, and she does not want him. Image transformation can target craving memories. Frank may picture episodes of intense craving for his wife that unfold positively, engaging in positive activities not related to her. Then, cues that trigger the craving for his wife can be identified such places, objects, and pictures of them can be taken. Frank can be exposed to these cues and practice new appraisals of the pictures.

Rational Emotive Imagery (REI) is another good method to develop memory-focused interventions (Maultsby 1971). REI (Maultsby 1971) is an important method used in REBT to consolidate the cognitive restructuring of irrational beliefs. Although I discuss it as an exposure method, when it is used to change embodied IBs associated with past memories of A (adversity), it can be a powerful memory-focused intervention. In this case, A is represented by a memory associated with craving (e.g., for Frank it could be craving for having a holiday with his wife). REI consists in vividly imaging the memory (e.g., craving for being with his wife), then letting dysfunctional emotions (feeling depressed) to unfold by thinking IBs (she should not leave me), and then restructuring IBs (e.g., even if I do not want her to leave me, she can do it) and experiencing the new functional emotions (sadness).

In a REI focused on embodied IBs, the therapist asks Frank to observe his feelings in response to the memory of being with his wife (e.g., vividly picture being together) and stay with the feelings of craving until they subside (rate them on a 0–10 scale), include the new appraisals (she left, even if we were to be together it will not be the same, etc.) and then observe new emotional feelings (at C).

7.4.6 Medication Treatment for Changing Embodied Rigid Appraisals

In opposition to disembodied beliefs, medication directly changes embodied IBs. Previous studies showed that just as little as a single dose of medication (d-fenfluramine) can change dysfunctional attitudes in 1 h after administration (Meyer et al. 2003). Yet no studies have intentionally tested whether medication results in direct changes of IBs. Indirect evidence suggests that individuals with depression that undergo pharmacotherapy display similar changes in IBs as those that undergo psychotherapy (David et al. 2008; Szentagotai et al. 2008). For instance, pharmacotherapy treatment (fluoxetine) resulted in changes in irrational beliefs measured by self-report scales (i.e., Attitude and Beliefs Scale). The analysis of the mechanisms of change for psychological therapies focused on changing IBs (REBT) and medication failed to identify a specific mechanism of change, all types of treatments resulting in changes in IBs (Szentagotai et al. 2008). Among the interpretations of these results, Szentagotai et al. (2008) suggested (in line with embodied IBs) that these results are because cognition (IBs), behavior, subjective feelings, and even some physiological modifications are strongly interrelated (e.g., as suggested by Ellis 1994). Embodied rigid appraisals suggest the reverse as well. Changing IBs results in changes of the brain mechanisms related to the dysfunctional embodiment. One study supports this affirmation. Iftene et al. (2015) found that psychological treatments focused on changing IBs (REBT) result in changes in biological markers such as serum concentrations of serotonin and norepinephrine (Iftene et al. 2015). Moreover, the psychological treatment focused on IBs seems to be as effective as SSRI (selective-serotonin reuptake inhibitor) medication (sertraline) to change the level of these biological markers in depressed children and adolescents (Iftene et al. 2015). Changes in these biological markers tentatively represent outcomes of changes in dysfunctional embodiments of embodied rigid appraisals.

When IBs are embodied, IBs result in disturbed emotions because of maladaptive central embodiments (simulations of dysregulated intense cravings and emotional responses). Given this idea, medication that successfully treats a dysregulated craving and emotional response should result in changes of IBs. There are several types of medication that can target cravings and stress-related mechanisms that induce craving (e.g., norepinephrine and glucocorticoid-induced dopamine/DA increases; see Chap. 5 for a detailed discussion). For instance, previous studies showed that increases in norepinephrine and glucocorticoids release can result in increased craving in some individuals as a response to stress (Douma and de Kloet 2020; Latagliata et al. 2018; Pascucci et al. 2007). Thus, medication that acts by this mechanism may reduce maladaptive craving and emotional embodiments. For instance, potential candidates are antidepressants that suppress the hyper-activation of noradrenergic neurons in locus coeruleus (Seki et al. 2018). It may be possible that a striatum dopaminergic overdrive based on noradrenaline input will be reduced. Furthermore, medications that reduce the hyper-activation of hypothalamic-pituitary-adrenal (HPA) axis and glucocorticoids release may also reduce a stress-induced craving (e.g., diazepam). In general, medication that optimizes the prefrontal regulatory function over motivation and emotion would largely result in reductions of the maladaptive embodiments of IBs (e.g., antidepressant medication; McRae et al. 2014).

This suggestion is in line with the results of clinical trials that indicate changes in the levels of self-reported irrational beliefs after antidepressant treatment (David et al. 2008). Furthermore, embodied irrational beliefs may be a neurocognitive marker able to help precision medication treatment in various emotional disorders. As stress sensitization produces neural sensitization to the effect of benzodiazepines (Kalman et al. 1997), easy-measured high levels of irrational beliefs may point to the patients that are responsive to these treatments.

When the treatment is focused on embodied IBs, medication is another way of changing IBs and their effect on emotions. It is also possible that medication can provide a quick relief from the effect of embodied IBs, especially in the case of acute stress. Although such effects can follow the administration of medication, this fact cannot be interpreted as no need for learning-based interventions. Changing verbal expressions of embodied irrational beliefs may be critical for backing up medication treatment. Verbal expression of demands may repeatedly trigger the mesolimbic salience system and maintain the sensitization of this system. Changing the verbal expression may offer the system time to "cool." Often, clients enjoy a "scratching metaphor" for illustrating this mechanism. "Saying *I need* or *I must* is like scratching a wound you want to heal. When you have a wound, no matter what and how good is the treatment you apply on the wound, if you scratch it, it will stay open. If you stop scratching it, you let your body heal. Then, medication can help a lot. So what do you think we have to say (and do) to stop scratching your emotional system?" Building linguistic and memory-based simulation-control mechanisms usually offers long-term stability over embodied simulations that are the foundation of IBs.

7.5 Summary

Embodied rigid appraisals are forms of appraisals based on an over-reactive mesolimbic dopaminergic system. When they are fully activated, they are experienced as cravings in response to adversities. The assessment of activated embodied IBs involves the assessment of the cognitive, affective, physiological, and behavioral components. Craving-focused measures may be adapted to assess embodied IBs. The treatment of embodied IBs extends beyond cognitive restructuring interventions. Interventions at physiological, behavioral, and cognitive levels are expected to reduce embodied IBs. New interventions such as exposure, memory re-scripting, and mindfulness meditation applied to changes of IBs may help the process of changing embodied IBs.

References

Anselme, P., & Güntürkün, O. (2019). Incentive hope: A default psychological response to multiple forms of uncertainty. *Behavioral and Brain Sciences, 42*, e35. 40-59.

Barlow, D. H., Farchione, T. J., Fairholme, C. P., Ellard, K. K., Boisseau, C. L., Allen, L. B., & Ehrenreich-May, J. (2011). *The unified protocol for transdiagnostic treatment of emotional disorders: Therapist guide*. Oxford University Press.

Barrett, L. F. (2017). *How emotions are made: The secret life of the brain*. Houghton Mifflin Harcourt.

Barsalou, L. W. (1999). Perceptual symbol systems. *Behavioral and Brain Sciences, 22*, 577–609.

Barsalou, L. W. (2008). Grounded cognition. *Annual Review of Psychology, 59*(1), 617–645.

Barsalou, L. W. (2017). Understanding contemplative practices from the perspective of dual-process theories. In J. C. Karremans & E. K. Papies (Eds.), *Mindfulness in social psychology* (pp. 30–49). Psychology Press.

Beck, A. T. (1976). *Cognitive therapy and the emotional disorders*. International Universities Press.

Berridge, K. C. (2018). Evolving concepts of emotion and motivation. *Frontiers in Psychology, 9*, 1647. https://doi.org/10.3389/fpsyg.2018.01647

Berridge, K. C., & Robinson, T. E. (2016). Liking, wanting, and the incentive sensitization theory of addiction. *The American Psychologist, 71*(8), 670–679. https://doi.org/10.1037/amp0000059

Bishop, S. R., Lau, M., Shapiro, S., Carlson, L., Anderson, N. D., Carmody, J., … Devins, G. (2004). Mindfulness: A proposed operational definition. *Clinical Psychology: Science and Practice, 11*, 230–241.

Burgess, P. (1986). Belief systems and emotional disturbance: Evaluation of the rational emotive model. Unpublished doctoral dissertation, University of Melbourne, Parkville, Melbourne, Australia.

Cabib, S., Campus, P., Conversi, D., Orsini, C., & Puglisi-Allegra, S. (2020). Functional and dysfunctional neuroplasticity in learning to cope with stress. *Brain Sciences, 10*(2), 127. https://doi.org/10.3390/brainsci10020127

Cabib, S., & Puglisi-Allegra, S. (2012). The mesoaccumbens dopamine in coping with stress. *Neuroscience & Biobehavioral Reviews, 36*(1), 79–89.

David, D. (2014). Some concerns about the psychological implications of mindfulness: A critical analysis. *Journal of Rat-Emotive Cognitive-Behavior Therapy, 32*, 313–324. https://doi.org/10.1007/s10942-014-0198-z

David, D., Coteț, C., Matu, S., Mogoașe, C., & Ștefan, S. (2017). 50 years of rational-emotive and cognitive-behavioral therapy: A systematic review and meta-analysis. *Journal of Clinical Psychology*, 1–15. https://doi.org/10.1002/jclp.22514

David, D., Szentagotai, A., Lupu, V., & Cosman, D. (2008). Rational emotive behavior therapy, cognitive therapy, and medication in the treatment of major depressive disorder: A randomized clinical trial, posttreatment outcomes, and six-month follow-up. *Journal of Clinical Psychology, 64*(6), 728–746. https://doi.org/10.1002/jclp.20487

David, D. O., DiGiuseppe, R., Dobrean, A., Păsărelu, C. R., & Balazsi, R. (2019a). The measurement of irrationality and rationality. In M. Bernard & W. Dryden (Eds.), *Advances in REBT*. Springer. https://doi.org/10.1007/978-3-319-93118-0_4

David, D. O., Sucală, M., Coteț, C., Șoflău, R., & Vălenaș, S. (2019b). Empirical research in REBT theory and practice. In M. Bernard & W. Dryden (Eds.), *Advances in REBT* (pp. 101–119). Springer. https://doi.org/10.1007/978-3-319-93118-0_5

Dharmadhikari, A. S., & Sinha, V. K. (2015). Psychological management of craving. *Journal of Addiction Research and Therapy, 6*, 230. https://doi.org/10.4172/2155-6105.1000230

DiGiuseppe, R., Doyle, K. A., Dryden, W., & Bacx, W. (2014). *A practioner's guide to rational emotive behavior therapy*. Oxford University Press.

DiGiuseppe, R., Leaf, R., Exner, T., & Robin, M. V. (1988). The development of a measure of rational/irrational thinking. Paper presented at the World Congress of Behavior Therapy, Edinburgh, Scotland.

Douma, E. H., & de Kloet, E. R. (2020). Stress-induced plasticity and functioning of ventral tegmental dopamine neurons. *Neuroscience and Biobehavioral Reviews, 108*, 48–77. https://doi.org/10.1016/j.neubiorev.2019.10.015

Drummond, D. (2000). What does cue-reactivity have to offer clinical research? *Addiction, 92*, 129–144.

Dryden, W. (2019). Rational emotive behavior therapy: Assessment, conceptualisation and intervention. In M. Bernard & W. Dryden (Eds.), *Advances in REBT* (pp. 165–210). Springer. https://doi.org/10.1007/978-3-319-93118-0_8

Dryden, W., & DiGiuseppe, R. (1990). *A primer on rational emotive therapy*. Champaign, IL: Research Press.

Ellis, A. (1958). Rational psychotherapy. *The Journal of General Psychology, 59*, 35–49.

Ellis, A. (1962). *Reason and emotion in psychotherapy*. Lyle Stuart.

Ellis, A. (1991). The revised ABC's of rational-emotive therapy (RET). *Journal of Rational-Emotive and Cognitive-Behavior Therapy, 9*, 139–172. https://doi.org/10.1007/BF01061227

Ellis, A. (1994). *Reason and emotion in psychotherapy*. Citadel.

Ellis, A. (2001). *Feeling better, getting better, staying better: Profound self-help therapy for your emotions*. Impact Publishers.

Ellis, A., David, D., & Lynn, S. J. (2010). Rational and irrational beliefs: A historical and conceptual perspective. In D. David, S. J. Lynn, & A. Ellis (Eds.), *Rational and irrational beliefs: Research, theory, and clinical practice* (pp. 3–22). Oxford University Press.

Felger, J. C. (2018). Imaging the role of inflammation in mood and anxiety-related disorders. *Current Neuropharmacology, 16*(5), 533–558. https://doi.org/10.2174/1570159X15666171123201142

Foa, E. B., & Kozak, M. J. (1986). Emotional processing of fear: Exposure to corrective information. *Psychological Bulletin, 99*(1), 20–35. https://doi.org/10.1037/0033-2909.99.1.20

Goldstein, A. N., & Walker, M. P. (2014). The role of sleep in emotional brain function. *Annual Review of Clinical Psychology, 10*, 679–708. https://doi.org/10.1146/annurev-clinpsy-032813-153716

Hayes, S. C., & Hofmann, S. G. (Eds.). (2018). *Process-based CBT: The science and core clinical competencies of cognitive behavioral therapy*. New Harbinger.

Hernandez, A. R., Hernandez, C. M., Campos, K., Truckenbrod, L., Federico, Q., Moon, B., … Burke, S. N. (2018). A Ketogenic diet improves cognition and has biochemical effects in prefrontal cortex that are dissociable from hippocampus. *Frontiers in Aging Neuroscience, 10*, 391. https://doi.org/10.3389/fnagi.2018.00391

Iftene, F., Predescu, E., Stefan, S., & David, D. (2015). Rational-emotive and cognitive behavior therapy (REBT/CBT) versus pharmacotherapy versus REBT/CBT plus pharmacotherapy in the treatment of major depressive disorder in youth: A randomized clinical trial. *Psychiatry Research, 225*(3), 687–694. https://doi.org/10.1016/j.psychres.2014.11.021

Jacka, F. N., Pasco, J. A., Mykletun, A., Williams, L. J., Hodge, A. M., O'Reilly, S. L., … Berk, M. (2010). Association of Western and traditional diets with depression and anxiety in women. *American Journal of Psychiatry, 167*, 305–311.

Kalman, B. A., Kim, P. J., Cole, M. A., Chi, M. S., & Spencer, R. L. (1997). Diazepam attenuation of restraint stress-induced corticosterone levels is enhanced by prior exposure to repeated restraint. *Psychoneuroendocrinology, 22*, 349–360.

Kujach, S., Byun, K., Hyodo, K., Suwabe, K., Fukuie, T., Laskowski, R., … Soyaab, H. A. (2018). Transferable high-intensity intermittent exercise improves executive performance in association with dorsolateral prefrontal activation in young adults. *NeuroImage, 169*, 117–125.

Latagliata, E. C., Puglisi-Allegra, S., Ventura, R., & Cabib, S. (2018). Norepinephrine in the medial pre-frontal cortex supports Accumbens Shell responses to a novel palatable food in food-restricted mice only. *Frontiers in Behavioral Neuroscience, 12*, 7. https://doi.org/10.3389/fnbeh.2018.00007

Leahy, R. L. (2015). *Emotional schema therapy*. Guilford Press.

Leventhal, H., & Scherer, K. R. (1987). The relationship of emotion to cognition: A functional approach to a semantic controversy. *Cognition and Emotion, 1*, 3–28.

Lindner, H., Kirkby, R., Wertheim, E., & Birch, P. (1999). A brief assessment of irrational thinking: The shortened general attitude and belief scale. *Cognitive Therapy and Research, 23*, 651–663.

Lowe, C., Reichelt, A., & Hall, P. (2019). The prefrontal cortex and obesity: A health neuroscience perspective. *Trends in Cognitive Sciences, 23*(4), 349–361. https://doi.org/10.1016/j.tics.2019.01.005

Macavei, B., & McMahon, J. (2010). The assessment of rational and irrational beliefs. In D. David, S. J. Lynn, & A. Ellis (Eds.), *Rational and irrational beliefs: Research, theory, and clinical practice* (pp. 115–147). Oxford University Press.

Marsden, J., Goetz, C., Meynen, T., Mitcheson, L., Stillwell, G., Eastwood, B., & Grey, N. (2017). Memory-focused cognitive therapy for cocaine use disorder: Rationale, design and protocol for an external pilot randomized controlled trial. *Contemporary Clinical Trials Communications, 8*, 264–273. https://doi.org/10.1016/j.conctc.2017.10.009

Marsden, J., Goetz, C., Meynen, T., Mitcheson, L., Stillwell, G., Eastwood, B., … Grey, N. (2018). Memory-focused cognitive therapy for cocaine use disorder: Theory, procedures and preliminary evidence from an external pilot randomized controlled trial. *eBioMedicine, 29*, 177–189. https://doi.org/10.1016/j.ebiom.2018.01.039

Marsden, J., Stillwell, G., James, K., Shearer, J., Byford, S., Hellier, J., … Mitcheson, L. (2019). Efficacy and cost-effectiveness of an adjunctive randomized psychosocial intervention in treatment-resistant maintenance opioid agonist therapy: A pragmatic, open-label, randomized controlled trial. *The Lancet Psychiatry, 6*, 391–402. https://doi.org/10.1016/S22150366(19)30097-5

Maultsby, M. (1971). Rational emotive imagery. *Rational Living, 6*(1), 24–27.

May, J., Andrade, J., Kavanagh, D. J., Feeney, G. F. X., Gullo, M. J., Statham, D. J., … Connor, J. P. (2014). The craving experience questionnaire: A brief, theory-based measure of consummatory desire and craving. *Addiction, 109*(5), 728–735. https://doi.org/10.1111/add.12472

McRae, K., Rekshan, W., Williams, L. M., & Gross, J. (2014). Effects of antidepressant medication on emotion regulation in depressed patients: An iSPOT-D report. *Journal of Affective Disorders, 159*, 127–132.

Mehta, N. D., Haroon, E., Xu, X., Woolwine, B. J., Li, Z., & Felger, J. C. (2018). Inflammation negatively correlates with amygdala-ventromedial prefrontal functional connectivity in association with anxiety in patients with depression: Preliminary results. *Brain, Behavior, and Immunity, 73*, 725–730. https://doi.org/10.1016/j.bbi.2018.07.026

Meyer, J. H., McMain, S., Kennedy, S. H., Korman, L., Brown, G. M., DaSilva, J. N., … Links, P. (2003). Dysfunctional attitudes and 5 HT2 receptors during depression and self-harm. *American Journal of Psychiatry, 160*, 90–99.

Moors, A., Ellsworth, P. C., Scherer, K. R., & Frijda, N. H. (2013). Appraisal theories of emotion: State of the art and future development. *Emotion Review, 5*(2), 119–124. https://doi.org/10.1177/1754073912468165

Papies, E. K., Pronk, T. M., Keesman, M., & Barsalou, L. W. (2015). The benefits of simply observing: Mindful attention modulates the link between motivation and behavior. *Journal of Personality and Social Psychology, 108*, 148–170.

Pascucci, T., Ventura, R., Latagliata, E. C., Cabib, S., & Puglisi-Allegra, S. (2007). The medial prefrontal cortex determines the accumbens dopamine response to stress through the opposing influences of norepinephrine and dopamine. *Cerebral Cortex, 17*, 2796–2804. https://doi.org/10.1093/cercor/bhm008

Persons, J. B. (2008). *The case formulation approach to cognitive-behavior therapy*. Guilford Press.

Robinson, T. E., & Berridge, K. C. (1993). The neural basis of drug craving: An incentive-sensitization theory of addiction. *Brain Research Reviews, 18*(3), 247–291. https://doi.org/10.1016/0165-0173(93)90013-P

Sayette, M. A., Shiffman, S., Tiffany, S. T., Niaura, R. S., Martin, C. S., & Shadel, W. G. (2000). The measurement of drug craving. *Addiction (Abingdon, England), 95*(Suppl 2), S189–S210. https://doi.org/10.1080/09652140050111762

Seki, K., Yoshida, S., & Jaiswal, M. K. (2018). Molecular mechanism of noradrenaline during the stress-induced major depressive disorder. *Neural Regeneration Research, 13*(7), 1159–1169. https://doi.org/10.4103/1673-5374.235019

Somoza, E., Dyrenforth, S., Goldsmith, J., Mezinskis, J., & Cohen, M. (1995). In search of a universal drug craving scale. Paper presented at the Annual Meeting of the American Psychiatric Association, Miami Florida.

Stalcup, S. A., Christian, D., Stalcup, J., Brown, M., & Galloway, G. P. (2006). A treatment model for craving identification and management. *Journal of Psychoactive Drugs, 38*, 189–202. https://doi.org/10.1080/02791072.2006.10399843

Stefan, S., & David, D. (2020). Mindfulness in therapy: A critical analysis. *International Journal of Clinical and Experimental Hypnosis, 68*(2), 167–182. https://doi.org/10.1080/00207144.2020.1720514

Szentagotai, A., David, D., Lupu, V., & Cosman, D. (2008). Rational emotive behavior therapy versus cognitive therapy versus pharmacotherapy in the treatment of major depressive disorder: Mechanisms of change analysis. *Psychotherapy: Theory, Research, Practice, Training, 45*(4), 523–538.

Szentagotai, A., Schnur, J., DiGiuseppe, R., Macavei, B., Kallay, E., & David, D. (2005). The organization and the nature of irrational beliefs: Schemas or appraisal? *Journal of Cognitive and Behavioral Psychotherapies, 2*, 139–158.

Tapper, K. (2017). Can mindfulness influence weight management related eating behaviors? If so, how? *Clinical Psychology Review, 53*, 122–134.

Tapper, K. (2018). Mindfulness and craving: Effects and mechanisms. *Clinical Psychology Review, 59*, 101–117. https://doi.org/10.1016/j.cpr.2017.11.003

Tiba, A. I., & Manea, L. (2018). The embodied simulation account of cognition in rational emotive behavior therapy. *New Ideas in Psychology, 48*, 12–20. https://doi.org/10.1016/j.newideapsych.2017.08.003

Toneatto, T. (1999). A metacognitive analysis of craving: Implication for treatment. *Journal of Clinical Psychology, 55*, 527–537.

Tsukamoto, H., Suga, T., Takenaka, S., Tanaka, D., Takeuchi, T., Hamaoka, T., … Hashimoto, T. (2016). Greater impact of acute high-intensity interval exercise on post-exercise executive function compared to moderate-intensity continuous exercise. *Physiology and Behaviour, 155*, 224–230.

Wells, A. (2009). *Metacognitive therapy for anxiety and depression*. Guilford Press.

Williams, J. M. G., Teasdale, J. D., Segal, Z. V., & Kabat-Zinn, J. (2007). *The mindful way through depression: Freeing yourself from chronic unhappiness*. Guilford Press.

Wu, M., Liang, Y., Wang, Q., Zhao, Y., & Zhou, R. (2016). Emotion dysregulation of women with premenstrual syndrome. *Scientific Reports, 6*, 38501. https://doi.org/10.1038/srep38501

Young, J. E., Klosko, J. S., & Weishaar, M. E. (2003). *Schema therapy: A practitioner's guide*. Guilford Press.

Index

A. Tiba, *Embodied Hot Cognitive Vulnerability to Emotional Disorders*,
https://doi.org/10.1007/978-3-030-53989-4

The manufacturer's authorised representative in the EU is Springer Nature Customer Service Centre GmbH, Europaplatz 3, 69115 Heidelberg, Germany. If you have any concerns regarding our products, please contact ProductSafety@springernature.com

Printed and bound by CPI Group (UK) Ltd, Croydon, CR0 4YY
30/09/2026
02225709-0005